REF
PR
4038
.P4
G39
2002

HWLCLT

Chicago Public Library

0178744263

Jane Austen and the theatre

LITERATURE AND LANGUAGE DIVISION
THE CHICAGO PUBLIC LIBRARY
400 SOUTH STATE STREET
CHICAGO, ILLINOIS 60605

D1064642

# JANE AUSTEN AND THE THEATRE

Jane Austen was fascinated by theatre from her childhood. As an adult she went to the theatre whenever opportunity arose. Scenes in her novels often resemble plays, and recent film and television versions have shown how naturally dramatic her stories are. Yet the myth remains that she was 'anti-theatrical', and readers continue to puzzle about the real significance of the theatricals in *Mansfield Park*. Penny Gay's book describes for the first time the rich theatrical context of Austen's writing, and the intersections between her novels and contemporary drama. Gay proposes a 'dialogue' in Austen's mature novels with the various genres of eighteenth-century drama: laughing comedy, sentimental comedy and tragedy, Gothic theatre, early melodrama. She re-reads the novels in the light of this dialogue to demonstrate Austen's analysis of the pervasive theatricality of the society in which her heroines must perform.

PENNY GAY is an Associate Professor of English at the University of Sydney, where she also teaches performance studies. Her 1994 book, *As She Likes It: Shakespeare's Unruly Women*, was the first feminist study of the performances of Shakespeare's comic heroines, and she has since published separate studies of *The Merchant of Venice* and *As You Like It*. She has also published extensively on Jane Austen.

# JANE AUSTEN AND THE THEATRE

PENNY GAY

*University of Sydney*

CAMBRIDGE
UNIVERSITY PRESS

PUBLISHED BY THE PRESS SYNDICATE OF THE UNIVERSITY OF CAMBRIDGE
The Pitt Building, Trumpington Street, Cambridge, United Kingdom

CAMBRIDGE UNIVERSITY PRESS
The Edinburgh Building, Cambridge CB2 2RU, UK
40 West 20th Street, New York, NY 10011-4211, USA
477 Williamstown Road, Port Melbourne, VIC 3207, Australia
Ruiz de Alarcón 13, 28014 Madrid, Spain
Dock House, The Waterfront, Cape Town 8001, South Africa

http://www.cambridge.org

© Penny Gay 2002

This book is in copyright. Subject to statutory exception
and to the provisions of relevant collective licensing agreements,
no reproduction of any part may take place without
the written permission of Cambridge University Press.

First published 2002

Printed in the United Kingdom at the University Press, Cambridge

*Typeface* Baskerville Monotype 11 / 12.5 pt.     *System* LATEX 2$_\varepsilon$   [TB]

*A catalogue record for this book is available from the British Library*

*Library of Congress Cataloguing in Publication data*

Gay, Penny, 1945–
Jane Austen and the theatre / Penny Gay.
p.   cm.
Includes bibliographical references and index.
ISBN 0 521 65213 8
1. Austen, Jane, 1775–1817 – Knowledge – Performing arts.   2. Theatre – England –
History – 19th century.   3. Theatre – England – History – 18th century.   4. Performing
arts in literature.   5. Theatre in literature.   I. Title.
PR4038.P4 G39   2002
823′.7 – dc21   2001052640

ISBN 0 521 65213 8 hardback

Ro178744263

LITERATURE AND LANGUAGE DIVISION
THE CHICAGO PUBLIC LIBRARY
400 SOUTH STATE STREET
CHICAGO, ILLINOIS 60605

## Contents

# Illustrations

# Prologue

Jane Austen was fascinated by theatre. As a child she read plays, she watched and took part in the family theatricals at Steventon. As an adult she went to the theatre whenever opportunity arose. Generations of readers have observed that many scenes in her novels resemble plays, developing the plot through brilliant, witty, and psychologically acute dialogue. Little has been made, however, of the intersections between her theatrical interests and experience and the six mature novels. At most a notion reigns that because of the weight given to the episode of the theatricals in *Mansfield Park* she was herself – or she became – 'anti-theatrical'.

This, as I shall argue in chapter 5, is a drastically simplified reading of a complex and assured text. Jonas Barish, authoritative historian of anti-theatrical prejudice (*The Anti-Theatrical Prejudice* (Berkeley and Los Angeles: University of California Press, 1981)), is right to conclude that 'hostility to impersonation . . . assuredly hangs in the air' in this novel. But when he goes on to claim that

uncomfortable personal memories . . . contributed to Jane Austen's defection from the theater. . . . The former believer is not merely giving up her childhood diversions in the barn, she is disavowing them, burning them in effigy, setting them down as forbidden games, (pp. 306, 304)

he is pursuing his thesis in the face of facts. Austen never 'defected' from the theatre. In fact, there is a good deal of evidence to the contrary, which, when combined with Austen's lively interest as a novelist in theatrical modes of behaviour, suggests that she found theatre – not just the dramatic text, but its embodiment in actors on a stage at a particular time and place – a curiously fascinating and thought-provoking experience. In this book I attempt to tease out both the theatrical context of Austen's writing, and how she deals in each of her major novels with a society that she perceives to be inescapably theatrical.

Most of this book was written during a Visiting Fellowship at Clare Hall, Cambridge; I would like to thank the Governing Body of Clare Hall for electing me to this privilege – the college and its President, Gillian Beer, created the perfect ambience for scholarly life and work. Several distinguished scholars have provided support, encouragement, and wonderfully useful comments and information for this project: I would particularly like to thank Margaret Kirkham, Kate Newey, and Juliet McMaster, and the anonymous theatre specialist who (along with Professor McMaster) read the manuscript for Cambridge University Press. The staff of the Cambridge University Library, the British Library, the Theatre Museum, and the V&A Picture Library have been admirably efficient and helpful. Special thanks must go, too, to Betty Brown and Ken Hall of Bath, who enabled me to spend a wonderful hour exploring the interior of the old Orchard Street Theatre (now a Masonic Hall). My editor, Sarah Stanton, has been an enthusiastic supporter of this project since it first gleamed as an idea. Parts of chapters 3 and 5 were first presented at Annual General Meetings of the Jane Austen Society of North America, and subsequently published in *Persuasions*; my thanks to the editors of that journal.

My colleagues at the University of Sydney, and the large Sydney membership of the Jane Austen Society of Australia, have enthusiastically followed the development of this project; JASA's President, Susannah Fullerton, was at an early stage a superbly helpful research assistant in tracking down the plays that we know Jane Austen saw or read. My family has contributed not only constant support but also expertise. My husband Robert Gay was a fount of information about eighteenth- and nineteenth-century music; my younger daughter Virginia brought her strong instincts for good theatre and good writing to bear on many issues; and my elder daughter Meg read the whole manuscript in draft with sharp and sympathetic editorial eyes. My profound thanks to them all.

As I complete this book I have an inescapable feeling that I have only scratched the surface of the terrain covered by 'Jane Austen and the Theatre'. I hope these first steps will encourage others to explore further in the rich fields of eighteenth-century drama and theatre, and the ways in which they engage in dialogue with the novels of the period.

# A note on in-text references

References to Jane Austen's six major novels are keyed to *The Novels of Jane Austen*, ed. R.W. Chapman, 3rd edn, vols. I–V (Oxford University Press, 1932–4, repr. 1973); and vol. VI, *Minor Works* (1954, revised B.C. Southam, Oxford University Press, 1975). Page references are cited in the text and abbreviated thus:

*Northanger Abbey* as *NA*
*Sense and Sensibility* as *S&S*
*Pride and Prejudice* as *P&P*
*Mansfield Park* as *MP*
*Emma* as *E*
*Persuasion* as *P*
*Minor Works* as *MW*

References to *Jane Austen's Letters* are to the edition by Deirdre Le Faye, 3rd edn (Oxford University Press, 1995), abbreviated in the text as *Letters*.

References to plays, unless otherwise noted, are to the transcriptions of early editions on the Chadwyck-Healey *English Drama* Full-Text Database, copyright © Chadwyck-Healey, 1997.

# CHAPTER ONE

# *Jane Austen's experience of theatre*

Despite being the home of a respectable country clergyman, Steventon parsonage was by no means divorced from things theatrical. Plays, both contemporary and classic, were evidently available for reading and for the production of home theatricals. Jane Austen's elder brothers perhaps brought the 'itch for acting' (*MP*, p. 121) home from Oxford, resulting in a series of domestic productions in 1782–90; but the reading of plays seems to have been part of the normal spectrum of home entertainment in a family where reading aloud was a regular after-dinner pastime. Cassandra and Jane's brief sojourn at the Abbey School, Reading (1785–6) was under the direction of the theatre enthusiast Mrs La Tournelle, and 'plays may have been a feature of Jane's and Cassandra's education', argues Claire Tomalin.[1] Whether or not this was the case, there is plenty of evidence that from childhood, Austen was reading plays, dissecting their characteristics, and delightedly reproducing them in her early experiments in writing.

## THE JUVENILIA

Austen's juvenilia, carefully collected by her into three 'volumes', include three spoof playlets, 'The Visit', 'The Mystery', and 'The first Act of a Comedy'. 'The Visit' (*MW*, pp. 49–54), like the other two, is set out in perfect compliance with the conventions of the printed drama, with stage directions including asides and instructions for actors' movements. The text of the playlet is a hilariously deadpan parody of society drama, in which polite clichés are exchanged and nothing of moment is said except by the resident Fitzgeralds, who blame all the shortcomings of the visit on the eccentricities of 'my Grandmother'.[2] This includes a surreal sequence in which Miss Fitzgerald says to the visitors, 'Bless me! there ought to be 8 Chairs and there are but 6. However, if your Ladyship will but take Sir Arthur in your Lap, & Sophy my Brother in hers, I beleive we shall do pretty well.' Which they proceed to do without turning a hair. The dinner, discussed with similar imperturbable politeness, includes 'fried Cowheel & Onion', red herrings, tripe, 'Liver & Crow', and suet pudding. All ends happily with arbitrary proposals of marriage insouciantly accepted.

'The Mystery' ('An Unfinished Comedy', *MW*, pp. 55–7), even shorter in its two pages, consists of an inspired riff on the trope of stage secrecy: the eight characters in the three scenes drop hints, nods and winks, and tantalising unfinished sentences – but nothing material is actually revealed to anyone, on or off stage:

DAPHNE. My dear Mrs Humbug how d'ye do? Oh! Fanny t'is all over.
FANNY. Is it indeed!
MRS. HUM. I'm very sorry to hear it.
FANNY. Then t'was to no purpose that I. . . .
DAPHNE. None upon Earth.
MRS. HUM. And what is to become of? . . .
DAPHNE. Oh! thats all settled. (*whispers* MRS. HUMBUG)

(*MW*, p. 56)

In 'The first Act of a Comedy' (*MW*, pp. 172–4) Austen expertly parodies the burletta or comic opera of the day:

CHLOE. Where am I? At Hounslow. Where go I? – To London. What to do? To be married –. Unto whom? Unto Strephon. Who is he? A Youth. Then I will Sing a Song.

   SONG.
   I go to Town
   And when I come down
   I shall be married to Strephon
   And that to me will be fun.
   CHORUS. Be fun, be fun, be fun,
   And that to me will be fun.

The parodies that these three playlets constitute are knowing, extremely accurate satire. Obviously well before she was an adult Jane Austen knew a great deal about contemporary theatre. There is even a theatrical in-joke in the final paragraphs of *Love and Friendship*: 'Philander & Gustavus, after having raised their reputation by their Performances in the theatrical Line at Edinburgh, removed to Covent Garden, where they still exhibit under the assumed names of *Lewis & Quick*'[3] (*MW*, p. 109). Elsewhere in the juvenilia Austen cites specific playwrights by name. In the 'History of England . . . By a partial, prejudiced, & ignorant Historian' she unabashedly draws much of her 'history' from Shakespeare's plays, which she expects her audience to recognise. 'Henry the 4th', for example, 'falling ill, his son the Prince of Wales came and took away the crown; whereupon the King made a long speech, for which I must refer the Reader to Shakespear's Plays, & the Prince made a still longer' (*MW*, p. 139). She had also by this stage (circa 1790) read and obviously appreciated Sheridan's hilarious satire of contemporary theatrical fashions, *The Critic* (1779): 'as [Sir Walter Raleigh] was an enemy of the noble Essex, I have nothing to say in praise of him, & must refer all those who may wish to be acquainted with the particulars of his Life, to Mr. Sheridan's play of the Critic, where they will find many interesting Anecdotes as well of him as of his freind Sir Christopher Hatton' (*MW*, p. 147). Brian Southam notes two other probable borrowings from *The Critic* in the juvenilia: the 'hints and mysteries' of scene ii of 'The Mystery' and the famous 'We fainted alternately on a Sofa' of *Love and Friendship* (Notes, *MW*, p. 458).

Southam has also argued persuasively for the presence of Jane Austen's authorial hand in 'Sir Charles Grandison', dating the final version of the manuscript around 1800 (after a start in about 1793). He assumes a later bout of family theatricals for which it was written, probably involving Austen's young niece Anna Lefroy. This very short five-act reduction of Richardson's massive novel is written in the style of the popular playwright Hannah Cowley, with a strong emphasis on the lives of women and most scenes taking place in drawing-rooms. 'The essence of the joke in Jane Austen's "Sir Charles Grandison"', Southam argues, 'is the reduction of a mammoth novel to a miniature play ... a comedy of abridgement.'[4] An amusing enough piece for home entertainment, it is however lame by comparison with the work of playwrights such as Cowley or Inchbald, depending as it does on the audience's knowledge of the original text (a favourite novel of Jane Austen's family); the pleasure arises from the contrast with Richardson's leisurely and circumstantial plotting. As Southam remarks, 'it was a play for the family to perform':[5] whether they did so in the year or so immediately preceding their removal to Bath is not known. More significant family entertainment at that time would have been provided by the reading aloud of early versions of *Sense and Sensibility*, *Northanger Abbey*, and *Pride and Prejudice*: Austen's original and mature drama was to be found in her novels.

## HOME THEATRICALS

'A love of the theatre is so general, an itch for acting so strong among young people', Austen wrote in *Mansfield Park* (p. 121) – an observation surely based on autobiographical experience. During the years 1782–9,

when Jane Austen was aged seven to fourteen, her older siblings regularly organised home theatricals.[6] Even at this early stage in her literary
career, Austen's taste clearly never ran to tragedy and high-flown sentiment: 'One of Edward's Mistresses was Jane Shore, who has had a
play written about her [by Nicholas Rowe, 1714], but it is a tragedy
& therefore not worth reading' (*MW*, p. 140). The young men of the
Austen family, however, clearly thought that they were capable of bringing off the bombastic style and sentiments of contemporary tragedy in
their first piece for the Steventon home theatricals, Thomas Francklin's
*Matilda*, which they produced in 1782. This is an inflated, unconsciously
comic historical-sensational drama, premiered by Garrick in 1775; it
offers plenty of opportunities for ranting by the proto-Mr Yateses of the
family – but surely little real entertainment for their audience.

As anyone who has been involved in amateur theatricals knows, comedy is a more reliable route to general satisfaction. The Austens soon
moved on to comedy, and stayed with it. The plays performed in the
Steventon home theatricals during Austen's childhood present a con-
spectus of late eighteenth-century fashionable comic theatre. Arguably
these performances, and – perhaps more importantly – the bustle and
excitement that inevitably accompanies 'putting on a show' (particularly
in amateur companies) had a profound influence on the young writer,
alerting her both to the seductive power of theatre and to the ambivalence of acting.

Sheridan's *The Rivals*, performed at Steventon in 1784, has kept its
place in the English dramatic repertory, and its significance will be examined in chapter 2. Susannah Centlivre's *The Wonder! A Woman Keeps a Secret*
(1714) was the play in which the Austens' cousin Eliza de Feuillide was the
flirtatious leading lady in 1787 – it was also the production of which we are
told that Mr Austen's 'barn is fitting up quite like a theatre, & all the young
folks are to take part'.[7] Given the large cast of *The Wonder*, this probably
included 'young folks' outside the family, a possibility which is discussed
with some anxiety in *Mansfield Park*. William Hazlitt thought this play 'one
of our good old English Comedies, which holds a happy medium between grossness and refinement . . . the dialogue [is rich] in *double entendre*,
which however is so light and careless, as only to occasion a succession
of agreeable alarms to the ears of delicacy'.[8] It does include some 'warm
parts' (to use Mary Crawford's phrase), such as this exchange:

DON FELIX. [Henry Austen's role?] . . . Give me your hand at parting however
    Violante, won't you? [*Here he lays his hand upon her knee several times.*] Won't
    you? – won't you? – won't you?

VIOLANTE. [*Half regarding him.*] Won't I do what?
DON FELIX. You know what I would have Violante. Oh! my heart!
VIOLANTE. [*Smiling.*] I thought my chains were easily broken. [*Lays her hand in to his.*]
DON FELIX. [*Draws his chair close to her and kisses her hand in a rapture.*] Too well thou knowest thy strength. Oh, my charming angel my heart is all thy own! forgive my hasty passion, 'tis the transport of a love sincere!

(Act v)

As well as contributing to the amorous raptures of Austen's *Love and Friendship*, the opportunities for physical contact here would not have been lost on 'Jane, a sharp-eyed girl of twelve'.[9]

Hannah Cowley's *Which is the Man?* and Garrick's *Bon Ton* had been under consideration for performance in 1787, at Eliza's instigation. The former, one of the most popular of the highly successful dramatist's works, will be discussed in chapter 5. Garrick's *Bon Ton, or High Life above Stairs* (1775) is a lively two-act comedy satirising the pretensions of well-off urbanites. Like many comedies of the period, it has a strong anti-Gallic tone[10] ('those monsters, foreign vices, and *Bon Ton*, as they call it') – a francophobia which Austen also exploits in her comic masterpiece *Emma*, as I shall argue in chapter 6.

*The Chances*, performed the following year, is Garrick's revision (1773) of Buckingham's rewriting of Beaumont and Fletcher's play. The revisions supposedly removed indecency, but it remains quite a risqué piece, especially in the character of Don John (played by Garrick in his version), a charming libertine who is finally converted by the love of a free-spirited witty young woman. The play also contains a proto-Mrs Malaprop – crossed perhaps with Lady Wishfort of *The Way of the World*: an affectedly genteel lady with a taste for liquor. Another play with a large cast, it too probably called for resources greater than the Austen family. Perhaps Henry, taken with the success of the previous year's opportunities for flirtation, was the prime mover in suggesting a play with a libertine for hero; in any case, Henry Crawford's character has a long ancestry. Fielding's *Tom Thumb*,[11] also performed in 1788, is a rollicking farce with a cast of giants and midgets; it parodies the excesses of Shakespearean tragedy in a way that must have appealed to the young Jane, herself writing parodies of contemporary fiction and drama. And like *The Chances*, it has its share of indecorum, not to say indecency: female drunkenness, gluttony, large breasts, and beds are staples of the rhyming dialogue.

The heroine Roxalana of Isaac Bickerstaff's *The Sultan* (1775; performed at Steventon in 1789) was a favourite role of the two great comic actresses of the day, Dorothy Jordan and Frances Abington. In chapter 4 I discuss the possible echoes in *Pride and Prejudice* of this comedy, which also provided the original plot for Mozart's *Die Entführung aus dem Serail*.[12] Another farce presented in the same year was James Townley's *High Life Below Stairs*, a moralising comedy in which servants ape the nobility, throwing a party while their master is away. He returns to share the revelry in disguise, and then dispense summary and harsh justice on their extravagance and 'impudence'. The charm of this popular farce must have lain in its classic carnival theme: the delights of a topsy-turvy world were exhibited on stage (including satire of the fopperies of the upper class), but the play concludes with everyone back in their place and the rebellious elements expelled.

Clearly the Austen family preferred comedy to the opportunities for ranting and risibility offered by contemporary tragedy; and like Edmund Bertram and Henry Crawford they probably thought of Shakespeare as more suitable for reading aloud than getting up as a performance. But 1789 saw the last of the Steventon theatricals: Tucker speculates that the elopement of a family connection, Thomas James Twisleton, with a young lady in September 1788, 'as a result of a liaison begun while they were acting in an amateur production of Jephson's tragedy *Julia* at the Freemason's Hall in London', may have induced some parental anxiety. Perhaps, he suggests, Mr and Mrs Austen felt that 'it was injudicious to encourage further amateur theatricals at the rectory for fear that something similar . . . might be duplicated in their own family'.[13] The erotic excitement generated by theatre finally had its effect, however: Henry Austen became Eliza de Feuillide's second husband in 1797.

VISITS TO LONDON AND BATH

The young Jane Austen, during intermittent visits to England's first and second fashionable cities in 1796, 1797, and 1799, undoubtedly went to the theatre, and may well have seen the great Sarah Siddons and her brother John Philip Kemble, reigning stars of the London stage. Of the plays mentioned in *Mansfield Park*, Siddons appeared in *Douglas*, *The Gamester*, and *The Rivals* (these plays are discussed in chapter 2 below), as well as the standard Shakespearean repertoire. The only plays Austen is actually known to have seen in this period were in 1799 at Bath: Kotzebue's *The Birth-Day* (adapted by Thomas Dibdin) and Colman's *Blue Beard, or, Female Curiosity!* – a 'pleasing spectacle', which had had a successful new production in London in January 1798.[14] *Blue Beard* was lightweight stuff based on the fairy tale (I discuss it further in chapter 3); but *The Birth-Day* represented a new kind of theatre, the sentimental 'German drama' that was to be so complained of by moralists in the next twenty years. Margaret Kirkham has drawn attention to the similarities of plot and theme between this domestic comedy and *Emma*,[15] but despite the play's possible role in providing Austen with ideas for her novel, it never comes near the ironic complexities of that text. (The parallels between the two are further discussed in chapter 6 below.)

## THE BATH YEARS, 1801–1806

On the Revd George Austen's retirement, he and his wife and their two daughters settled in Bath – not, according to most biographies, with any great enthusiasm on Jane's part. The pleasures of the theatre, however, may have provided some consolation for the loss of a quiet country life. What might Jane Austen have seen at the lively and prestigious Bath theatre in those five years? Mrs Siddons, Kemble, G.F. Cooke, R.W. Elliston all made appearances there during these years; it is inconceivable that Austen would have missed a chance to see 'good hardened real acting' (*MP*, p. 124) from these stars.

The theatre in Orchard Street (built 1749) was licensed as a 'Theatre Royal' in 1767 – the first such licence in the provinces; it indicated a recognition that by mid-century Bath had grown to be the second most fashionable city in the kingdom. This royal patent 'free[d] the theatre from the stigma, however notional by this time, of illegality'.[16] That is to say, the theatre was entitled to present, without fear of prosecution, 'legitimate' or spoken-word drama (which in London was confined by law to Drury Lane, Covent Garden, and the summer-season Haymarket).[17] The Bath audience – largely consisting of visiting fashionable Londoners and country gentry – 'had long maintained the character of being the most elegant and judicious in the kingdom; and the "School" [for young actors], which gradually formed under their influence and the exertions of Mr. Palmer [the entrepreneurial manager] obtained the pre-eminence in the eyes of the Dramatic Tyro and the London critic'.[18] It was, in fact, the most important and successful playhouse outside London; between 1779 and 1817 it expanded its business profitably to the theatre in King Street, Bristol, transporting the company several times a week over the twelve miles that separated the two cities.

1  Interior of the Orchard Street Theatre, Bath

The capacity of the Orchard Street Theatre would have been about 900–1,000 people, in pit, boxes, first gallery, and upper gallery. The seating divisions mirrored class divisions in the audience: 'the wealthy and privileged occupying the boxes; the "bucks", "critics" and other men about town in the pit; citizens and their wives from the middle classes in the middle gallery . . . ; the lower classes, often noisy and uninhibited, in the upper gallery'.[19] As the only extant illustration of its interior shows (Figure 1), a full house was a crowded house: the auditorium was only 40 feet wide and about 45 feet deep. By 1805 it was clearly too small and awkwardly sited: its location was at the now less fashionable end of the town, opposite South Parade, and so close to the river as to be in constant danger of floods. The new Theatre Royal, nearly twice the size of the old one, was opened in October 1805 on the more central Beaufort Square.

Only nine letters have survived from Jane Austen's years in Bath (and several of them are solely to do with Mr Austen's death): not enough for us to make any inferences about how often Austen attended the Bath theatre. Mr Austen died in January 1805, which event would undoubtedly have limited the Austen ladies' theatre-going for the remainder of their stay in Bath. But that Austen was indeed familiar with the inside of the Orchard Street Theatre can be inferred from the detailed description in *Northanger Abbey*, chapter 12:

it was a play she wanted very much to see. . . . She was not deceived in her own expectation of pleasure: the comedy so well suspended her care, that no one observing her during the first four acts would have supposed she had any wretchedness about her. On the beginning of the fifth, however, the sudden view of Mr. Henry Tilney and his father joining a party in the opposite box recalled her to anxiety and distress. The stage could no longer excite genuine merriment, no longer keep her whole attention. Every other look upon an average was directed towards the opposite box; and for the space of two entire scenes did she thus watch Henry Tilney, without being once able to catch his eye. No longer could he be suspected of indifference for a play; his notice was never withdrawn from the stage during two whole scenes. At length, however, he did look towards her, and he bowed, but such a bow! No smile, no continued observance attended it: his eyes were immediately returned to their former direction. Catherine was restlessly miserable; she could almost have run round to the box in which he sat, and forced him to hear her explanation. (*NA*, p. 92)

In a theatre only 40 feet wide, Catherine and Henry are opposite each other at a distance of perhaps 32 feet. No wonder she feels snubbed.

We can make educated guesses about what Jane Austen is likely to have seen in her five years in Bath. Margaret Kirkham lists the Bath performances of the plays mentioned in *Mansfield Park*: all but *The Gamester*[20] were performed several times during 1801–6; notably *Lovers' Vows* (fifteen performances) and *The Heir at Law* (ten performances).[21] It is very likely that Austen saw these plays. Kirkham also cites performances of 'other plays of special interest to students of Austen' which were performed with some frequency in Bath: Cumberland's *The West Indian*, Thomas Dibdin's *Nelson's Glory* and *The Birth-Day*.[22] Apart from Shakespeare, the most popular playwrights in Bath were Cobb, Holcroft, Dibdin, and Morton; to whom we can add the German dramatist Kotzebue, whose works were represented in translation (*Lovers' Vows*, *The Stranger*, *Pizarro*, *The Birth-Day*).

What does this tell us about Jane Austen's theatrical experience? Broad farce, good-humoured or sentimental comedy, and the drama of sensation which was to mutate into melodrama make up the spectrum of popular theatre available in the early years of the nineteenth century. Shakespeare is represented largely by those plays which offer strong roles for male actors: *Hamlet*, *Macbeth*, *Othello*, *Richard III*, *The Merchant of Venice*. Shakespeare's comedies, which, with Restoration drama, to us seem the nearest ancestors of the witty banter of Elizabeth Bennet or Emma Woodhouse, were in the new century less commonly played. Hare's *Bath Calendar* lists only a small number of performances of *As You Like It*, *Much Ado about Nothing*, and *The Merry Wives of Windsor*. *Twelfth Night* and *A Midsummer Night's Dream* were not performed at all during the Austens' residence in Bath.[23] That Austen read all these plays is virtually certain: references can be found to them in the novels, juvenilia, and letters, and plays as domestic reading material were almost as popular as novels.[24] But that she saw theatrical embodiments of Rosalind, Beatrice, or Viola is less likely. Her condoling with Cassandra on her not seeing the most famous Shakespearean comedienne of her day, the forty-year-old Dora Jordan, suggests that she knew what her sister was missing (*Letters*, 8–9 January 1801). (Austen certainly saw Jordan late in her career, in 1814, in *The Devil to Pay* at Covent Garden.) In fact she is more likely to have encountered the witty young woman as stage heroine in the plays of Hannah Cowley, Elizabeth Inchbald, and Isaac Bickerstaff – plays which have largely disappeared from our map of eighteenth-century drama.

During a visit by Jane to her brother and his family at Godmersham, the Austen tradition of family theatricals was revived; and according to Fanny Austen's diary Jane Austen took part in these unrehearsed performances (presumably readings).[25] *The Spoilt Child* (Bickerstaff)[26] and *Innocence Rewarded* (untraced) were the plays. Austen was always a lively reader-aloud: on another occasion, remembered her niece Caroline, she took up 'a volume of Evelina and read a few pages of Mr. Smith and the Brangtons [sic] and I thought it was like a play. She had a very good *speaking* voice . . . '.[27] A Hampshire gentleman remembered being present at a 'Twelfth-day party where Jane Austen drew the character of Mrs. Candour [from *The School for Scandal*] and assumed the part with great spirit'.[28] It is reasonable to conclude from evidence such as this that Austen took pleasure in acting, in the dramatic embodiment of such characters as she herself created in her fiction and which she delighted to recognise in the fiction of her sister novelists.

### SOUTHAMPTON, 1807–1809

Jane Austen, her mother, her sister, and Martha Lloyd moved to a house in Castle Square, Southampton in early 1807. Claire Tomalin notes that when a family party came to visit the Austen ladies in September 1807 they 'went to the theatre to see John Bannister in *The Way to Keep Him*, Arthur Murphy's perennially popular satire on women who stop bothering to please their husbands after marriage'.[29] The theatre at Southampton (in French Street, not far from Castle Square) was smaller and less prestigious than Bath's Orchard Street Theatre;[30] it was mainly used by provincial companies, although Tucker indicates that 'the celebrated Mr. and Mrs. Charles Kemble played there for a few nights in August 1808'.[31] In a letter of 20 November 1808, Austen writes, '*Our* Brother [James, it is presumed] we may perhaps see in the course of a few days – & we mean to take the opportunity of his help, to go one night to the play. Martha ought to see the inside of the Theatre once while she lives in Southampton, & I think she will hardly wish to take a second veiw [sic].' The implication – borne out in the novels – that one needs a gentleman as escort and assistant on any venture to the theatre, suggests that Jane's theatre-going would certainly have been curtailed after the death of her father.

### THE CHAWTON YEARS, 1809–1817

Once she was settled at Chawton Cottage, Austen's only theatre-going would have been during visits to London. Her surviving letters indicate that she saw a wide range of contemporary theatre. In 1811 she saw

Bickerstaff's *The Hypocrite*, adapted from Molière's *Tartuffe*, which played
at the Lyceum. In 1813 she saw *Midas*, a burletta by Kane O'Hara,
and *The Clandestine Marriage* (Garrick and Colman), both at Covent
Garden; and again at the Lyceum *Don Juan*, a pantomime by Delpini,
and Beazley's *Five Hours at Brighton (The Boarding House)* (Austen's party
missed the first act of this two-act musical farce – 'none the worse' she
commented, *Letters*, 15–16 September 1813). They also saw *The Beehive*,
a musical farce by Millingen, 'rather less flat & trumpery', Austen remarked. In 1814 she saw the new acting sensation Edmund Kean in *The
Merchant of Venice* at Drury Lane; at Covent Garden there was *Isabella*
(Garrick's adaptation of Southerne's *The Fatal Marriage*), the farce *The
Devil to Pay* with Dora Jordan, Arne's opera *Artaxerxes*, and *The Farmer's
Wife*, a new musical by Charles Dibdin Jnr.

Austen's occasional comments on these theatre-going experiences in
her letters, written at the same time as she was working on her mature
novels, are of great interest. She clearly valued the spoken drama over
the lightweight burlettas[32] and musicals which were the most common
genre of entertainment. A night at the theatre, even one of the royal
patent houses (Covent Garden and Drury Lane) which had the sole right
to present 'legitimate'[33] drama, offered a pot-pourri, up to five hours
worth of entertainment. A German visitor wrote with some amazement:

Each evening two plays must be given, one in five acts and an afterpiece, often
also in two or three acts. Usually at the end some farce is played, on rare
occasions a short opera, often some absurdity based on one of the new English
novels, full of night and horror. No-one is concerned whether the afterpiece has
been chosen to be appropriate to the main play or contrasts with it so violently
[as to offend] any person of refined sensibility. It is enough that the spectator
gets value for his money.[34]

Of course there was no obligation to attend the entire evening; pre-
booked boxes were held only until the end of the first act of the mainpiece. After the third act everyone was let in at half-price, a custom
which, Johanna Schopenhauer said, was 'unpleasant for the better part
of society. With a great hubbub all the creatures of the night . . . swarm
in . . . the worst of company – of course in the prescribed dress – spreads
through the whole house. For this reason women never go to the theatre
without men to accompany them.'[35]

Austen had hoped to see the legendary Sarah Siddons, now in the
twilight of her career, as Constance in *King John* at Covent Garden in
April 1811, but was frustrated in her plans by inaccurate information

that Siddons had cancelled – 'I should particularly have liked seeing her in Constance, & could swear at her with little effort for disappointing me' (*Letters*, 25 April 1811).[36] Instead she and her brother Henry 'went to the Lyceum, & saw the Hypocrite, an old play taken from Moliere's *Tartuffe*, & were well entertained. Dowton & Mathews were the good actors. Mrs Edwin was the Heroine – and her performance is just what it used to be.'[37] Bickerstaff's *The Hypocrite* is a lively and well-constructed five-act comedy, which considerably reduces the element of farce found in Molière's *Tartuffe*, and increases the psychological and social complexity of the characters. It is notable particularly for a witty and unpredictable heroine, whose relation with her lover is reminiscent of that of Millamant to Mirabell in Congreve's *The Way of the World*. She is active in the plot to catch the hypocrite, and also has the play's last moralising speech, a commonsense denunciation of hypocrisy (while being careful not to decry 'true piety'). It is not hard to see why Austen would have enjoyed this.

## SPECTACLE AND THE ENLARGEMENT OF THE PATENT THEATRES, 1790–1800s

When Jane Austen went to the Covent Garden or Drury Lane theatres during visits to London in 1811–14 she would have had a materially different experience from her earlier visits to the theatre in Bath and Southampton. Both London patent theatres, enlarged radically in the 1790s (Figure 2), had been sumptuously rebuilt after fires: Covent Garden in 1809 (and further altered 1812–13), Drury Lane in 1812. Drury Lane's capacity after the rebuilding of 1794 was 3,611; this was slightly reduced, to around 2,800, after the 1809 fire. Covent Garden's rebuilding competed for a similarly huge audience.

In these remodellings the doors onto the forestage (the proscenium) were finally eliminated for dramatic use (they were used only for curtain calls). Actors performed further upstage, 'within the scene'. The loss of intimacy is testified by numerous observers of the period. Richard Cumberland, the dramatist, wrote in his 1806 memoirs:

Since the stages of Drury Lane and Covent Garden have been so enlarged in their dimensions as to be henceforward theatres for spectators rather than play-houses for hearers, it is hardly to be wondered at if their managers and directors encourage those representations, to which their structure is best adapted. The splendour of the scenes, the ingenuity of the machinist and the rich display of dresses, aided by the captivating charms of music, now in a great degree supersede the labours of the poet.[38]

2 Interior of Drury Lane Theatre after the rebuilding of 1794 (By permission of the V&A Picture Library)

Sir Walter Scott found 'the paltry-puppet show exhibition' of these spectacles ridiculous:

The persons of the performers are, in these huge circles, so much diminished, that nothing short of the mask and buskin could render them distinctly visible to the audience. Show and machinery have therefore usurped the place of tragic poetry; and the author is compelled to address himself to the eyes, not to the understanding or feelings of the spectator . . . we have enlarged our theatres, so as to destroy the effect of acting, without carrying to any perfection that of pantomime and dumb show.[39]

Austen's impatience with much London theatre – 'I beleive the Theatres are thought at a low ebb at present' (*Letters*, 25 September 1813) – may well have been the result of this market-driven fashion for extravagant spectacle. As Robert D. Hume comments, 'Given the difficulty of hearing dialogue clearly in such barns we cannot be surprised that ranting melodrama flourished while wit comedy languished.'[40] Elizabeth Inchbald, adapter of *Lovers' Vows*, prefaced her own domestic comedy *To Marry or Not to Marry* (1805),

The stage delights the eye far oftener than the ear. Various personages of the drama, however disunited, amuse the looker-on; whilst one little compact family presents a sameness to the view, like unity of place; and wearies the sight of a British auditor fully as much. Incidents, too, must be numerous, however unconnected, to please a London audience: they seem, of late, to expect a certain number, whether good or bad. Quality they are judges of – but quantity they *must have*.[41]

A not dissimilar development, though on a smaller scale, was seen in the new Theatre Royal which opened at Bath in October 1805, seven months before the Austens left Bath for Southampton. An opulently seated audience now gazed upon a picture-frame within which (as well as the older domestic comedies) the new spectacular drama of heightened passions and violent experiences was shown. By contrast, in the Orchard Street Theatre Royal, the audience would have been witness to performances which, because of the room-like structure of the forestage with its doors of entrance on either side and audience boxes above, had the appearance of representing artificially exaggerated but still recognisable behaviour of 'real people', sharing a space with the audience. Donald C. Mullin comments:

The forestage was within the enclosure of the auditorium, in the same room as the audience. The scenes and related special effects were outside the audience chamber. The proscenium, for lack of a better word, marked the boundary between the closely observable world of daily life on the forestage and the world of exoticisms, surprises, or flights of fancy in the scenic space.[42]

The Orchard Street Theatre did pride itself on scenic effects, as the illustration of its interior indicates (Figure 1) – and as its investment in the crowd-pleasers *The Castle Spectre* and *Blue Beard* testifies (see chapter 3). But the theatre was nevertheless small by the standards of the London patent houses – the distance from the 'front boxes' (behind the pit) to the stage was about 45 feet. Its forte was *intimacy*, not separation, between actor and audience; the effect was that theatre's artificiality could be acknowledged across the footlights, a shared pleasure in theatricality which implicated the audience, making them almost as much participants as consumers. The prologues and epilogues to eighteenth-century plays reinforced this collusive relation by means of a set of witty couplets in which a principal actor 'came forward' and reminded his audience of their necessity to the success of the performance. Frequently he or she would comment on contemporary fashionable behaviours, that is, on the audience's own involvement in theatricality.[43] Cowley's epilogue to *The Belle's Stratagem* (1780) offers a typical example of this familiar address:

> Nay, cease, and hear me – I am come to scold –
> Whence this night's plaudits, to a thought so old?
> To gain a Lover, hid behind a Mask!
> What's new in that? or where's the mighty task?
> For instance, now – what Lady Bab, or Grace,
> E'er won a Lover – in her *natural* Face?

The experience of theatre-going in the smaller eighteenth-century theatres thus had much in common with the dangerous domestic intimacy of home theatricals. In the extract from chapter 12 of *Northanger Abbey* quoted above, Henry Tilney, in the audience, is as much part of the spectacle for Catherine as the actors on stage. The auditorium was fully lit in this period, and the audience went almost as much to be seen as to see; to be gazed on and to gaze, equally at the stage and other members of the audience.[44] Interestingly enough, Austen commented on a visit to the unaltered and relatively small Lyceum[45] in 1813, where they sat in a stage box, 'One is infinitely less fatigued than in the common way' (*Letters*, 15–16 September 1813). This, I imagine, refers to the weariness that arises when one is in a constrained social situation where the rewards are too few to compensate for the lack of ease – as in the huge new theatres. On this evening, there was some interesting acting to be seen, and at close range: of this performance of Delpini's pantomime *Don Juan* – based on

Gluck's successful ballet of 1761, and using his music – Austen remarked, 'I must say that I have seen nobody on the stage who has been a more interesting Character than that compound of Cruelty & Lust' (*Letters*, 15–16 September 1813). This piece was described in playbills as 'A Tragic Pantomimical Entertainment';[46] it included songs and dancing, but virtually no spoken words – only a few in the climactic scene between Don Juan and the Ghost of the Commandant who comes to urge him to repent. In one of the published versions of the pantomime's scenario, Delpini remarks on the dramatic effectiveness of 'the Pantomime, or continued representation by means of dumb shew ... At the time the eye is delighted, the understanding is employed in those sentiments and that language which is wisely left for the spectator to supply.'[47] Austen had, in fact, just months earlier finished supplying language for her own version of the fascinating mythical figure of Don Juan, in the character of Henry Crawford. My guess is that she had not before encountered this powerful dramatic embodiment of the rebel against the Father's law, and she was struck by the coincidence between the Don and her own imaginative creation of the modern libertine. Henry Crawford (whose ancestry is more directly traceable to Richardson's Lovelace) is undoubtedly a 'compound of cruelty and lust', overlaid – as in the near-contemporary Mozart version[48] – with performative charm, civility, and sexual vitality.

By contrast, her visit to Covent Garden the following evening elicited these comments: 'the Clandestine Marriage was the most respectable of the performances, the rest were Sing-song and trumpery, but did very well for Lizzy & Marianne, who were indeed delighted; – but *I* wanted better acting. – There was no Actor worthy naming. – I beleive the Theatres are thought at a low ebb at present' (*Letters*, 25 September 1813). Garrick and Colman's *The Clandestine Marriage* (1766) is a mainpiece comedy, with an exasperatingly sentimental plot,[49] but a good cast of Fieldingesque supporting characters. Still, Austen wanted 'better acting'.

'ACTING SELDOM SATISFIES ME'

The best acting was provided at last in March 1814 when Austen saw Edmund Kean in what was to become one of his most famous roles, Shylock (Figure 3). He had made his London debut in this role just six weeks earlier. Even at Drury Lane, where they could only manage to get 'the 3d & 4th row' in a 'front box' (behind the pit) his genius and originality were evident: 'I cannot imagine better acting', said Austen, 'but the part was too short, & excepting him & Miss Smith, & *she* did not

MR. KEAN,

*in the character of Shylock*

*Engraved by H. Meyer, from a picture in ivory of the same size, painted from the life in March 1814, by W. H. Watts*

3  Edmund Kean as Shylock, 1814 (By permission of the V&A Picture Library)

quite answer my expectation, the parts were ill filled & the Play heavy' (*Letters*, 6 March 1814).

William Hazlitt reviewed 'Mr Kean's Shylock' at his first appearance at Drury Lane in January 1814:

For voice, eye, action, and expression, no actor has come out for many years at all equal to him . . . There was a lightness and vigour in his tread, a buoyancy and elasticity of spirit, a fire and animation . . . in giving effect to the conflict of passions arising out of the contrasts of situation, in varied vehemence of declamation, in keenness of sarcasm, in the rapidity of his transitions from one tone and feeling to another, in propriety and novelty of action, presenting a succession of striking pictures, and giving perpetually fresh shocks of delight and surprise, it would be difficult to single out a competitor.[50]

Revisiting the production a fortnight later, Hazlitt added to his encomium on Kean: 'His style of acting is, if we may use the expression, more significant, more pregnant with meaning, more varied and alive in every part, than any we have almost ever witnessed. The character never stands still; there is no vacant pause in the action; the eye is never silent . . . he reminds us of the descriptions of the "far-darting eye" of Garrick.'[51] Such was the rage for Kean that tickets had to be booked a fortnight ahead. 'I shall like to see Kean again excessively, & to see him with You too', Jane told Cassandra, who was expected in town – 'it appeared to me as if there were no fault in him anywhere; & in his scene with Tubal there was exquisite acting' (*Letters*, 6 March 1814).[52]

After Kean's performance, 'We were much too tired to stay for the whole of Illusion (Nourjahad) which has 3 acts; – there is a great deal of finery & dancing in it, but I think little merit.'[53] This oriental 'melo-dramatic spectacle' was a more typical Drury Lane offering; Austen was disappointed that Robert Elliston, whose work she had admired earlier in Bath, was performing in this piece, 'not at all calculated for his powers. There was nothing of the *best Elliston* about him. I might not have known him, but for his voice.' Elliston had begun his career in the Bath theatre, and was its star from 1793–1804 – years when Jane Austen undoubtedly saw him. Elliston was renowned for his good voice and lively manner, and was at his best in comedy, but as we have seen, that repertoire was no longer fashionable – indeed, barely playable, in the huge barns of spectacle that the London patent theatres had become.

Cassandra being Jane's chief correspondent, information about their activities is thin when they are together. We do not know if Austen saw

Kean again with Cassandra – though in the next letter she is inviting her to 'Prepare for a Play the very first evening, I rather think Covent Garden, to see [Charles] Young in Richard' (*Richard III*, presumably; *Letters*, 9 March 1814).[54] We do know that Austen went twice to Covent Garden before Cassandra's arrival, seeing Arne's opera *Artaxerxes* (popular since its premiere in 1762) on 7 March, and the Charles Dibdin burletta *The Farmer's Wife* the following night. Both starred the popular soprano Catherine Stephens:

her merit in singing is I dare say very great; that she gave *me* no pleasure is no reflection upon her, nor I hope upon myself, being what Nature made me on that article. All that I am sensible of in Miss S. is, a pleasing person & no skill in acting. (*Letters*, 9 March 1814)

Again we note the importance for Austen of 'skill in acting'. The ballad farce *The Devil to Pay*, on the same bill as *Artaxerxes*, amused Austen more, possibly because it featured Dora Jordan, now at the end of her career, but still able to shine in the comic role of the cobbler's wife (Figure 4).[55] Similarly, 'Mathews, Liston & Emery', three well-known comic actors in *The Farmer's Wife*, provided 'some amusement' in this new comic opera whose plot is driven by the Henry Crawford-like attempts of Sir Charles Courtly to seduce the virtuous Emma.

  Austen's last experience of professional theatre, as far as we know, was during a visit to London in November 1814. At Covent Garden she saw the celebrated new actress Eliza O'Neill (aged twenty-three), famed for her ability to draw the audience's tears in tragic parts. The play was *Isabella*, Garrick's revision (1757) of Southerne's *The Fatal Marriage*, in which the heroine eventually goes mad and stabs herself. It was one of Sarah Siddons's most famous roles (I discuss it in chapter 2), but as that queen of 'she-tragedies' had at last retired, Miss O'Neill was attempting to show herself worthy of the crown. For Austen,

I do not think she was quite equal to my expectation. I fancy I want something more than can be. Acting seldom satisfies me. I took two Pocket handkerchiefs, but had very little occasion for either. She is an elegant creature however & hugs Mr Younge delightfully. (*Letters*, 29 November 1814)

Posterity has agreed with this judgement of Eliza O'Neill; Hazlitt was commenting only eighteen months later, 'She whined and sang out her part in that querulous tone that has become unpleasant to us by ceaseless repetition . . . We half begin to suspect that she represents the bodies, not the souls of women, and that her *forte* is in tears, sighs, sobs, shrieks,

4 Dorothy Jordan as Nell in *The Devil to Pay*; frontispiece to Catherine E. Oxberry (ed.), *Oxberry's Dramatic Mirror*, London, 1828 (By permission of the British Library, 1508/1431)

and hysterics.'[56] Like Hazlitt, Austen clearly preferred 'good hardened real acting' (Edmund Bertram's phrase, *MP*, p. 124) – whether comic or tragic – of a standard that fully engages the audience's intelligence, emotional interest, and sympathy. Spectacle, cheap sentimentality, or the 'exotic and irrational entertainment' (as Dr Johnson called it) of opera, merely made her impatient.

Although it is scant, the biographical material here surveyed demonstrates that Austen had considerable opportunity to experience a range of contemporary theatre, and that on occasion she actively sought out the theatre experience. Arguably, this interest contributed to her sense of the theatricality of everyday life, especially as it was lived among the gentry. Much of Austen's social life took the form of rituals in theatricalised spaces: the ball or public assembly, the dinner-party, the morning or afternoon call, the after-dinner entertainment expected of young ladies; and church, where young women were for once not performers but admiring audience of the theatre of religious ceremony and exhortation. Performances of gender, class, and status are all unavoidable in these social situations, and Austen as the creator of fictions of contemporary social life found her analysis assisted by the techniques, style, and rich vein of metaphor provided by the theatre.

### THE PROBLEM OF THEATRICALITY

Notwithstanding this love of good theatre, 'theatrical' is always a pejorative term for Austen, an easy way of dismissing foolish affectation. In the juvenilia's 'A Collection of Letters',

'. . . on a sudden he interrupted me in the midst of something I was saying, by exclaiming in a most Theatrical tone –
Yes I'm in love I feel it now
And Henrietta Halton has undone me – ' (*MW*, p. 167)

In the unfinished but mature work *The Watsons*, Austen anticipates a theme that will recur in *Mansfield Park*. Mr Watson says of the clergyman hero Mr Howard,

'He reads extremely well, with great propriety & in a very impressive manner; & at the same time without any Theatrical grimace or violence. – I own, I do not like much action in the pulpit – I do not like the studied air & artificial inflexions of voice, which your very popular & most admired Preachers generally have . . . Mr. H. read like a scholar & a gentleman.' (*MW*, pp. 343–4)

However, in the completed novels Austen never uses the word 'theatrical' to describe a character's behaviour. This, I suggest, is because her sense of the pervasive theatricality of contemporary genteel society is so complex that she will spend much of each novel teasing out its implications. The easy dismissal provided by a pejorative label will not do.

In the epilogue to *The Belle's Stratagem*, Hannah Cowley claimed that contemporary society constituted a world of masks, even more theatrical than the theatre itself:

> . . . should I shew your features to each other,
> Not one amongst ye'd know his Friend, or Brother.
> 'Tis plain, then, all the world, from Youth to Age,
> Appear in Masks – Here, only, on the Stage,
> You see us as we are: *Here* trust your eyes;
> Our wish to please, admits of no disguise.

Stage actors, Cowley implies, are paradoxically more sincere than the audience which comes to watch them. The social world, the parade of gentry that Austen represents in her novels, operates with a particularly large set of obviously coded, that is, 'theatrical', behaviours, in dress, deportment, and etiquette. Like Cowley's epilogue-speaker, Austen looks *from* the stage of her public art *at* her society, the consumers of that art which mirrors themselves. If patriarchal society – such as that of eighteenth-century England – objectified women such that even the marriage-plot of the ('feminine') novel is a tool of oppression, then a woman who turns her own gaze back on this society is actively deconstructing the authority it claims to have.

Looking and gazing are always, of course, acts of the gendered body, that is, they are coloured by the historical and material conditions of their moment. As Elin Diamond pertinently asks of performances, 'what body is in view, what body is viewing?'[57] Within the novels, as the characters watch, note, and judge each other, they do so as part of a shifting and intersecting matrix of discourses. As Judith Butler argues, gender – the 'given' of the marriage plot – is always performative,

an identity instituted through a *stylized repetition of acts* . . . The acts by which gender is constituted bear similarities to performative acts within theatrical contexts . . . [The body] is a materiality that bears meaning . . . and the manner of this bearing is fundamentally dramatic. By dramatic I mean only that the body is not merely matter but a continual and incessant *materializing* of possibilities.[58]

By emphasising the *theatricality* of this apparently natural but compulsively repeated process, Austen is making her own contribution to the deconstruction of it. This, I believe, goes a long way towards explaining the characteristic irony of her narratorial persona. Consider, for instance, 'What did she say? – Just what she ought, of course. A lady always does' (*E*, p. 431); or, 'I purposely abstain from dates on this occasion, that every one may be at liberty to fix their own, aware that the cure of unconquerable passions, and the transfer of unchanging attachments, must vary much as to time in different people' (*MP*, p. 470). Austen's 'I' is a voice as conscious as that of the actress who usually spoke a play's epilogue: what she has been presenting for our entertainment (and perhaps edification) is a fable constrained by 'a culturally restricted corporeal space . . . enact[ing] interpretations within the confines of already existing directives'.[59] It is not too fanciful to consider Austen's formulation of '3 or 4 families in a country village' as 'the very thing' to work with (*Letters*, 9–18 September 1814), to be an intuitive grasp of this philosophical point – of particular relevance, as each of her novels demonstrates, to young marriageable women. The country village is particularly easy to read as a culturally restricted corporeal space, or stage, *theatrum mundi*; the three or four families provide, in fact, the average makeup of the cast of a comedy of the period.

If, then, we cannot escape our own theatricality, we must also recognise that the notion of a stable identity is a utopian fiction (in the simplest terms, it produces the one-note characters – villains and heroines – of melodrama; and the simple dénouements of its plots). Diamond points out that, even if we think of ourselves as 'audience',

we are continually taking in objects we desire, continually identifying with or imitating these objects, and *continually being transformed by them* . . . What this suggests is that the borders of identity, the wholeness and consistency of identity, is [sic] transgressed by every act of identification.
. . . The ego, this representative of reason and common sense, is a theatrical fiction, permeable, transformable, a precipitate of the subject's psychic history with others.[60]

In seeing that theatre stages the instability of identity – and reinforces it in the process of audience 'identification' – Diamond helps us to understand the symbiotic relation between Jane Austen's realistic novels about female identity, her deconstructive irony, and the rich and varied theatre of her day.

Theatre in England has always exhibited the lineaments of carnival; carnival itself is society at play – play which may be licensed, but is always in danger of transgression.[61] This danger is to be found in every one of Jane Austen's mature fictions (not to mention its riotous and uncontrolled presence in the juvenilia): Catherine Morland's grotesque Gothic imaginings; Marianne and Willoughby's indulgence in precipitate passion; the sexy and flirtatious presence of the militia in Meryton and Brighton (with the particularly carnivalesque episode of the girls dressing up one of the men in women's clothes); Mansfield Park's theatricals; the perpetual trickster Frank Churchill; Louisa's leap from the Cobb. These are all events in the novels which alert us to their interest in the theatricality of everyday life. In putting each novel into dialogue with specific examples of late eighteenth- and early nineteenth-century drama – Gothic theatre, comedy of manners, the drama of sensibility and melodrama – I attempt in the following chapters to highlight the ironic steadiness of Austen's gaze at her society.

# CHAPTER TWO

# Sense and Sensibility: *comic and tragic drama*

The title of Jane Austen's first published novel suggests the sort of duality, or antithesis, dear to the Augustan mind. Just such a duality was the basis of Oliver Goldsmith's anonymous essay published in 1773, 'An Essay on the Theatre; or, a Comparison between Laughing and Sentimental Comedy'. This short piece presents a broadside attack on the 'Weeping Sentimental Comedy, so much in fashion at present', by which Goldsmith means

[plays] in which the virtues of Private Life are exhibited, rather than the Vices exposed; and the Distresses, rather than the Faults of Mankind, make our interest in the piece . . . In these Plays almost all the Characters are good, and exceedingly generous; they are lavish enough of their *Tin* Money on the Stage, and though they want Humour, have abundance of Sentiment and Feeling.[1]

As with most binaries, this one serves an ideological purpose rather than representing the messiness of the real situation in contemporary drama. As Richard Bevis has shown in his extensive survey of eighteenth-century comedy,[2] most plays were 'mixed', adding in a fair proportion of 'low' comedy or satire of folly even when several principal characters are models of virtue. Goldsmith's own *She Stoops to Conquer*, which premiered a few months after the essay's publication, introduces knockabout farce and satire into its fable, but it cannot resist the fashionable cultural imperative, giving a prominent place to a sentimental couple, Constance and Hastings (I discuss this seminal play in more detail below).

The drama's contribution to the eighteenth-century debate about sensibility was extensive, beginning with the 'reform' of comedy instituted in response to the objections of such moralists as Jeremy Collier to the licentiousness of Restoration comedy (*A Short View of the Immorality, and Profaneness of the English Stage*, 1698). Richard Steele's *The Conscious Lovers* (1723) is the *locus classicus* of this new style of reformed comedy, in which poetic justice operates perfectly (the good are rewarded, the bad punished or reformed), and, perhaps more importantly, scenes of pathos and the utterance of high-flown sentiments by the hero and heroine are an expected element in the drama's affective power.[3] Steele's Preface defends his innovations on the grounds of audience approval of the experience:

any thing that has its Foundation in Happiness and Success, must be allow'd to be the Object of Comedy, and sure it must be an Improvement of it, to introduce a Joy too exquisite for Laughter, that can have no Spring but in Delight . . . To be apt to give way to the Impressions of Humanity is the Excellence of a right Disposition, and the natural Working of a well-turn'd Spirit.

Steele's play has all the elements of the mid-century's 'weeping comedy', as well as a remnant of robust humour in the less central characters. Indiana and Bevil Junior are a high-minded pair of unacknowledged lovers embroiled in plot complications which have Bevil willing to engage himself to Lucinda, in order to obey his father (Lucinda however loves Bevil's friend Myrtle); and Indiana, an apparent orphan, unwilling to spoil Bevil's chances of a rich marriage. In the end it emerges that Indiana is the long-lost daughter of Lucinda's father's first marriage, and all ends happily – duels averted by civilised explanation, fortunes spread evenly among all worthy recipients.

SIR JOHN BEVIL. Now, Ladies and Gentlemen, you have set the World a fair
    Example: your Happiness is owing to your Constancy and Merit: And the
    several Difficulties you have struggled with, evidently shew
        Whate'er the generous Mind it self denies,
        The secret Care of Providence supplies.

It is the sententiousness of such utterances, and the apparently bloodlessly correct behaviour of such characters, that come under attack in Goldsmith's essay and his subsequent dramatic practice. The plot of *She Stoops to Conquer* revolves around the figure of Charles Marlow, who suffers from crippling shyness when expected to make fashionable sentimental conversation with a young lady of his own class, but who can rattle on impudently with 'females of another class'.[4] Kate Hardcastle, a resourceful and witty young woman, pretends to be a serving-maid at an inn in order to captivate him. Goldsmith's anatomy of the repressive conventions of class is wickedly acute; and although the plot of his play contributed nothing to Austen's *Sense and Sensibility*, it is arguable that her self-conscious Edward Ferrars would have recognised himself in Marlow. Both complain of their education in establishments that kept them from acquaintance with the sophisticated manners of society; both are conscious of their social awkwardness. Marlow calls it, interestingly, 'The

Englishman's malady' and asks his more sophisticated friend Hastings, 'where could I have learned that assurance you talk of? My life has been chiefly spent in a college, or an inn [of court], in seclusion from that lovely part of the creation that chiefly teaches men confidence' (Act II).[5] Edward, echoing Marlow, says:

' . . . I never wish to offend, but I am so foolishly shy, that I often seem negligent, when I am only kept back by my natural aukwardness. I have frequently thought that I must have been intended by nature to be fond of low company, I am so little at my ease among strangers of gentility!' (*S&S*, p. 94)

'Low company' is not a phrase Austen generally uses, and Edward is probably here deliberately evoking Goldsmith's critique of snobbery in the popular comic figure of Tony Lumpkin.[6] It is a pleasing thought that the novel's tyrannical mother Mrs Ferrars might be construed by contemporary readers to be as foolish and ignorant as Goldsmith's country snob Mrs Hardcastle.

Richard Brinsley Sheridan continued the attack on sentimentality and sententiousness in *The School for Scandal* (1777) in the contrasted figures of Charles and Joseph Surface – the good-hearted ne'er-do-well and his hypocritical brother – and, in more complex fashion, in the sprawling comedy of manners *The Rivals* (1775). Jack Absolute's masquerade as the sentimental Ensign Beverly in order to woo the novel-addicted Lydia Languish is a critique of the hypocrisy that parades as the New Sensitive Masculinity, and it interestingly prefigures Austen's exploration of masculinity in *Sense and Sensibility*. If we read the eloquent but effete Willoughby as 'Beverly', and the frank and honest Colonel Brandon as 'Absolute', it fits to have them 'both' wooing the heroine of sensibility, and the plain soldier finally winning (Sheridan makes high comedy of the actor having to woo Lydia in both characters while her aunt Mrs Malaprop chaperones, Act III, scene iii).

In these comedies we also see two types of young femininity: the culturally correct young woman, dutiful and pious; and the witty, more earthy heroine descended from Restoration and Shakespearean comedy. In negotiating new positive models of womanhood, playwrights found this binary opposition dramatically useful – just as Austen was to do in *Sense and Sensibility*. In Goldsmith's *She Stoops to Conquer* Kate Hardcastle's vitality and wit are emphasised by the contrast with her friend Constance Neville. Constance is no dull prude – from their very first scene her wit matches Kate's, and in the course of the plot she shows enterprise and courage. But in the last act's complications, when the plan of eloping with

Hastings has been frustrated, she is deflated as a complex character, and she reverts to the dramatic stereotype suggested by her Christian name:

CONSTANCE. . . . My spirits are so sunk with the agitations I have suffered, that I am unable to face any new danger. Two or three years' patience will at last crown us with happiness.

HASTINGS. Such a tedious delay is worse than inconstancy. Let us fly, my charmer. Let us date our happiness from this very moment. Perish fortune. Love and content will increase what we possess beyond a monarch's revenue. Let me prevail.

CONSTANCE. No, Mr Hastings, no. Prudence once more comes to my relief, and I will obey its dictates. In the moment of passion, fortune may be despised, but it ever produces a lasting repentance. I'm resolved to apply to Mr Hardcastle's compassion and justice for redress.

(Act v)

In their brief utterances in the play's final scene, the pair continue in this sentimental vein. Kate Hardcastle's last speech, by contrast, embodies her earthy wit and the laughter that has characterised her throughout the play (anticipating Elizabeth Bennet's relationship with her lover):

KATE. In which of your characters, sir, will you give us leave to address you? As the faltering gentleman, with looks on the ground, that speaks just to be heard, and hates hypocrisy: or the loud, confident creature, that keeps it up with Mrs Mantrap, and old Miss Biddy Buckskin, till three in the morning; ha, ha, ha!

(Act v)

Unique as Kate is in her self-confidence and her willingness to play-act in order to get her man, she is basically as good and virtuous as her friend Constance. She is not punished for transgressing the codes of femininity; rather, she is rewarded for her enterprise with the man of her choice (who also happens to be her father's choice). There is no darkness in this comedy.

In Sheridan's *The Rivals* the two friends Lydia Languish and Julia Melville present similarly contrasted heroines. Lydia is energetic and witty but also a devotee of popular romantic novels, disappointed when her love life fails to equal them:

LYDIA. Why, is it not provoking; when I thought we were coming to the prettiest distress imaginable, to find myself made a mere Smithfield bargain of at last – There had I projected one of the most sentimental elopements! – so becoming a disguise! – so amiable a ladder of Ropes! – Conscious Moon – four horses – Scotch parson – with such surprise to Mrs Malaprop – and such paragraphs in the News-papers! – O, I shall die with disappointment.[7]

This scene in the play follows immediately on the powerful and entirely serious – not sentimental – scene in which the sensible and intelligent Julia breaks off with Faulkland on the grounds of his insulting refusal to trust in her love for him. She then has to listen, broken-hearted, to the frivolous fantasies of her cousin, who airily claims, 'whatever vexations you may have, I can assure you mine surpass them' (Act v). The emotional situation is similar to Elinor's throughout much of *Sense and Sensibility*. Edward Ferrars puts Elinor through the same kind of uncertainty and distress, and Marianne is oblivious to her sister's sufferings.[8] But in both novel and play, both young women are rewarded by the Muse of Comedy with their true loves in a world in which the threat of violence, even death, has been averted by good sense – the men's attempt to solve issues by duelling is frustrated (in Sheridan) or inconclusive (in Austen). The play's last speech is Julia's, uncharacteristically sententious but, despite its floweriness, redolent of good sense:

> while Hope pictures to us a flattering scene of future Bliss, let us deny its pencil those colours which are too bright to be lasting. – When Hearts deserving Happiness would unite their fortunes, Virtue would crown them with an unfading garland of modest, hurtless flowers; but ill-judging passion will force the gaudier Rose into the wreath, whose thorn offends them, when its Leaves are dropt!

Forty years later, Jane Austen and her spokeswoman Elinor are defended by a habit of irony from uttering such a florid curtain line, but it is surely the case that what is expressed here is the 'moral' of *Sense and Sensibility*, the resolutions of its final chapter. It is a pleasing coincidence that Elinor is the sister who draws and paints, thus providing an echo of Julia's metaphorical turn here. It is Marianne – much more dangerously than Lydia, addicted to the texts of sensibility – who has been tempted by the 'Rose' of passion and a budding sexuality, and who has suffered the prick of the 'thorn' left in her soul and marked on her body by her emotional involvement with Willoughby. Austen, that is to say, writes a more fragile and complex comedy (in the 'feeling' tradition instituted by Steele) than the stage could countenance. When Goldsmith concluded his critique of Sentimental Comedy with the withering comment that 'It is . . . the most easily written. Those abilities that can hammer out a Novel, are fully sufficient for the production of a Sentimental comedy',[9] he could not have guessed that within forty years the dominant literary form would be a transformed version of that despised and predominantly female art. And as I argue below, the female playwrights of the latter part of the century undoubtedly contributed to the novel's transformation and its triumph in the work of Jane Austen.

The Sentimental Comedy, as Goldsmith complained, in utilising 'a Pathetic Scene or two, with a sprinkling of tender melancholy Conversation through the whole', was claiming some of the affective ground hitherto only available to tragedy. But tragedy, according to classical rules (and as Goldsmith also points out), could only deal with 'the Calamities of the Great'; if the rising bourgeoisie were to find their emotional lives represented on the stage, it would be more credible in contemporary dress and speech. By 1815 Hazlitt was able to define 'Sentimental comedy' as 'the equivocal reflection of tragedy in common life'.[10] In Steele's *The Conscious Lovers*, the character of Indiana the orphan is modelled on the distressed heroines of Restoration tragedy, still popular throughout the eighteenth century. She is the passive victim of events; her only activity is the utterance and bodily performance of her distress (significantly, she finds herself affected by the opera *Griselda*, 'her forlorn Condition, her Poverty, her Solitude, her Resignation, her Innocent Slumbers', Act II). Action to relieve the situation is not an option in this model of femininity. The only difference between Indiana and the heroines of tragedy is that the former speaks in prose – though it is a flowery, 'literary' prose that momentarily removes the play into a rarefied sphere far from its contemporary setting. For example, from the climactic final scene:

INDIANA. If you say this from what you think of me, you wrong your self and him – Let not me, miserable tho' I may be, do injury to my benefactor – No, sir, my treatment ought rather to reconcile you to his virtues – If to bestow, without a prospect of return; if to delight in supporting, what might, perhaps, be thought an object of desire, with no other view than to be her guard against those who would not be so disinterested; if these actions, Sir, can in a careful parent's eye commend him to a daughter, give yours, Sir, give her to my honest, generous Bevil – What have I to do but sigh, and weep, to rave, run wild, a lunatick in chains, or hid in darkness, mutter in distracted starts, and broken accents, my strange, strange story!
. . . All my comfort must be to expostulate in madness, to relieve with frenzy my despair, and shrieking to demand of Fate, why – why was I born to such variety of sorrows?
. . . No – 'twas Heaven's high will, I should be such – to be plunder'd in my cradle! Toss'd on the seas! and even there, an infant captive! to lose my mother, hear but of my father – To be adopted! lose my adopter! then plung'd again in worse calamities!

(Act V)

The ellipses represent Sealand's attempts to stem this flow of pathetic expostulation, but Indiana, who elsewhere shows taste and good sense, is not to be stopped (she still has to exclaim upon the virtues of her rescuer, Bevil Junior) as the play approaches its sensational dénouement – which of course the audience has anticipated, since Sealand has helpfully provided his side of the story in Act 1. Father, daughter, and aunt are united at last in a pathetic tableau, to be embellished by lovers, friends, and almost every character except the comic servants (who have already demonstrated other, more earthy, means to pleasure).

Although it is difficult to take this sort of extravagant display of sensibility seriously in the cynical twenty-first century, it must be recognised as an important effort to redirect comedy away from the male-centred licentiousness of the Restoration and into the more 'feminine' territory of domestic life and feelings; in that way it begins the century's long march towards the triumph of the woman-centred novel. Further, the generically mixed nature of sentimental comedy prompts us to reconsider the equally popular and even more 'unrealistic' genre of tragedy. It is here, in fact, that we can locate the roots of much of the emotional power of *Sense and Sensibility*.

That Sarah Siddons was considered the greatest actress of the last quarter of the eighteenth century was largely due to her affective power in the performance of what were known as 'she-tragedies', plays in which – in contrast to the traditional but often tedious narratives of the falls of great men – the focus was on a woman caught in a situation not of her own making, the only exit from which was madness and/or death (Figure 5). Sir Joshua Reynolds famously painted Siddons as the Tragic Muse in 1784.[11] Lady Macbeth, one of Siddons's most famous roles, is of course the *locus classicus* of this genre. Hazlitt wrote of her sleepwalking scene (immortalised in numerous paintings and sketches), 'In coming on . . . her eyes were open, but the sense was shut. She was like a person bewildered, and unconscious of what she did. She moved her lips involuntarily; all her gestures were involuntary and mechanical.'[12] Siddons was equally admired in her lifetime for her Constance in *King John* (which Austen regretted missing – see above, p. 13). Of this bravura role Siddons wrote that she would listen offstage to the deal being arranged between King John and the King of France: 'The sickening sounds of that march [of celebration] would usually cause the bitter tears of rage, disappointment, betrayed confidence, baffled ambition, and, above all, the agonizing feelings of maternal affection to gush into my eyes.'[13] Another of Siddons's famous roles, Belvidera in Otway's *Venice Preserv'd*, ends with a

5 Sarah Siddons in Southerne's *Isabella, or The Fatal Marriage*

fine pseudo-Jacobean mad scene (with ghosts) and death for the heroine. Calista in Rowe's *The Fair Penitent* concludes with suicide following guilt over one night of passion with 'the gay Lothario'; interrupted by her husband in a subsequent scene with Lothario, she utters the immortal line, 'Distraction! Fury! Sorrow! Shame! and Death!' The last scene of Hannah More's *Percy* contains the stage direction, 'As Douglas goes to stab himself, enter Edwina [Siddons] distracted, her hair dishevell'd, Percy's Scarf in her hand.' After a Lady Macbeth-like scene of guilt, she dies on stage. Lady Randolph in Home's *Douglas*, distracted at the death of her long-lost child, throws herself off a cliff.[14]

G.J. Bell recorded Siddons's reaction to the famous speech in this play, 'My name is Norval' (remembered as a 'spouting piece' by Tom Bertram in *Mansfield Park*): 'The idea of her own child seems to have been growing, and at this point overwhelms her and fills her eyes with tears. Beautiful acting of this sweet feeling throughout these speeches.'[15] Of her first London appearance in *Isabella*, the *Public Advertiser* wrote ecstatically, 'the Look at the Child, when she gives her hand to Villeroy!, Her expressive Deportment at the banquet!, Her Fainting!, Her Death!'[16] The affective power of Siddons's 'Look' was clearly something unprecedented in English theatre. The young William Charles Macready, himself to become a great tragic actor of the next generation, partnered Siddons in the quintessential sentimental tragedy, Moore's *The Gamester* (considered, briefly, for production at Mansfield Park); he wrote of her performance:

The climax to her sorrows and sufferings was in the dungeon, when on her knees, holding her dying husband, he dropped lifeless from her arms. Her glaring eyes were fixed in stony blankness on his face; the powers of life seemed suspended in her; her sister and Lewson gently raised her, and slowly led her unresisting from the body, her gaze never for an instant averted from it; when they reached the prison door she stopped, as if awakened from a trance, uttered a shriek of agony that would have pierced the hardest heart, and, rushing from them, flung herself, as if for union in death, on the prostrate form before her.[17]

The published script of this 1753 play carries no stage directions indicating that this is how the last scene should be performed: it is all Siddons's invention, her embodiment of an extreme agony. This performance was in the season of 1811–12, the very period in which *Sense and Sensibility* was published; Siddons had been playing the role for thirty years, and had clearly defined it, as she had her other roles, for a generation.

Michael Booth concludes his study of Siddons with the comment,

Sarah Siddons was the first English stage performer to affect audience behaviour so powerfully, and by the nature and style of her characterisations of suffering women the first to reach out and arouse, in an almost uncontrollable outflow of feeling, the sympathetic emotions of the female part of her audience.[18]

All the evidence of contemporary response suggests that Siddons's triumphs as a tragic actress stemmed from the affective responses produced by her complete embodiment of these women – their suffering is not merely declaimed in blank verse but readable on her body. In fact the body is often more important as a signifier than the broken utterances which constitute the words given to the character (this is why Lady Macbeth's sleepwalking scene is so central to the genre): 'attitudes',[19] gestures, facial expressions, and gazes are commented on much more frequently at this time than at any other period of dramatic criticism.

An observation by the Romantic critic Leigh Hunt interpellates Mrs Siddons into the aesthetic of theatrical 'naturalness' – and indicates its potentially dangerous convergence of life and art:

If Mr Kemble studiously meditates a step or an attitude in the midst of passion, Mrs Siddons never thinks about either, and therefore is always natural because on occasions of great feeling it is the passions should influence the actions. Attitudes are not to be studied, as old Havard used to study them, between six looking glasses: feel the passion, and the action will follow . . .[20]

It is not hard to see Marianne Dashwood 'performing' her most profound life-experiences according to this Siddonian model. Arguably, Marianne's story is congruent with the expectations and atmosphere created by 'she-tragedy' – the true drama of sensibility – until at the last moment it is turned by her author towards the model of sentimental comedy.

MARIANNE DASHWOOD, TRAGEDIENNE

That Marianne is the heroine of her own drama is made clear early in the novel by her highly theatrical farewell to Norland – a more than faintly ridiculous performance in the real world:[21]

'Dear, dear Norland!' said Marianne, as she wandered alone before the house, on the last evening of their being there, 'when shall I cease to regret you! – when learn to feel a home elsewhere! – Oh! happy house, could you know what I suffer in now viewing you from this spot, from whence perhaps I may view you no more! – And you, ye well-known trees! – but you will continue the same. No leaf will decay because we are removed, nor any branch become motionless although we can observe you no longer! – No; you will continue the same; unconscious of the pleasure or the regret you occasion, and insensible of any change in those who walk under your shade! – But who will remain to enjoy you?' (*S&S*, p. 27)

Austen indulgently provides Marianne with a 'curtain' here – the end of a chapter – but alas, trees neither applaud nor pay hard cash; Marianne is her own, and only, audience.

She is determined, however, to cast other people in the drama of her life. Her complaints about Edward Ferrars's failings as a romantic ideal suggest that she is ready to fall in love with the first young man with thespian good looks that she meets: '[Edward] is not the kind of young man – there is something wanting – his figure is not striking; it has none of that grace . . . His eyes want all that spirit, that fire . . . ' (*S&S*, p. 17). With all the enthusiastic idealism of a teenager besotted with a rock star, she claims, 'I could not be happy with a man whose taste did not in every point coincide with my own. He must enter into all my feelings; the same books, the same music must charm us both.' In the real world this is a near impossibility; but a good *actor* of 'sensibility', as Willoughby will show himself to be, can pick up cues, and respond with immediate conviction.

The masculine ideal of mid-century sensibility was embodied in David Garrick: his revolution in acting style, called 'natural' at the time, was achieved *as a performance* – paradoxically (as Diderot wrote), without the actor's personal emotional involvement. Hannah More wrote of Garrick's Hamlet,

To the most eloquent expression of the eye, to the handwriting of the passions on his features, to a sensibility which tears to pieces the hearts of his auditors, to powers so unparalleled, he adds a judgment of the most exquisite accuracy, the fruit of long experience and close observation, by which he preserves every gradation and transition of the passions, keeping all under the control of a just dependence and natural consistency. So naturally, indeed, do the ideas of the poet seem to mix with his own, that he seemed himself to be engaged in a succession of affecting situations, not giving utterance to a speech, but to the instantaneous expression of his feelings, delivered in the most affecting tones of voice, and with gestures that belong only to nature.[22]

As William Worthen comments, 'The actor's performance becomes a model for social activity outside the theater . . . [it] epitomizes the process of polite social interaction.'[23] Marianne's complaint against Edward is ultimately that he is *not* a good actor: 'Oh! mama, how spiritless, how tame was Edward's manner in reading to us last night! . . . To hear those beautiful lines which have frequently almost driven me wild, pronounced with such impenetrable calmness, such dreadful indifference!' (*S&S*, pp. 17–18). There is something asexual about Edward Ferrars – unassertive and under his mother's thumb, he is the wooed rather than the wooer (as indeed is his foppish brother Robert); he does not play the role of masculine lover as the charismatic Willoughby effortlessly does – for as long as that role is financially rewarding. Only at the end of the novel will Marianne sorrowfully realise the inherent illusiveness of this social dynamic: 'if I could be satisfied on one point, if I could be allowed to think that he was not *always* acting a part, not *always* deceiving me . . .' (*S&S*, p. 344).

When Willoughby arrives so opportunely and romantically to rescue Marianne, he of course fills the demands of her imagination for a 'star'[24] so that soon 'she had no eyes for any one else. Every thing he did, was right. Every thing he said, was clever' (*S&S*, p. 54). Their indulgence in the pleasures of elegant taste – 'They read, they talked, they sang together; his musical talents were considerable; and he read with all the sensibility and spirit which Edward had unfortunately wanted' (*S&S*, p. 48) – confirms her fantasy. In singing together, they are like a pair of lovers in an opera; in reading together, they are re-enacting a primal scene of erotic sensibility – Paolo and Francesca, or, closer to current fashions, Werther and Charlotte reading Ossian.[25] In *Love and Friendship* Laura complains, in a comic anticipation of Marianne's strictures on Edward, 'They said he was Sensible, well-informed, and Agreable; we did not pretend to Judge of such trifles, but as we were convinced he had no soul, that he had never read the Sorrows of Werter, & that his Hair bore not the slightest resemblance to Auburn, we were certain that Janetta could feel no affection for him, or at least that she ought to feel none' (*MW*, p. 93).[26]

It is undoubtedly significant that before Willoughby's inexplicable desertion of Marianne they had been reading *Hamlet* together. It is difficult to resist the inference that the page was left open at Hamlet's 'Get thee to a nunnery' scene with Ophelia. Marianne's teenage fantasy of romantic love has got out of hand, and by the end of chapter 16 she has become a fully-fledged tragic heroine; her behaviour from this point until chapter 43 follows the trajectory of the deserted and distressed woman of eighteenth-century tragedy. Just as Marianne's 'fall' is literally enacted through her body (her twisted ankle, Willoughby's masterful carrying of her in his arms), so her tragic status after his departure is written on her body. She becomes noticeably less articulate, but at the same time an easily readable image of the suffering woman. Austen's stage directions are precise:

> They saw nothing of Marianne till dinner time, when she entered the room and took her place at the table without saying a word. Her eyes were red and swollen; and it seemed as if her tears were even then restrained with difficulty. She avoided the looks of them all, could neither eat nor speak, and after some time, on her mother's silently pressing her hand with tender compassion, her small degree of fortitude was quite overcome, she burst into tears and left the room. (*S&S*, p. 82)

In fact Marianne slips into this role with ease, as though she has been waiting all her young life to play it. Her unconscious methods here echo those of Sarah Siddons, in a kind of thespian economy:

> She played over every favourite song that she had been used to play to Willoughby, every air in which their voices had been oftenest joined, and sat at the instrument gazing on every line of music that he had written out for her, till her heart was so heavy that no further sadness could be *gained;* and this *nourishment* of grief was every day *applied* . . . In books too, as well as in music, she *courted the misery* which a contrast between the past and the present was certain of giving. (*S&S*, p. 83; my emphases)

She indulges in 'solitary walks and silent meditations' to which the reader, like her family, is spectator (we are not taken inside her mind, as we might be by another novelist), and must try to interpret the meaning. ' "Why do you not ask Marianne at once," said [Elinor], "whether she is, or is not engaged to Willoughby?" ' (*S&S*, p. 84). Her mother's 'romantic delicacy' considers such a question unaskable: essentially, she is recognising the taboo which forbids the audience's interruption of the actor's performance.

Marianne's public rejection by Willoughby at the grand London evening party is another highly theatrical scene, but one over which Marianne now has no control; he is the better actor. Attempting to gain Willoughby's notice, 'she started up, and pronouncing his name in a tone of affection, held out her hand to him' (*S&S*, p. 176). Again the directions for the actors in Austen's drama are precise: Willoughby tries 'to avoid her eye, . . . determined not to observe her *attitude*' (my emphasis), and speaks only to Elinor. Marianne's frantic speeches then are as extreme (and indecorous) as those reported of Rowe's Calista:[27]

'Good God! Willoughby, what is the meaning of this? Have you not received my letters? Will you not shake hands with me?'

He could not then avoid it, but her touch seemed painful to him, and he held her hand only for a moment. During all this time he was evidently struggling for composure. Elinor watched his countenance and saw its expression becoming more tranquil.

Lothario-like, he is cool, insulting:

'I did myself the honour of calling in Berkeley-street last Tuesday, and very much regretted that I was not fortunate enough to find yourselves and Mrs. Jennings at home. My card was not lost, I hope.'

Marianne's response expresses the 'wildest anxiety':

'But have you not received my notes? . . . Here is some mistake I am sure – some dreadful mistake. What can be the meaning of it? Tell me, Willoughby; for heaven's sake tell me, what is the matter?'

Although Willoughby displays some 'embarrassment' he is far more in control of the situation than she is; he turns away 'with a slight bow' and rejoins his current object of courtship. The narrative continues to focus on Marianne's Siddons-like embodiment of extreme and indecorous distress: 'Marianne, now looking dreadfully white, and unable to stand, sunk into her chair, and Elinor, expecting every moment to see her faint, tried to screen her from the observation of others, while reviving her with lavendar water' (*S&S*, pp. 176–7). Elinor is conscious that what has hitherto been a private drama has become public – the large and splendid London party is to all intents a theatre, in which Willoughby has been acting the gay Lothario while Marianne appears as the seduced and abandoned Calista. Momentarily drawn in as the tragic heroine's confidante, Elinor attempts to 'screen' her from the public gaze.

Although after this big scene the drama returns to the private and domestic stage, it is no less intensely readable in Marianne's bodily attitudes. The morning after, Elinor wakes to see 'Marianne, only half-dressed, . . . kneeling against one of the window-seats . . . and writing as fast as a continual flow of tears would permit her' (*S&S*, p. 180). Austen's text positions Marianne obsessively in the bedroom, as though unable to drag herself away from the barren bed and its failed promise of bliss:

on opening the door, [Elinor] saw Marianne stretched on the bed, almost choked by grief, one letter in her hand, and two or three others lying by her. (*S&S*, p. 182)

Marianne, seated at the foot of the bed, with her head leaning against one of its posts, again took up Willoughby's letter . . . (*S&S*, p. 190) no attitude could give her ease; and in restless pain of mind and body she moved from one posture to another, till growing more and more hysterical, her sister could with difficulty keep her on the bed at all . . . (*S&S*, p. 191)

Austen's imagination is working theatrically here; she is writing directions for a character's movement on a small, claustrophobic stage; she forces us, like Elinor, to watch an embodied performance of physical and mental agony.

The visit to Cleveland enables Marianne once again to indulge herself in private performances on a fine picturesque set:

from its Grecian temple, her eye . . . could fondly rest on the farthest ridge of hills on the horizon, and fancy that from their summit Combe Magna might be seen. In such moments of precious, of invaluable misery, she rejoiced in tears of agony to be at Cleveland . . . (*S&S*, pp. 302–3)

But the fifth-act climax of Marianne's dramatic trajectory is yet to come. Her illness threatens her with death, as we expect of a tragedy heroine. Elinor, Colonel Brandon, Mrs Jennings, the doctor – principal onlookers – all expect it. Marianne does not die, but she does have a scene of 'distraction', however brief:

Marianne, suddenly awakened by some accidental noise in the house, started hastily up, and with feverish wildness, cried out –
'Is mamma coming? –'
'Not yet,' replied the other, concealing her terror, and assisting Marianne to lie down again, 'but she will be here, I hope, before it is long. It is a great way, you know, from hence to Barton.'
'But she must not go round by London,' cried Marianne, in the same hurried manner, 'I shall never see her, if she goes by London.'
Elinor perceived with alarm that she was not quite herself . . . (*S&S*, pp. 310–11)

Marianne recovers; Austen chooses to remain within the genre of comedy: her ironic view of her society would not have allowed her to venture any further down the path of 'she-tragedy'. She was only too aware of its potential absurdities: witness the deaths and runnings-mad, the exclamations and faintings of many hilarious pages of the juvenilia – *Love and Friendship* most famously perhaps, which here anticipates, but in a very different tone, the situation of Elinor and Marianne at Cleveland:

Her disorder turned to a galloping Consumption & in a few Days carried her off. Amidst all my lamentations for her (& violent you may suppose they were) I yet received some consolation in the reflection of my having paid every attention to her, that could be offered, in her illness. I had wept over her every Day – had bathed her sweet face with my tears & had pressed her fair Hands continually in mine –. 'My beloved Laura (said she to me a few Hours before she died) take warning from my unhappy End & avoid the imprudent conduct which has occasioned it . . . beware of fainting-fits . . . Though at the time they may be refreshing & Agreable yet beleive me they will in the end, if too often repeated & at improper seasons, prove destructive to your Constitution . . . My fate will teach you this . . . I die a Martyr to my greif for the loss of Augustus . . . One fatal swoon has cost me my Life . . . Beware of swoons Dear Laura . . . A frenzy fit is not one quarter so pernicious; it is an exercise to the Body & if not too violent, is I dare say conducive to Health in its consequences – Run mad as often as you chuse; but do not faint –'[28] (*MW*, p. 102)

By the mid-eighteenth century the novel and the sentimental drama were feeding on each other. Marianne's story in many ways echoes Richardson's monumental novel *Clarissa* (1749), though Austen's novel is briefer, funnier, and ultimately happier. And as Margaret Anne Doody and Jocelyn Harris have pointed out at length, Richardson thought of his novel as a *drama*.[29] In both *Clarissa* and *Sense and Sensibility*, the heroine's suffering is written on her body and expressed through it, in the same way that the late eighteenth-century aesthetic of acting was embodied in the tragedy performances of Sarah Siddons. Marianne's story, however, ultimately conforms to the model of sentimental comedy. She suffers, survives, reforms, is rewarded. She has one last scene in the novel before she is silenced by comedy's conventional closure. It is the perfect performance of a repentant heroine (though not tragedy's Fair Penitent, who is obliged to die):

'There, exactly there' – pointing with one hand, 'on that projecting mound, – there I fell; and there I first saw Willoughby.'
Her voice sunk with the word, but presently reviving she added,
'I am thankful to find that I can look with so little pain on the spot! – shall we ever talk on that subject, Elinor?' – hesitatingly it was said. – 'Or will it be wrong? – I *can* talk of it now, I hope, as I ought to do.' (*S&S*, p. 344)

There follows in due course a long self-reflective speech in which Marianne draws the moral of her experience. Amidst all the good sense and deep feeling which Austen gives Marianne here, there is nevertheless a vein of theatricality in her utterance, which allows the reader a modicum of ironic detachment (Marianne is still, after all, only seventeen):

'. . . I cannot express my own abhorrence of myself. – Whenever I looked towards the past, I saw some duty neglected, or some failing indulged. Every body seemed injured by me . . . I shall now live solely for my family. You, my mother, and Margaret, must henceforth be all the world to me; you will share my affections entirely between you. From you, from my home, I shall never again have the smallest incitement to move; and if I do mix in other society it will be only to shew that my spirit is humbled, my heart amended, and that I can practise the civilities, the lesser duties of life, with gentleness, and forbearance . . .' (*S&S*, p. 346)

### ELINOR, THE HEROINE OF A MODERN COMEDY

Elinor's story also has its dramatic models, though in a less affecting form than contemporary tragedy. In comedy too the closeness between drama and the novel had continued to develop, and not just in terms of the broad 'humours' comedy that Henry Fielding, playwright-turned-novelist, employed. Richard Brinsley Sheridan's mother, Frances Sheridan, was a novelist and playwright, successful in her day (and admired by Hannah More, who said of the son's work, 'I love him for the sake of his amiable and ingenious mother'[30]). Her final (unfinished) play, *A Journey to Bath*, created the prototypes of her son's Mrs Malaprop and Mrs Candour. More interesting for our purposes, however, is her successful play *The Discovery* (1763): despite its uses of a conventional comic topos – the discovery of a long-lost daughter, which makes all the right marriages possible – it is most remarkable for its crisp, clear, naturalistic dialogue and the psychological complexity of its characters and their relationships. In short, the play has novelistic qualities. Rather than depending on strongly farcical, satirical, or sentimental characters and scenes, it proceeds with considerable subtlety. Two unhappy marriages are saved through a little intrigue, the good sense of the two women concerned, and their determination to talk things through with their husbands. (The epilogue, written to be spoken by Hannah Pritchard, the first actress of Lady Medway, includes the ironical complaint, 'the character will seem so flat, / Give *me* threats, tears, hysterics, and all that'.) The young lovers, Colonel Medway and Clara Richly, are each enmeshed in family situations which cause considerable stress: the Colonel is pressured by his father to marry Clara's much richer sister and thus save the family from bankruptcy – dutifully, but with genuine protests, he agrees. Clara is disliked and bullied by her sister for no particular reason except that she is quiet and unfashionable. The scene in which the lovers accidentally meet, expecting to give each other up, is moving and emotionally realistic – despite the rhetoric of sensibility which it utilises – because we have already encountered the characters' psychological complexity:

COLONEL MEDWAY. Oh Clara, why did I give you up? what have I got to compensate for your loss?

MISS RICHLY. Your virtue! the consciousness of having acted right – You have broke no oaths, no promises to me; nay, I have often told you I would never be your's but with your father's consent; for sunk as I am in fortune, I would not meanly creep into a family that rejected me. And for this reason, I would neither give, nor receive a vow; but left you at full liberty to make a better choice, when your duty or your interest should urge you.

COLONEL MEDWAY. That last word, madam, carries a reproach in it, which I cannot bear from you.

MISS RICHLY. Do not mistake me, Sir; I have not the least suspicion, that interest has the smallest share in this action – I wish it had – for then perhaps I should part with you with less reluctance, than now I own I have power to do – but we must not touch upon this string – My sister loves you, and I hope will make you happy.

After a few more speeches in this vein – speeches which do not require actors to attitudinise, for spoken with the utmost sobriety of gesture and utterance they would still be heart-rending – Clara exits with the line, 'I am going to quit her house directly, and this, sir, for my own, for my sister's, and for your sake, is the last time we must ever meet – forget me, sir, and try – I conjure you try to be happy –.'[31]

This exchange anticipates the tension of the scenes between Elinor and Edward when it seems that Edward must marry Lucy Steele; it is not unlikely that Austen, a keen reader of plays, was aware and indeed appreciative of Mrs Sheridan's work. There is a prototype of Miss Bates in her second play, *The Dupe* [1763], the circumstantially talkative Mrs Friendly: though *The Dupe* was not successful on stage it sold well as a 'closet' (i.e. reading) comedy. Certainly Austen would have agreed with the self-defence of Mrs Sheridan's prologue to *The Discovery*, which anticipates *Northanger Abbey*'s praise, in chapter 5, of the work of 'sister novelists':

> . . . Our humble scenes no charms of art can boast,
> But simple nature, and plain sense at most:
> Perhaps some character – a moral too –
> And what is stranger still – the story's new:
> No borrow'd thoughts throughout the piece are shewn,
> But what our author writes is all her own.
>     By no sly hint, or incident she tries
> To bid on modest cheeks the blush arise:
> The loosest thoughts our decent scenes suggest,
> Virtue herself might harbour in her breast;
> And where our harmless satire vents its spleen,
> The soberest prude may laugh, without a skreen.

But not to mirth alone we claim your ear,
Some tender scenes demand the melting tear;
The comic dame, her different powers to prove,
Gives you the dear variety you love;
Sometimes assumes her graver sister's art,
Borrows her form, and tries to touch the heart.[32]

In *Sense and Sensibility* Austen follows this model to the letter. Her comic scenes are 'harmless satire' of the silliness of much of fashionable society. Robert Ferrars is just such a pompous fop, revealing his foolishness in his speeches, as is Sir Anthony Branville (Garrick's role) in *The Discovery*. And where 'straight' sentimental comedies never venture beyond the clichés of courtship in depicting adult relationships, both Frances Sheridan and her son (in *The School for Scandal*'s Teazles) depict dysfunctional marriages, where husband and wife either snipe at each other or wilfully misunderstand each other. Similarly *Sense and Sensibility*'s chapter 20 works as a staged set-piece introducing the Palmers' marital relationship, a situation of contempt on his side and Pollyannaish prattle on hers:

'. . . My love,' applying to her husband, 'don't you long to have the Miss Dashwoods come to Cleveland?'

'Certainly,' – he replied with a sneer – 'I came into Devonshire with no other view.'

'There now' – said his lady, 'you see Mr. Palmer expects you; so you cannot refuse to come.' (*S&S*, p. 113)

Frances Sheridan writes scenes between women that go beyond the amusing scenes in Goldsmith or Sheridan which display the charms of the company's ingénues; hers are moments in which women jockey for power – subtly competing for a lover, or for economic and social control. *The Discovery*'s Mrs Knightly and Miss Richly are an example. Mrs Knightly (Clara's elder sister) interrupts a tête-à-tête between Clara Richly and Colonel Medway. After some minutes of carefully double-edged chat, with attempts at gallantry by the Colonel, these lines occur:

MRS KNIGHTLY. You see, Colonel, the mysterious speech you have made has the fate of all oracles, to be interpreted different ways, and, perhaps, none of them right – Nay, I am inclined to think it bears a still nearer resemblance to them, and that you, like the priests of old, delivered what you said without any inspiraton of a god.

COLONEL MEDWAY. There, Madam, your comparison fails, for I assure you I am at this instance under the influence of a very powerful one.

MRS KNIGHTLY. I vow I don't believe you; do you, Clara?

MISS RICHLY. I never had any reason to doubt the Colonel's veracity, sister.

MRS KNIGHTLY. What, then, you think he is really in love?

MISS RICHLY. Didn't you hear him acknowledge it?

COLONEL MEDWAY. Nay, madam, if you won't take *my* word for it, I can't see what reason you have to believe any one's else.

MRS KNIGHTLY. Why no, that's true – But where a matter of faith doesn't concern one's self, infidelity, you know, can be of no great consequence one way or another.

. . .

MISS RICHLY. Very true, sister; but scepticism is a dangerous, as well as an uneasy state, in *some* cases.

MRS KNIGHTLY. And a state of *security*, Miss Clara, the casuists in *love*, as well as religion, are agreed, is not always the safest. But I don't know how we fell upon this odd topic.

MISS RICHLY. Nor I, I am sure.[33]

After some lines more of this, Colonel Medway understandably takes the opportunity to leave ('I see by your pursuing this subject, that you have a design of getting my secret out of me') – as Edward Ferrars was to do in a not dissimilar situation.

In Austen's version of the tensions underlying polite chat in drawing-rooms, Lucy Steele comes to triumph over Elinor ('My dear friend, I come to talk to you of my happiness. Could any thing be so flattering as Mrs. Ferrars's way of treating me yesterday? . . . ', etc. (*S&S*, pp. 238–9)), only to have their tête-à-tête interrupted by the arrival of Edward himself. Edward is painfully embarrassed; Lucy sits 'with a demure and settled air, . . . determined to make no contribution to the comfort of others'; and Elinor desperately makes the polite small-talk that a 'normal' occasion demands: 'almost every thing that *was* said, proceeded from Elinor, who was obliged to volunteer all the information about her mother's health, their coming to town, &c. which Edward ought to have enquired about, but never did' (*S&S*, p. 241). Further embarrassment is produced by the rapturous and naive entrance of Marianne, who claims Edward as a close member of the family – implicitly Elinor's lover – and Austen rounds off the scene by having Edward leave in great discomfort. 'Lucy, who would have outstaid him had his visit lasted two hours, soon afterwards went away' also, leaving first the two sisters, then Elinor alone and perplexed. There is a strong impression as the chapter closes that we have been watching a scene in a drawing-room drama, complete with significant exits and entrances – that is, that Austen's imagination is working dramatically.

The scenes in which Colonel Brandon commissions Elinor to offer Edward a living on his behalf (chapters 39 and 40) form another delicately patterned sequence of the comedy and tension of social life. Brandon's and Elinor's conversation is overheard and misunderstood by Mrs Jennings – so keen is she to get them engaged to each other – which leads to a classic scene of dialogue at cross-purposes between Elinor and Mrs Jennings. This is contrasted with the painful scene in which Elinor has to convey the offer to Edward – a virtual elegy to their unspoken love. It concludes with the narrator's 'direction' of the two actors' contrasted performances:

> Elinor did not offer to detain him; and they parted, with a very earnest assurance on *her* side of her unceasing good wishes for his happiness in every change of situation that might befall him; on *his*, with rather an attempt to return the same good will, than the power of expressing it. (*S&S*, p. 290)

What is notable about this passage, and others between Elinor and Edward, is the narrative emphasis on what is said – or repressed – that is, on speech, that medium of polite intercourse, rather than on the less controllable behaviour of the body such as we have seen in Marianne's story. Elinor, we might say, even under stress is the articulate heroine of comedies such as those written by Frances Sheridan and Hannah Cowley; she resists the role of the tragedienne. A radical change is effected, however, in the novel's last few chapters. The catalyst is the extraordinary scene in which Willoughby arrives at Cleveland – a coup de théâtre – to tell his side of the story and assert his continuing love for Marianne. This is an encounter which has to my knowledge no parallel in contemporary drama, yet it is intensely dramatic.[34]

It begins with precise stage directions:

> Elinor, starting back with a look of horror at the sight of him, obeyed the first impulse of her heart in turning instantly to quit the room, and her hand was already on the lock, when its action was suspended by his hastily advancing, and saying, in a voice rather of command than supplication,
> 'Miss Dashwood, for half an hour – for ten minutes – I entreat you to stay.' (*S&S*, p. 317)

After their first brief exchange, 'she walked silently towards the table, and sat down. He took the opposite chair, and for half a minute not a word was said by either.' Willoughby is 'sitting in an *attitude* of deep meditation' (my emphasis) and appears not to hear Elinor's invitation to begin explaining himself. In a moment, as he begins to speak disconnectedly, he rises up and 'walk[s] across the room'; and as his confession – a performance of self-justification not at all contradictory of his self-indulgent character – develops circumstantial details, Elinor responds not only with words but with her own physical expression: she 'turn[s] her eyes on him with the most angry contempt' (*S&S*, p. 320); she 'colour[s]' (p. 322) in response to his eloquent blush. While her 'heart' is 'softened' towards Willoughby in the course of his recital, she attempts to override this evidence of the affective qualities of his performance by speaking from her rational and moral centre. But it is not easy, in the face of such a masterly and intimate performance:

> 'You are very wrong, Mr. Willoughby, very blameable', said Elinor, while her voice, in spite of herself, betrayed her compassionate emotion; 'you ought not to speak in this way, either of Mrs. Willoughby or my sister . . .' (*S&S*, p. 329)

When Willoughby finally declares, 'Now you know all', there is a silent pause from both participants. Elinor, to whose thoughts we are privy, reflects on Willoughby's spiritual state in the gravest language of eighteenth-century moralism; of what is going on in Willoughby's head we know nothing, but it becomes clear that he wants a satisfying end to the scene, with appropriate focus on its star, himself:

> From a reverie of this kind she was recalled at the end of some minutes by Willoughby, who, rousing himself from a reverie at least equally painful, started up in preparation for going, and said:
>     'There is no use in staying here; I must be off.'
>     'Are you going back to town?'
>     'No – to Combe Magna. I have business there; from thence to town in a day or two. Good bye.'
>     He held out his hand. She could not refuse to give him her's; – he pressed it with affection.
>     'And you *do* think something better of me than you did?' said he, letting it fall, and leaning against the mantelpiece, as if forgetting he was to go. (*S&S*, p. 281)

The apparently careless attitude here is a display of the actor's sexual charisma: the carefully rationed physical contact, then the elegant pose for his audience's appreciative gaze – how could anyone want him to leave? Having gained the assurance that his audience – Elinor and the fascinated reader – has been won over by his performance (she 'assured him . . . that she forgave, pitied, wished him well – was even interested in his happiness'), Willoughby can make an exit as dramatic as his entrance:

> ' . . . But I will not stay to rob myself of all your compassionate good-will by showing that where I have most injured I can least forgive. Good bye, – God bless you!'
>     And with these words, he almost ran out of the room. (*S&S*, p. 332)

Superbly dramatic as this chapter is, what is even more interesting is its role in repositioning Elinor as the centre of the novel's metadrama; not as yet another variation on the dramaturgic cliché of the suffering woman (which Marianne's story conforms to), but as a woman who both thinks and feels, who is capable of both vocal and bodily expression.[35] Willoughby's undoubted physical charisma has in a sense drawn Elinor back into her body, that aspect of herself that she has so consciously repressed since losing the hope of fulfilment of her desire for Edward.

> Willoughby – he whom only half-an-hour ago she had abhorred as the most worthless of men – Willoughby, in spite of all his faults, excited a degree of commiseration for the sufferings produced by them, which made her think of him as now separated for ever from her family with a tenderness, a regret, rather in proportion, as she soon acknowledged within herself – to his wishes than to his merits. She felt that his influence over her mind was heightened by circumstances which ought not in reason to have weight; by that person of uncommon attraction, that open, affectionate, and lively manner which it was no merit to possess; and by that still ardent love for Marianne, which it was not even innocent to indulge. But she felt that it was so, long, long before she could feel his influence less. (*S&S*, p. 333)

When Elinor hears the supposed news of Edward's marriage, Austen shows us her reaction by a variation of the trope that has previously defined her. Elinor has been the maker of static and framed drawings (in contrast to her sister's interest in dynamic arts such as music and drama). But any artistic production can be perturbed by the emotional state of a body and mind that will not be repressed:

> In Edward, – she knew not what she saw, nor what she wished to see; – happy or unhappy – nothing pleased her; – she turned away her head from every sketch of him. (*S&S*, pp. 357–8)

Edward's arrival in this same chapter – less melodramatic, but equally unexpected – forces both protagonists into being unconscious performers in a drama not of 'sensibility', with its repertoire of attitudes, but of the 'nature' that the greatest actors of the eighteenth century devoted their art to simulating on stage. Austen builds a tense scene that demonstrates the interdependence of the body and the emotional life: the white and stammering lover, the awful silences, the trivial chat that hides an unbearable suspense:

> Not a syllable passed aloud. They all waited in silence for the appearance of their visitor. His footsteps were heard along the gravel path; in a moment he was in the passage, and in another he was before them.

His countenance, as he entered the room, was not too happy, even for Elinor. His complexion was white with agitation, and he looked as if fearful of his reception and conscious that he merited no kind one. Mrs. Dashwood, however, conforming, as she trusted, to the wishes of that daughter by whom she then meant, in the warmth of her heart, to be guided in everything, met him with a look of forced complacency, gave him her hand, and wished him joy.

He coloured, and stammered out an unintelligible reply. Elinor's lips had moved with her mother's and when the moment of action was over, she wished that she had shaken hands with him too. But it was then too late, and with a countenance meaning to be open, she sat down again and talked of the weather.

Marianne had retreated as much as possible out of sight to conceal her distress; and Margaret, understanding some part, but not the whole, of the case, thought it incumbent on her to be dignified, and therefore took a seat as far from him as she could, and maintained a strict silence.

When Elinor had ceased to rejoice in the dryness of the season, a very awful pause took place. It was put an end to by Mrs. Dashwood, who felt obliged to hope that he had left Mrs. Ferrars very well. In a hurried manner he replied in the affirmative.

Another pause. (*S&S*, p. 359)

As the information finally emerges from the embarrassed Edward that it is his brother who is married, his unconscious action is the sort of physicalisation that a modern Method actor would be pleased to come upon:

He rose from his seat and walked to the window, apparently from not knowing what to do; took up a pair of scissars that lay there, and while spoiling both them and their sheath by cutting the latter to pieces as he spoke, said, in an hurried voice,

'Perhaps you do not know – you may not have heard that my brother is lately married to – to the youngest – to Miss Lucy Steele.' (*S&S*, p. 360)

We 'see' Edward's action as a sign of his total failure of gentlemanly decorum, destroying the ladies' delicate instrument; we might also register as we watch this scene in our mind's eye that he is cutting through the sheath of convention that has bound both himself and Elinor. Certainly the combination of words and action has a liberating effect on Elinor:

Elinor could sit it no longer. She almost ran out of the room, and as soon as the door was closed, burst into tears of joy, which at first she thought would never cease. Edward, who had till then looked anywhere rather than at her, saw her hurry away, and perhaps saw – or even heard, her emotion . . . (*S&S*, p. 360)

This exit from the stage is the most violent physical movement Elinor performs in the course of the novel. As a vital expression of the body's energies, it is akin to Marianne's running down the hill at Barton, but it is accompanied by no equivalent fall, since all we have read and watched of Elinor's story up to this point justifies this final outburst of feeling. She has lived her family and social life watchfully and dutifully, and suffered inwardly. This moment of physicalisation is not the careless first cause of a series of life events, but literally their dénouement, their unknotting. It comes at the right moment in the novel's drama to provide great audience satisfaction. The rest of the novel is simply mopping-up – unnecessary on stage, vital if the novel as Austen conceives it is to retain its cool ironic frame.

One of Elinor's more engaging characteristics is that she shares her author's penchant for irony – for example, to the gushing Marianne, 'It is not every one who has your passion for dead leaves' (*S&S*, p. 88). In this style Elinor is congruent with the witty heroines of Frances Sheridan, or of Hannah Cowley and Elizabeth Inchbald in later generations. As a participant member of a theatrical society, Elinor throughout the novel has had to perform the social roles required of her. It is she who is unfailingly polite to the variously unattractive Middletons, Mrs Jennings, Fanny and John Dashwood, Mrs Ferrars, and the Steele sisters, while Marianne refuses, as such 'hypocritical' behaviour doesn't fit her notion of her role as the heroine of sensibility. At a crucial moment this diplomacy enables Elinor to find out what she desperately needs to know from Lucy Steele regarding her engagement to Edward (chapters 23 and 24). She acts with superb ironic control in a situation drawn from the comedic model, rather than imitating her sister's tendency to play in her own solo tragedy. And her conscious performance here gives her both the power and the knowledge that she desires:

Lady Middleton proposed a rubber of casino to the others. No one made any objection but Marianne, who, with her usual inattention to the forms of general civility, exclaimed, 'Your ladyship will have the goodness to excuse me – you know I detest cards. I shall go to the pianoforte; I have not touched it since it was tuned.' And without further ceremony, she turned away and walked to the instrument.

Lady Middleton looked as if she thanked heaven that *she* had never made so rude a speech.

'Marianne can never keep long from that instrument, you know, ma'am,' said Elinor, endeavouring to smooth away the offence; 'and I do not much wonder at it, for it is the very best-toned pianoforte I ever heard.'

The remaining five were now to draw their cards.

'Perhaps,' continued Elinor, 'if I should happen to cut out, I may be of some use to Miss Lucy Steele, in rolling her papers for her; and there is so much still to be done to the basket, that it must be impossible, I think, for her labour singly, to finish it this evening. I should like the work exceedingly, if she would allow me a share in it.'

...In a firm, though cautious, tone Elinor thus began:

'I should be undeserving of the confidence you have honoured me with, if I felt no desire for its continuance, or no further curiosity on its subject. I will not apologise therefore for bringing it forward again.'

'Thank you,' cried Lucy warmly, 'for breaking the ice; you have set my heart at ease by it; for I was somehow or other afraid I had offended you by what I told you that Monday.'

'Offended me! How could you suppose so? Believe me,' and Elinor spoke it with the truest sincerity, 'nothing could be farther from my intention than to give you such an idea. Could you have a motive for the trust that was not honourable and flattering to me?' (*S&S*, pp. 144–6)

As the heroine of such scenes of social comedy, Elinor displays all the requisite alertness, wit, and intelligence. As the passionately fond sister and the silently broken-hearted lover, she and her author take the novel beyond sensibility and into a kind of female interior drama that the stage of the early nineteenth century had no place for. Hannah Cowley prefaced her last play, *The Town Before You* (1795) with this complaint:

The following is rather the Comedy which the Public have chosen it to be, than the Comedy which I intended...The patient developement of character, the repeated touches which colour it up to Nature, and swell it into identity and existence (and which gave celebrity to Congreve), we have now no relish for. The combinations of interest, the strokes which are meant to reach the heart, we are equally incapable of tasting. Laugh! Laugh! Laugh! is the demand. Not a word must be uttered that looks like instruction, or a sentence which ought to be remembered.

From a Stage, in such a state, it is time to withdraw, but I call on my younger contemporaries, I invoke the rising generation, to *correct* a taste which, to be gratified, demands neither genius or intellect, – which asks only a happy knack at inventing TRICK, I adjure them to restore to the Drama SENSE, OBSERVATION, WIT, LESSON! and to teach our Writers to respect their own talents.

In appealing for 'ELEGANCE and FEELING' to take their place on the national stage – a stage which, as I pointed out in chapter 1, was growing ever more distant from its increasingly huge audience – Cowley might have been anticipating that subtle and intimate comedy of the novel of which Jane Austen was to become the foremost practitioner. But, as we shall see in chapter 3, the male dominance of the public stage – theatrical, political, pedagogical, cultural – was not going to disappear.

# CHAPTER THREE

# Northanger Abbey: *Catherine's adventures in the Gothic theatre*

To the prodigious applause with which this piece was received, if we add its *hysterical effects* on several ladies, it must be considered as a *chef d'oeuvre* in its way. Nothing, at one period of the play, was to be heard but hysterical affections in the boxes, nothing to be seen but delicate ladies crying and fainting, and nothing to be smelt but *hartshorn* and *thieves vinegar*; with which articles it would not be amiss if the orange women were to provide themselves, and dispense them to the ladies on reasonable terms with their fruit and play-bills at all future representations of *The Castle Spectre*.

*Bath Chronicle*, 26 April 1798

The period of Jane Austen's adult life coincided with the heyday of the Gothic drama,[1] a style of play and theatrical presentation which used exotic and spectacular locations to extend the effects produced by the emotionally extreme situations of the theatre of sensibility. For the Georgian theatregoer, Paul Ranger writes, 'the successful gothic drama was one which theatrically exploited locations, dialogue and spectacle. There was little that was new in the incidents of the plot . . . Locations, however, set the emotional tone of the piece.'[2] By 1797, 'Monk' Lewis's *The Castle Spectre*, set in a vaguely medieval time and place, verged on being a self-conscious parody of every element characteristic of Gothic drama, thus guaranteed to produce the response of hysterics in minds 'craving to be frightened' (*NA*, p. 200). It promised 'dungeons damp, Drear forests, ruin'd aisles, and haunted towers' for settings; 'Lightning and Thunder, Flames, Daggers and Rage'[3] for effects. And, of course, the Spectre – of which more below.

The Bath Theatre Royal in Orchard Street did not (being small, probably could not) depend upon scenic spectacle to attract an audience: the records for the years 1799–1805 indicate that the majority of its offerings were the standard eighteenth-century comedies, tragedies, and farces.[4] *The Castle Spectre* and *Blue Beard* were its two staple 'Gothic' pieces. We know that Austen saw the latter piece (on Saturday 22 June 1799), and it is not unlikely that she saw the former, a classic of its kind, which played regularly at the theatre during the time she lived in Bath.

Ranger's study, *'Terror and Pity reign in every Breast'* takes its title from a 1757 journal article on contemporary theatre, but by Jane Austen's day sophisticated audiences responded as much to the entertainment as to the affective value of such pieces, whose extreme situations were easy targets for burlesque. In the same year as *The Castle Spectre* was bringing on hysterical fits in the more susceptible Bath ladies, the Gothic extravaganza *Blue Beard, or, Female Curiosity!* premiered in London. This was a musical oriental extravaganza starring Michael Kelly, a friend of Mozart, as its singing hero,[5] and featuring as much spectacle as possible, including cut-out elephants in later revivals. Intended principally to amuse and produce admiration rather than hysterics, this show played knowingly with one of the principal Gothic tropes, 'female curiosity' – particularly in the Blue Chamber scene:

> exhibit[ing] various tombs, in a sepulchral building; – in the midst of which ghastly and supernatural forms are seen; – some in motion, some fix'd – In the centre is a large Skeleton seated on a tomb, (with a Dart in his hand) and over his head, in characters of Blood is written: '*THE PUNISHMENT OF CURIOSITY*'.
>
> (stage direction, Act I, scene iii)

The climax of *Blue Beard* both reflects and comments on the fashion for Gothic sensationalism: *this* is what could happen to such young women as the indomitably curious heroines of Radcliffe's novels.[6] It is exactly this quality of heroineship, of course, that Austen is affectionately guying in *Northanger Abbey*.

Gothic drama was a home-grown entertainment, stemming from two sources: the development of theatres which specialised in scenic effects, and the great success of the Gothic novel in England. Just as today successful novels are made into films with all possible speed, so the popular novels of Ann Radcliffe and Matthew 'Monk' Lewis were seized upon by the hack writers whose business it was to keep the theatres supplied with new crowd-pullers. In March 1794 *Fontainville Forest*, James Boaden's adaptation of Ann Radcliffe's Gothic novel, *The Romance of the Forest* (1791), had its premiere performances at the Theatre Royal Covent Garden. Boaden was a young lawyer with theatrical pretensions; in due course, he was to become the authoritative biographer of such greats of the Georgian theatre as John Philip Kemble and

Sarah Siddons.[7] But at this stage in his career (he was twenty-eight), Boaden was seizing the opportunity to ride to fame on the back of a far more talented woman novelist, the leading writer of English Gothic novels. Ann Radcliffe was in a league well above that represented by the list of 'horrid' novels supplied by Isabella Thorpe (via her friend Miss Andrews) to the ingénue Catherine Morland (*NA*, p. 40), but her evocation of the Burkean sublime in the landscapes of mountains, forests, castles, ruined abbeys, caves, and tunnels, in which her heroines underwent their adventures, most powerfully defined the genre's characteristic trappings.

Of Radcliffe's four Gothic novels, only the sprawling *Mysteries of Udolpho* seems not to have been adapted for the stage. After the success of *Fontainville Forest*, Boaden also adapted Radcliffe's *The Italian* as *The Italian Monk* (1797);[8] and the most horrid of them all, Matthew Lewis's *The Monk*, as *Aurelio and Miranda* (1798). Henry Siddons, son of the great Sarah, followed hard on the success of *Fontainville Forest* by adapting Radcliffe's *The Sicilian Romance* for the Covent Garden stage in May 1794. The latter text – a three-act 'opera' (though in fact it only contains half a dozen songs) – bears a minimal relation to Radcliffe's novel, but it does feature an incarcerated wife in a suitably gloomy cave. What Radcliffe thought of the simplification of her complex psychological texts is unrecorded, but the fact of their adaptation by male writers in search of commercial theatre successes invites us to consider the gendered relations between author, genre, and public during this period (an issue that Austen herself was strongly aware of, as her defence of the novel in chapter 5 of *Northanger Abbey* shows). As I will argue in the following comparison between Radcliffe's novel *The Romance of the Forest* and Boaden's dramatic adaptation *Fontainville Forest*, the theatricality of Gothic itself is gendered, assigned a different function and value according to whether it valorises a male or a female perspective. And Austen's commentary on this social dynamic in *Northanger Abbey* is acute.

ADAPTING RADCLIFFE

Austen wrote the first version of *Northanger Abbey* in the 1790s, during the period of most of the 'crossovers' between Gothic novel and Gothic drama. Austen, critics argue, parodied Radcliffe, and the 'horrid' novels of which she was the most accomplished creator, in order to show that 'the anxieties of common life' (*NA*, p. 201) could provide just as entertaining and more instructive reading. Boaden's aim was distinctly different – not parody, but adaptation of Radcliffe's novel into overtly theatrical form. Boaden's own story of this undertaking, told from the perspective of thirty years later, is revealing:

Mr. Boaden had read the Romance of the Forest with great pleasure, and thought that he saw there the ground-work of a drama of more than usual effect. He admired, as every one else did, the singular address by which Mrs. Radcliffe contrived to impress the mind with all the terrors of the ideal world; and the sportive resolution of all that had excited terror into very common natural appearances; indebted for their false aspect to circumstances, and the overstrained feelings of the characters.

But, even in romance, it may be doubtful, whether there be not something *ungenerous* in thus playing upon poor timid human nature, and agonizing it with false terrors . . . Perhaps, when the attention is once secured and the reason yielded, the passion for the marvellous had better remain unchecked; and an interest selected from the olden time be entirely subjected to its gothic machinery. However this may be in respect of romance, when the doubtful of the narrative is to be exhibited in the *drama*, the decision is a matter of necessity. While *description* only fixes the inconclusive dreams of the fancy, she may partake the dubious character of her inspirer; but the pen of the dramatic poet must turn everything into shape, and bestow on these 'airy nothings a local habitation and a name.'9

Determined, thus, to introduce on the stage a 'real' Phantom, Boaden experimented with the most effective way of presenting such a figure, given that the most famous dramatic ghost, that of Hamlet's father, regularly produced incredulity with its 'heavy, bulky, creaking substantiality'.10 Finally he decided on a tall thin figure seen behind a bluish-grey gauze scrim; the sepulchral voice of another actor in the wings uttered the spectre's few lines. This was quite consciously theatre of affect: the Phantom, dressed in

a dark blue grey stuff, made in the shape of armour, and sitting close to the person . . . the breathless silence, while he floated along like a shadow, – proved to me, that I had achieved the great desideratum; and the often-renewed plaudits, when the curtain fell, told me that the audience had enjoyed
'That sacred terror, that severe delight,'
for which alone it is excusable to overpass the ordinary limits of nature.11

As this passage shows, Boaden was fully aware of the manipulation of the audience's or reader's emotions which is basic to the effectiveness of the Gothic. He was also conscious of the difference between the phenomenological experience of the reader and that of the theatre audience. In a note to the printed text of *Fontainville Forest*,12 he remarks that he has retained 'passages expunged in the performance' (for reasons of dramatic pace), as 'The Stage and the Closet are very different mediums for our observance of effects.' This is an acute comment which bears also on the relation between novel and drama. The *situation* of reading is different from that of the audience in the theatre: the one private, closeted, almost indeed self-imprisoned in a masochistic place of pleasurable terror, the theatre of the mind (Henry Tilney expresses this well: 'The Mysteries of Udolpho when I had once begun it, I could not lay down again; – I remember finishing it in two days – my hair standing on end the whole time' (*NA*, p. 106)); the other public, communal, with a much clearer division between the audience and the performers – bodies like ourselves, not imagined, but seen, and somehow safe because of theatre's generic guarantee of a satisfying dénouement (even if in the process it does occasionally produce hysterics in enthusiastic ladies).

Evidence of this intuition of the safety of the theatre-experience comes in Boaden's prologue. 'The moderns', he claims, 'Demand intrigue, and banquet on surprize' – sensation is a right and an uncomplicated pleasure. There is one possible complication, however:

> Caught from the Gothic treasure of Romance,
> [Our Author] frames his work, and lays the scene in France.
> The word, I see, alarms . . .

In 1794, France at the height of the Terror was in reality a very alarming prospect, a genuinely 'horrid' phenomenon of the modern world:

> Deprav'd by cruelty, by pride inflam'd,
> By traitors madden'd, and by sophists sham'd . . .

Boaden goes on to conclude, however, that no such terrifying prospect blights the lucky world of the British audience, and that consequently there is no need for the stage to act as propaganda vehicle – or to do anything other than entertain a complacent audience:

> Britons, to you, by temperate freedom crown'd,
> For every manly sentiment renown'd,
> The Stage can have no motive to enforce
> The principles, that guide your glorious course;
> Proceed triumphant – 'mid the world's applause,
> Firm to your King, your Altars, and your Laws.[13]

Despite the theatrical bombast, there is a parallel here with Henry Tilney's somewhat more complex formulation of the distinctly ungothic qualities of modern British life:

'. . . What have you been judging from? Remember the country and the age in which we live. Remember that we are English, that we are Christians. Consult your own understanding, your own sense of the probable, your own observation of what is passing around you – Does our education prepare us for such atrocities? Do our laws connive at them? Could they be perpetrated without being known, in a country like this, where social and literary intercourse is on such a footing; where every man is surrounded by a neighbourhood of voluntary spies, and where roads and newspapers lay every thing open? . . .' (*NA*, pp. 197–8)

The point is that Austen, like Boaden, is writing in a period of constant threat from the anarchic country across the Channel; *Northanger Abbey* is based in a valorisation of Englishness (for all its pettiness and gossip) just as firmly as *Emma* is.[14] For English (Protestant) Christians the enemy is always foreign and Catholic. Radcliffe herself reinforces this model deliberately by having Adeline find refuge in the home of a Swiss Protestant pastor, and by giving her a taste for English literature which anticipates Henry Tilney's incorporation of 'literary intercourse' into the national system of surveillance:

> She had become a tolerable proficient in English while at the convent where she received her education, and the instruction of La Luc, who was well acquainted wth the language, now served to perfect her. He was partial to the English; he admired their character, and the constitution of their laws, and his library contained a collection of their best authors, particularly of their philosophers and poets . . . her taste soon taught her to distinguish the superiority of the English from that of the French. . . . She frequently took a volume of Shakespear or Milton . . .[15]

– a rather avant-garde taste for a dweller in the Swiss Alps in the middle of the seventeenth century! Boaden, however, omits the Savoy section of the story and the Protestant La Luc family with whom Adeline finds secure refuge. He sets his version of Radcliffe's story in the pre-Reformation period, 'the beginning of the Fifteenth Century': distant, exotic, and unproblematically Catholic for an English audience of the late eighteenth century.

Other alterations that Boaden makes to Radcliffe's text in the interests of dramatic simplicity (almost, indeed, of classical dramatic unity) include the restriction of the action to Fontainville Abbey and its environs – so that the heroine Adeline is deprived of one of her most attractive characteristics, the ability to travel intrepidly, often after a daring escape from the evil Marquis or his henchmen. Further, the object of her affections is not the sensitive (and Protestant) Theodore La Luc, who along with the rest of his family doesn't appear, but the scion of the humble La Motte family, young Louis, who in the original novel after pining for Adeline ends up with 'a lady of some fortune at Geneva'.[16] He it is who in true sentimental heroic style rescues both his beloved and his mother at the play's fifth-act climax:

> *Enter* LOUIS.
> LOUIS. Hold off your hands, you servile Ministers,
> Or my quick rage shall trample you to earth.
> MARQUIS. Audacious stripling! . . . (etc.)

In the second act of the play, Louis arrives at the Abbey and finds his parents in hiding; in his second scene – things move quickly on stage – he declares his love for the newly met Adeline (who at least has enough Radcliffean good sense to beg him not to speak of it at this inappropriate juncture). As soon as he leaves the stage Adeline begins a soliloquy:

> The night is rough, and through these shatter'd casements,
> The wind in shrilling blasts sweeps the old hangings.
> Whether the place alone puts such thoughts in me,
> I know not; but asleep, or waking, still
> Conviction haunts me, that some mystery
> Is wrapt within these chambers, which my fate
> Will have me penetrate. – The falling gust
> With feeble tone expires like dying sighs –
> The tap'stry yonder shakes, as tho' some door
> Open'd behind it [*takes her lamp*] Ha! 'tis so; the bolt,
> Tho' rusty, yields unto my hand; I'll see
> To what it leads. – How, if I sink with fear?
> And so benumb'd, life freeze away in horror?
> No matter, powerful impulse drives me onward,
> And my soul rises to the coming terror.
>
> (Act II, scene iv)

The scene 'changes to a melancholy Apartment. The Windows beyond reach, and grated. – An old Canopy in the distance, with a torn Set of Hanging-Tapestry.' Adeline, entering, treads on a rusty dagger ('Yes, murder has been busy!' she concludes, Catherine-like), then intrepidly touches the tapestry, which falls down to reveal the mysterious paper ('What scroll thus meets me in the falling lumber?'). Picking it up, she hastily exits before her light is extinguished – this is, after all, a theatre and the audience must be able to *see* her horrid experiences.

In the next scene, the following morning, Mme La Motte's arrival in her room delays her reading of the document. Here Boaden appropriates one of the most original of Radcliffe's devices – the proto-Freudian dreams that Adeline has at the end of volume I, in which her unconscious mind supplies her with quasi-supernatural images of her murdered father and a mysterious figure in black who leads her to him. 'Think no more of them', says Mme La Motte, no psychotherapist, but a motherly figure not unlike Mrs Morland: 'such illusions . . . do usurp the pow'rs, that make life happy, / And thickly cloud the sunshine of the mind' – advice that might well have been given to Catherine Morland, except that her dreams are waking fantasies, and require the sterner correction of a clergyman.

When Boaden's Adeline does finally read the rolled-up manuscript discovered in the 'Secret Apartment', her reading of its dreadful tale is interrupted by the famous 'Phantom': at first just a voice 'heard within the chamber'; then 'faintly visible', calling 'O, Adeline!'; then, climactically, to end the Act:

> ADELINE. Great God of mercy! could there none be found
>   To aid thee? Then he perish'd –
> PHANTOM. Perish'd here.
> ADELINE. My sense does not deceive me! awful sounds!
>   'Twas here he fell!
> *The phantom here glides across the dark part of the Chamber,*
> *Adeline shrieks, and falls back. The Scene closes upon her.*

In Radcliffe's novel, of course, this moment of horror is firmly contained within the heroine's disturbed consciousness – its objective cause is revealed to be Peter the servant who has been trying secretly to attract her attention. Radcliffe, that is to say, no more believes in the 'reality' of the supernatural than does Austen. But in Boaden's theatre of affect, 'illusion' must be shared by the audience: the Phantom is even named in the cast list (Mr Follet); and no doubt the star actress Mrs Pope prided herself on a fine shrieking faint.

Austen and Radcliffe share an interest in the situation of the vulnerable young woman, and her perception of the dangers that threaten her; while Austen ironises this naive habit of mind, Radcliffe empathises with it and finally allows relief from anxiety through rational explanation. These are women-centred novels written by women. But in the Gothic drama of the last decade of the eighteenth century (mostly written by men), 'sensation' is expected and reason is discounted. The Gothic theatre, in fact, operates as a public institution to provide strictly rationed relief from the repressive strictures of Enlightenment models of behaviour. As Boaden remarks, 'Perhaps, when the attention is once secured *and the reason yielded*, the passion for the marvellous had better remain unchecked.'[17]

Not only does the audience see the Phantom which causes Adeline's dramatic faint, it is treated also, from this point onwards in the play, to soliloquies of passion, guilt, and self-recrimination by the villainous Marquis, played by the leading 'heavy' actor of the company. As Act IV begins, the Marquis is discovered alone on stage, accompanied by all the technical effects available to the late eighteenth-century theatre:

> *Violent Thunder and Light'ning, the Abbey rocks, and through the distant Windows one of the Turrets is seen to fall, struck by the Light'ning.*
>
> *Enter the Marquis, wild and dishevell'd.*

> MARQUIS. Away! Pursue me not! Thou Phantom, hence!
>   For while thy form thus haunts me, all my powers
>   Are wither'd as the parchment by the flame,
>   And my joints frail as nerveless infancy.
>
>                                   [*Light'ning.*]
>
>   See, he unclasps his mangled breast, and points
>   The deadly dagger. – O, in pity strike
>   Deep in my heart, and search thy expiation;
>   Have mercy, mercy! [*falls upon his knee.*] Gone! 'tis all illusion!
>   My eyes have almost crack'd their strings in wonder,
>   And my swoln heart so heaves within my breast,
>   As it would bare its secret to the day . . .
>
>                                   (Act IV, scene i)

We might surmise that the phantom haunting Boaden's text here really goes by the name of Shakespeare's Richard III, one of the century's most popular male roles (his 'nightmare' scene is famously represented in Hogarth's portrait of Garrick as Richard). The ranting soliloquy by the villain was an expected part of the evening's entertainment: Mr Yates's favourite part of the Baron in *Lovers' Vows*, a play which was at the height of its popularity when Boaden wrote *Fontainville Forest*, is a fine example from the same period.

Radcliffe, by contrast, never shows us the Marquis alone – as far as she is concerned, he is simply the most extreme embodiment of all the threatening father-figures in her heroine's adventures. Much of his dangerous image, in fact, arises from his inscrutability – just as Catherine Morland cannot fathom much of what General Tilney says or the motives for his behaviour. Boaden does not have time within the constraints of a two-hour drama to dwell on the inscrutability of the Marquis; instead, this character fulfils a role which was to become very common in the melodramas of the following century, the dyed-in-the-wool villain. His attempt on Adeline's virtue is a dramatic climax whose sensationalism was an expected part of the 'strong' drama of the period:

> MARQUIS. I have heard too much; and my impetuous love
> Now grasps its choicest good – In vain this struggle!
> How lovely is this terror! By my transport
> It heightens the bewitching charm of beauty,
> And lends ten thousand graces to that bosom.
> ADELINE. Help! help! for mercy's sake.
> MARQUIS. You call in vain.
> None dare intrude. Know, here, that I command;
> No power on earth shall snatch you from my arms.
>
> [*He pursues her, and seeing the picture of her mother, snatches it from her bosom.*]
>
> Ha! what is this? Hell! do my eyes deceive me?
> My brother's wife! Even as she liv'd once more!
> ADELINE. Then my father's murderer stands before me.

– which no doubt caused a *sensation* in the audience.[18] In Radcliffe, the Marquis's sexual importunacy amounts (like John Thorpe's) to not much more than a tacky setting for a proposed seduction: it gets as far as 'he threw his arm round her, and would have pressed her towards him, but she liberated herself from his embrace . . . [and] entreated he would leave her to repose'[19] – which he does, and she promptly escapes. The real threat is in the mind: Adeline's dreams, La Motte's realisation that the proposed violation which he had facilitated would have been incestuous. Austen, of course, displaces the threat of rape onto the comic caddishness of John Thorpe and the failed 'abduction' to Blaise Castle; and Catherine learns eventually to distrust the workings of the waking imagination, and has dreamless sleeps. But for Boaden, simplified conventional gender behaviours are sufficient to provide for the entertainment of his audience. Thus Adeline remains a passive victim, to be rescued by the young hero; and the Marquis not only offers the audience thrilling soliloquies of guilt and violence which break the taboos of the novel's feminine-identified culture[20] –

> MARQUIS. When can ambition lay him down secure
> Of ill-got power, and dread no retribution?
> . . . Furies of Hell!
> To tempt me thus with damning *incest* too!
> And bid me crush the form I would enjoy!
>
> (Act v, scene i)

– he also provides a satisfying on-stage suicide, which keeps him in the foreground as the ultimate star of the show. In both Radcliffe and Austen, by contrast, the repentance of the villainous father-figure happens off-stage, and is reported by the narrator, who is much more interested in the fast-approaching 'perfect felicity' of her *jeune premier* couple.

Thus the Gothic theatre, of which *Fontainville Forest* is a central example, is at once transgressive and conservative: deliciously – and safely – taboo-breaking but ultimately refusing to disturb the structure of patriarchal society by providing either Radcliffe's psychological or Austen's social analysis. Nevertheless, the convention that gives a play's epilogue to the principal actress of the company provides a coincidental rapprochement between the masculinist ideology underlying the play and the proto-feminism of Austen (whose heroine's admirable qualities are summed up in her mother's comment, '...it is a great comfort to find that she is not a poor helpless creature, but can shift very well for herself' (*NA*, p. 237)). Where Austen offers a tongue-in-cheek 'moral' – 'I leave it to be settled by whomsoever it may concern, whether the tendency of this work be altogether to recommend parental tyranny, or reward filial disobedience' (*NA*, p. 252) – Boaden ends his play proper with Adeline's pious appeal to the Almighty, which draws on the traditional association of the feminine with natural morality: 'the great Avenger of perverted nature / Before us has display'd a solemn lesson'. But he provides a counter-image of femininity in the epilogue written for the same actress, Mrs Pope. It is witty and ironical, appealing to a sophisticated audience which recognises the conventionality of the images and experiences it has been enjoying in the theatre:

> Well, heav'n be prais'd, I have escap'd at last,
> And all my woman's doubts and fears are past.

She is represented as questioning the success of any playwright's 'modern ghost' compared with that of *Hamlet*:

> Know you not, Shakspeare's petrifying pow'r
> Commands alone the horror-giving hour?
> ...You mean to sanction then your own pale sprite,
> By his 'that did usurp this time of night.'

This allows the young playwright, responding punningly to this call to humility, to claim instead (as she reports him) a small place in the great tradition of theatrical sensationalists:

> 'Why should your terror lay my proudest boast,
> Madam I die, if I give up the ghost.'

This clever conceit (in both senses of the word) creates a persona for the author, James Boaden, separate from the sensationalist text of his play. It is not unlike the persona presented by Henry Tilney as he spins a tale to fascinate and pleasurably terrify his female audience. Henry's entertainment of Catherine on the way to Northanger (chapter 20) is consciously a performance in which he shows that one can simply assemble the standard elements of the Gothic in any combination: they will continue to delight audiences who are willing to subject themselves to it. Henry Tilney and James Boaden, I am sure, would have enjoyed each other's company at the theatre; but both Jane Austen and Ann Radcliffe saw themselves as authors of rather more complex imaginative adventures.

What Boaden's adaptation of Radcliffe shows is that English Gothic theatre of the late eighteenth century is *male*, i.e. constructed so that beautiful helpless heroines are the object of a male gaze, and masculine villains and heroes, both, are empathetic figures – vessels of fantasy identification for the male members of the audience. The heroes and villains perform cultural stereotypes which reinforce, in an entertaining and pleasurable way, dominant discourses, here basically the discourse of patriarchy. But actresses throughout the century regularly seized the opportunity offered by public performance to transgress patriarchal boundaries – for example, by continuing to play with the eroticism opened up through cross-dressing; by behaving in their private lives with equivalent freedom and mobility to their male contemporaries; by even becoming 'stars' and crowd-pullers in their own right, thus skewing the centre of a play towards its tragic or comic heroine.

### THE THEATRE AND THE REAL WORLD IN *NORTHANGER ABBEY*

*Northanger Abbey* famously boasts a heroine who disobeys the stereotype provided by the sentimental novel and drama, and whose energy and forthrightness are much more akin to the transgressive and histrionic heroines of Austen's juvenilia. As Douglas Murray puts it, 'During Catherine's early years, no one has warned her from her unladylike interest in "cricket, base ball, riding on horseback, and running about the country", and neither her mother nor anyone else has insisted that she spend a proper number of hours in lady-like pursuits.' It has been 'a girlhood which has not prepared her to attract the attention and approbation of strangers'.[21]

It is when Catherine travels to Bath and thence to Northanger that she has to contend with a concerted effort by the dominant culture to mould her into a 'true', i.e. conventional heroine such as is depicted in Boaden's re-writing of Radcliffe's Adeline. For Bath, as Murray points out, is a theatre, a perfect system of social surveillance, to which young women come in order to be 'looked at' with a view to marriage:

> It is arguable that some of the most penetrating, the most discriminating, and the most paralyzing gazes of the Enlightenment were aimed at young women in Bath, a public space where the persons and the behavior of girls were subject to the perpetual scrutiny of relatives, neighbors, strangers, and potential marriage partners. Enlightenment Bath was, in fact, planned as a site of ceaseless, unavoidable gazing . . .

Murray instances the open squares, the Circus, and the Royal Crescent, 'all in effect amphitheaters or colosseums, with hundreds of rooms, like private boxes, from which those passing on the stage below may readily be seen'. Austen, who had visited Bath on various occasions before she lived there, was undoubtedly aware of the architectural uniqueness of this city planned as a theatre for fashion and intrigue. The interior public spaces – the Assembly Rooms, the Pump-Room, the theatre – are even more consciously used in her novels as stages for self-display and gazing at others. And if one such as Isabella Thorpe chooses to reverse the gaze and actively pursue handsome young men, she can be admired for a temporary transgression of the gender codes, though finally of course she is only too eager to return to them and play the heroine of sensibility: James Morland 'is the only man I ever did or could love' (*NA*, p. 216), she claims – after being unceremoniously dumped by Captain Tilney.

Catherine's encounter with theatricality thus begins in Bath (we do not hear of home theatricals at Fullerton parsonage forming part of Catherine's haphazard education). Not only does she attend the theatre for the first time – in her first week there, as she assures Henry Tilney – but Bath's theatrical *modus vivendi* is constantly foregrounded:

> Every morning now brought its regular duties; – shops were to be visited; some new part of the town to be looked at; and the Pump-room to be attended, where they paraded up and down for an hour, looking at every body and speaking to no one. (*NA*, p. 25)

Dress, or costume, is therefore important; garments – even everyday wear – are strongly semiotically coded. Mrs Allen noticing that her lace is richer than Mrs Thorpe's, Isabella in pursuit of a new hat or determined 'to be dressed exactly like [Catherine]. The men take notice of *that* sometimes you know' (*NA*, p. 42); the ritual of evening dress and fancy dress – all indicate that one is a performer, even when one thinks to be no more than a looker-on. Once Catherine has met Henry Tilney, and can expect to meet him again in the public rooms, 'what gown and what head-dress she should wear on the occasion became her chief concern' (*NA*, p. 73). And although Austen as narrator takes time to moralise iron-ically at this point, claiming that men never notice what women wear ('Woman is fine for her own satisfaction alone'), we have already seen that Henry Tilney does not conform to the generality of 'the men', and has a most unmasculine interest in muslins.

Austen begins her persistent use of theatrical metaphor with Cather-ine's first public appearance – a ball at the Upper Rooms:

> now was the time for a heroine, who had not yet played a very distinguished part in the events of the evening, to be noticed and admired. Every five minutes, by removing some of the crowd, gave greater openings for her charms. She was now seen by many young men who had not been near her before. Not one, however, started with rapturous wonder on beholding her, no whisper of eager inquiry ran round the room, nor was she once called a divinity by any body. (*NA*, p. 23)

In this milieu defined by the male gaze, Catherine will not have the easy path to stardom that many a more beautiful young woman had. The positive side of this is that she will not easily be seduced into the performance of a theatrical femininity largely marked by its excessive sensibility, such as is displayed by Isabella Thorpe. She will retain more of her androgynous vitality, commonsense, and integrity – despite her temporary fall into the dangers presented by the Gothic imagination. But that is yet to come: meanwhile, in Bath, we see her unconsciously shifting, as she tries on adult roles, between socially defined femininity and her native commonsense.

The latter is tested by her introduction to Henry Tilney, whom she meets in a most unromantic way – through the historically real master of ceremonies, Mr King. Importantly, this introduction does not partake of the prevalent scopophilia of Bath's theatrical culture: Catherine has not been picked out for her beauty. It is her vitality and eagerness to learn that attracts Henry's mentoring attention, so that in due course his quasi-effeminacy and foppishness will be transformed into his proper masculine social role – that of a responsible clergyman. With the evi-dence that we later glean, it would seem highly likely that Henry Tilney has come to Bath, at the age of 'four or five and twenty' (*NA*, p. 25) not only to see his family, whom he sees all the time, but to find a wife (Mr Elton goes successfully to Bath with the same intention). Henry Tilney, like those other Henries, Austen and Crawford, is by nature an actor. He has a fondness for writing his own scenarios and directing them, controlling the performances of others, most notably his sister and Catherine. Psychoanalysts might argue that this is an act of sublimation: he does this in order to create an artificial position of power for himself, since he has no power in the 'real' world of Northanger Abbey governed by his tyrannical father. He does have a separate existence, and a socially respectable role, as a clergyman, though in the novel it is embryonic, immature – Woodston parsonage is only partly furnished; Henry only occasionally officiates there; he has no wife to complement his parish work. All this will change after the novel's end, after Henry has finally acted (in the non-theatrical sense)[22] as an independent adult by disobeying his father, instead of remaining silent and constrained in his presence. We can usefully look not only at Catherine's but at Henry's development in the novel from the perspective of their involvement in and response to theatricality.

Henry does not present as a clergyman, but rather as a 'very gentlemanlike young man' (*NA*, p. 25). How does such a young man, with the added personal advantages of 'fluency and spirit', perform in the theatre of Bath? Dull and correct he cannot afford to be, if he hopes to attract interest on this crowded stage – so Henry creates for himself a mask, slipping in and out of various consciously framed roles. There is the 'simpering' young man about town, 'forming his features into a set smile':

> 'Have you been long in Bath, madam?'
> 'About a week, sir,' replied Catherine, trying not to laugh.
> 'Really!' with affected astonishment. (*NA*, p. 26)

– and so on, through the accepted catalogue of trite enquiries. (My guess is that Mr Elton follows this script with solemn exactitude.) There is the rather more amusing (to him) and unreadable (to Catherine) character of the 'queer, half-witted man' – decoded, one who doesn't properly perform masculinity, but talks in an unpredictable way about sprigged muslin, journals, and other areas of feminine expertise. But this does not constitute Henry as basically effeminate, since he frequently steps outside these self-conscious performances to offer Catherine a third, more 'rational' image of himself, as a witty and opinionated young man of the world, a producer of bon mots and Spectatorial observations:

'As far as I have had opportunity of judging it appears to me that the usual style of letter-writing among women is faultless, except in three particulars.'

'And what are they?'

'A general deficiency of subject, a total inattention to stops, and a very frequent ignorance of grammar.' (*NA*, p. 27)

Henry has yet to accept that this too is a performance, that, as Catherine reflects, 'he indulge[s] himself a little too much with the foibles of others' (*NA*, p. 29). The reader learns with some surprise, at the end of this chapter, that Henry Tilney is a clergyman. The pervasive theatricality of Bath encourages him to try out other, less sober roles.

The point is made clear not by the obvious contrast with the 'rattle' John Thorpe, who is a caricatured type of boorish male common enough in Austen's sister novelists, but by that with the more quietly and realistically drawn James Morland and Eleanor Tilney. James Morland is a sincere and naive young lover, who cannot recognise Isabella Thorpe's exclamatory sensibility for what it is, a performance to trap a likely suitor. Like all the Morlands, he is a 'plain matter of fact [person], who seldom aimed at wit of any kind' (*NA*, pp. 65–6). It is clear that Henry Tilney, on the other hand, does aim at wit, with its attendant dangers of misleading linguistic play. His sister Eleanor is no performer herself – 'she seemed capable of being young, attractive, and at a ball, without wanting to fix the attention of every man near her, and without exaggerated feelings of extatic delight or inconceivable vexation on every little trifling occurrence' (*NA*, p. 56). She is often shown as a deflator of Henry's self-dramatising tendencies, for example during the conversation on the walk to Beechen Cliff: 'You are more nice than wise. Come, Miss Morland, let us leave him to meditate over our faults in the utmost propriety of diction, while we praise Udolpho in whatever terms we like best' (*NA*, p. 108). It is Eleanor who closes this conversation with the affectionate reprimand to Henry, 'Be more serious' (*NA*, p. 114). But 'seriousness' in his courtship will not seem necessary to Henry until the moment when he realises that his performance as impromptu inventor of a Gothic drama has drastically misled the naive Catherine.

The walk to Beechen Cliff is the climax of a series of scenes in which Austen increasingly foregrounds theatricality as a way of seeing, a product of the urban sophistication that Catherine is meeting for the first time. Fittingly, the first such scene takes place at the Bath theatre, on the day after John Thorpe's aborted abduction of Catherine and her unintended rudeness to the Tilneys. Miss Tilney as a consequence has apparently refused to receive Catherine's visit: Catherine 'knew not how such an offence as her's might be classed by the laws of worldly polite-ness . . . Dejected and humbled, she had even some thoughts of not going with the others to the theatre that night' (*NA*, p. 92). But as it is 'a play she wanted very much to see' (and this will be her *third* visit to the theatre), she proceeds there with the Allens. Unfortunately we are not told which play 'so well suspend[s] her care', but significantly it is a comedy, not one of the fashionable Gothic or German plays. In this Catherine accords with her author's taste. But even more significantly, when real life in the form of Henry Tilney supervenes, Catherine can no longer concentrate on the stage. She is more anxious to 'catch his eye' than to follow the play; Henry, by contrast, displays a proper aficionado's interest: 'his notice was never withdrawn from the stage for two whole scenes'. And while Catherine does not think to put on an affectation of indifference, Henry is offended, and shows it in his polite but cool behaviour. Catherine is a quick learner: she is able to read Henry's feelings – more, perhaps, than he admits to himself – from his facial expression:

> 'Nay, I am sure by your look, when you came into the box, you were angry.'
> 'I angry! I could have no right!'
> 'Well, nobody would have thought you had no right who saw your face.'
> He replied by asking her to make room for him, and talking of the play.
> (*NA*, p. 95)

This is the drama of emotional life in the real social world: as readers, we appreciate the more Austen's achievement by her setting this scene in the frame of a visit to the theatre, and showing the inauthenticity of its 'representation of human life' (charming though it be) against reality.

Among the many important themes canvassed in chapter 14's walk with the Tilneys to Beechen Cliff, the setting itself is significant, and emphasised as such. On arriving at the top of the hill above the city, the Tilneys discuss the view 'with the eyes of persons accustomed to drawing, and decid[ing] on its capability of being formed into pictures' (*NA*, p. 110). This, as Austen's ironical narratorial voice makes clear, is a distorting of reality through sophisticated habits of looking: 'It seemed as if a good view were no longer to be taken from the top of an high hill, and that a clear blue sky was no longer proof of a fine day.' Instead, with the Tilneys' employment of fashionable jargon – 'fore-grounds, dis-tances, and second distances – side-screens and perspectives – lights and shades' – we are alerted to the theatricalising of the English landscape. Gilpin's terminology for the 'picturesque' landcape is identical to that of the scene-painters of the late eighteenth-century theatre, most notably De Loutherbourg,[23] who developed the 'stage picture' behind the frame of the proscenium arch into an oversize version of the romantic Gothic landscapes of fashionable painting. The seductive difference is that in the theatre, or in a theatricalised landscape, you see people moving, *acting*.

The danger of such a sophisticated, fashionably educated perception as Henry Tilney's is that it encourages seeing the whole world as a stage set. Catherine is all too eager to learn this new way of seeing: she 'was so hopeful a scholar, that when they gained the top of Beechen Cliff, she voluntarily rejected the whole city of Bath, as unworthy to make part of a landscape' (*NA*, p. 111). Henry, as pedagogue, is 'delighted with her progress', though 'fearful of wearying her with too much wisdom at once'. 'Wisdom' is an ironical epithet here, as the sentence's descent through other masculine areas of expertise to 'silence' makes clear. In short, what Henry so complacently offers as instruction to Catherine is at best unhelpful and at worst radically misleading.

Ironically enough, Catherine's learning from her Bath experiences to watch and observe people's behaviour, when applied to the 'altered' behaviour of Isabella Thorpe (chapter 19), is discounted by Henry Tilney as of no significance in the 'real' world, but simply another game or performance: 'real jealousy can never exist between them . . . they know exactly what is required and what can be borne; and you may be certain, that one will never tease the other beyond what is known to be pleasant' (*NA*, p. 152). Henry has failed to read either the money-hungry Isabella or the naive James Morland correctly, while knowing exactly what role his more familiar brother is playing, that of the flirtatious young officer, who believes it is his professional right (in his splendid regimental costume) to attract the female eye.

'Henry Tilney must know best' is Catherine's conclusion to this interlude. 'She blamed herself for the extent of her fears, and resolved never to think so seriously on the subject again' (*NA*, p. 153). No wonder, then, that she is more than ready to view Northanger Abbey and its chief inhabitant as participants in a Gothic drama, when Henry further compounds his role as pedagogue with that of the composer of theatrical scenarios – a fictional James Boaden, young man about town-cum-dramatist. Henry, like Boaden, has institutional and cultural power to support him as he tells the story that will garner him applause. Boaden had a theatre, as argued earlier, that privileged the male actor; Henry's father, the General, orders Catherine to travel tête-à-tête with Henry so that he can perform to a captive audience of one. The irony detectable in his speeches does not detract from the pleasure he patently takes in his virtuoso performance of a collage of Gothic plots from Radcliffe: he is finally 'too much amused by the interest he had raised, to be able to carry it farther; he could no longer command solemnity either of subject or voice, and was obliged to entreat her to use her own fancy in the perusal of Matilda's woes' (*NA*, p. 160).

Despite her earnest assurances to Henry that she will not confuse fantasy and real life, Catherine does follow his instruction (again) and use her own fancy as she encounters the world of Northanger, obsessively theatricalising it despite every appearance that would contradict this. It is true that Nature, in the form of the satirical novelist, does assist by providing a violent storm for Catherine's first night at the abbey; but it is only when she sees the piece of furniture that had formed a stage property in Henry's scenario that she begins actively to take part in the Gothic drama that he – more immediately than Mrs Radcliffe – has written for her: 'Henry's words, his description of the ebony cabinet which was to escape her observation at first, immediately rushed across her . . . it was certainly a very remarkable coincidence!' (*NA*, p. 168). And she goes on to enact just such a performance of the Gothic heroine as she might have seen on stage or created in the theatre of her mind. But of course, she is in the real world, not a fashionable theatre, as the laundry-list so pointedly demonstrates (Gothic heroes and villains never need such mundane things).

Just in case the reader has not noticed Henry's culpability, the next morning (on discovering her error) Catherine is shown reflecting, 'it was in a great measure his own doing, for had not the cabinet appeared so exactly to agree with his description of her adventures, she should never have felt the smallest curiosity about it' (*NA*, p. 173). However, Henry is not in the same way directly to blame for Catherine's more egregious and embarrassing misinterpretation of what she sees, her construction of the General as a Gothic villain. Her own reading here coincides, we may say with the benefit of psychoanalytic theory, with a barely unconscious fear of the General as powerful father-figure within the patriarchal structure of late eighteenth-century English society. He *is* an emotional and social tyrant, as the simple folk of rural Fullerton instinctively perceive on her return home. But Catherine's mind is by now so coloured by theatrical ways of seeing that it is fatally easy for her to think of her surmises about the General's crimes in terms of 'the guilty scene to be acting': 'it struck her that, if judiciously *watched*, some rays of light from the General's lamp might glimmer through the lower windows, as he passed to the prison of his wife' (*NA*, pp. 188–9; my emphasis). Such scenes to thrill the *watching* audience were nightly created by the new technologies of scenery and lighting in the theatres of this period.[24]

As Catherine finally realises, she has been both audience and performer in her own private theatre:

> it had been all a voluntary, self-created delusion, each trifling circumstance receiving importance from an imagination resolved on alarm, and every thing forced to bend to one purpose by a mind which, before she entered the Abbey, *had been craving to be frightened.* (*NA*, pp. 199–200; my emphasis)

Henry's reprimand to Catherine, the moment when we at last hear him as cleric and pastor in defence of the English and Christian way of life (an implied contrast to that of French Catholics, atheists, and revolutionaries), carries nevertheless a sting in its tail which indicates the pervasiveness of watching others' behaviour, once the culture has developed the habit: 'a country like this, where social and literary intercourse is on such a footing; where every man is surrounded by a neighbourhood of voluntary spies . . .' (*NA*, pp. 197–8). It is this sort of 'spying', and the gossip that arises from it, which make it all too easy for General Tilney in turn to take up the role of stage villain ('his performances have been seen' by the reader, the narrator comments in the penultimate chapter (*NA*, p. 247)). His excessive courtliness in paying attention to one he believes to be an heiress, followed by the 'actual and natural evil' (*NA*, p. 227) of his discourteous repudiation of her, sending her, incidentally, on a real-life replay of the Gothic heroine's unaccompanied flight across the country, mark him as an inauthentic person, an actor (specialising in 'heavy' roles) who occupies sites of power but has no other relation with his co-performers.

The novel ends back in the country, well away from the theatrical sets of Bath or Northanger. After her rite-of-passage adventures, Catherine will move from one *locus amoenus* to another – from her sensible parents' village rectory to her husband's. The great world, with its deceptive shows, its surveillance and intrigue, need not impinge on the small world of Woodston, where the Reverend Mr Tilney will put his charm and intelligence to good effect as a clergyman and local landlord, and his wife will put her energy unpretentiously into doing good works. These are social roles, uses of the energies circulating around and in theatricality, which Austen can unambiguously approve.

If, as I have argued, both Henry and Catherine have grown beyond their gender-constructed obsessions with the specifically theatrical, this 'moral', nevertheless, is presented in a text which shares many of the characteristics of the genre it supposedly repudiates. Sparkling dialogue between energetic young people, dramaturgically brilliant scenes, a delighted recognition of fiction's artifice shared between author and audience: these will recur notably in *Pride and Prejudice* and *Emma*. The difference between Austen and Henry Tilney (or James Boaden) as authors is that she refuses to incorporate cheap sensation and conventional sensibility into her text, except to laugh at it. She knows that her own 'performance' is superior. The word is used twice in the famous defence of the novel that she makes in chapter 5. By the second occurrence Austen is writing in the first-person plural:

From pride, ignorance, or fashion, our foes are almost as many as our readers ... there seems almost a general wish of decrying the capacity and undervaluing the labour of the novelist, and of slighting the performances which have only genius, wit, and taste to recommend them. (*NA*, p. 37)

Unlike his author, Henry Tilney as creative writer displays some wit, but little genius and poor taste. He will be better employed turning his undoubted facility with language into eloquent sermons, performing a role from within the confines of a rural pulpit which will nurture the souls of his unfashionable audience.

# CHAPTER FOUR

# Pride and Prejudice: *the comedienne as heroine*

The last season of home theatricals at Steventon was early in 1789, when Jane Austen was in her fourteenth year. The plays were the farce *High Life Below Stairs* and Isaac Bickerstaff's *The Sultan* (a play which premiered the year Austen was born, 1775). In the latter, 'Miss Cooper performed the part of *Roxalana* & Henry *the Sultan*.'[1] Roxalana, the lively young Englishwoman who challenges the entrenched masculine superiority of the Sultan, was a favourite role with both of the star comediennes of the late eighteenth century, Frances Abington and Dora Jordan. Readers of Austen's 1813 novel *Pride and Prejudice* will find the relationship between Roxalana and the Sultan in this two-act comedy strikingly familiar.

Roxalana spends a good deal of the play laughing, Elizabeth-like, at the great man: 'Upon my word, you have made a very delicate speech, and I admire the gravity with which it was uttered'; 'Now, sir, farewell. If I find you profit by my first lesson, I may, perhaps, be tempted to give you another.' Early in the piece he soliloquises about her in these terms:

> She's not handsome, that is, what is called a beauty; yet her little nose, cocked in the air, her laughing eyes, and the play of her features, have an effect altogether – yet, methinks, I have a mind to sift Roxalana's character; mere curiosity, and nothing else. It is the first time we have seen in this place a spirit of caprice and independence ...
>
> (Act 1)

Like Darcy, he is attracted against his will by the vitality and unconventionality of his involuntary guest. Finally the omnipotent Sultan is reduced to pleading, 'Tell me who you are; what species of inconstant being, at once so trifling and so respectable, that you seduce my heart while you teach me my duty.' In her reply challenging him to marry her, Roxalana exhorts him: 'Make the people happy, and they will not prevent your being so. They would be pleased to see you raise to the throne one that you love, and would love you, and would be beloved by your people' (Act II). 'It is enough', replies the Sultan; 'my scruples are at an end.' He admits that his pride has been based on 'prejudices' about Roxalana's social inferiority; a good Enlightenment ruler, he recognises 'the light of [her] superior reason', and concludes, 'my love is no longer a foible; you are worthy of empire'. Roxalana, the independent, witty, yet high-principled young Englishwoman, has won the love *and respect* of a mighty man who admits 'hitherto I have known only flatterers'.

Bickerstaff's little play also has its version of the flattering Miss Bingley and Mrs Hurst: the grand Elmira and the accomplished Ismena, both desperate to gain the Sultan's attention and affection. In Austen's domestic updating of this dramatic fable, Elizabeth spells out the emotional dynamic in her final recorded conversation with Darcy:

'. . . Now be sincere; did you admire me for my impertinence?'
'For the liveliness of your mind, I did.'
'You may as well call it impertinence at once . . . The fact is, that you were sick of civility, of deference, of officious attention. You were disgusted with the women who were always speaking and looking, and thinking for *your* approbation alone. I roused, and interested you, because I was so unlike *them* . . .' (*P&P*, p. 380)

We can well imagine that a fortnight or so's absorption during the Steventon home theatricals' exploration of similar dynamics in *The Sultan* could stimulate the imagination of the thirteen-year-old writer in the family. Her reading of Shakespearean and contemporary comedy would have reinforced the possibilities of working on this model of love-story in her chosen form, the novel.

Bickerstaff's popular play, to which I shall return, was technically only a 'farce', an afterpiece; it did not carry the commercial consequence of a mainpiece. Hannah Cowley was one of the playwrights who, taking their cue from Goldsmith's crusade to bring laughter back into the mainpiece drama, provided much of the wit and satire of the Restoration comedies, without their licentiousness. She was also one of the most successful, in a writing career spanning nearly twenty years (1776–95). As Sheridan did in *The School for Scandal*, and as Congreve and others had done before him, Cowley satirised gossip-mongers and self-promoters. Her play *Which is the Man?* (1782) was proposed by Eliza de Feuillide for performance at the Steventon theatricals of Christmas 1788. Even though it was not finally performed, the young Jane Austen certainly became familiar with it: she refers to it in the juvenilia and in later letters.[2] The most successful of Cowley's plays was *The Belle's Stratagem* (1780); it was the eleventh most popular mainpiece overall in London performances 1776–1800, and the fourth most popular new piece in this period.[3] It contains such familiar types as Courtall, 'a vain boaster of female favours', and Flutter, 'a noted liar'; Mrs Racket, 'a fashionable widow', Miss Ogle, the companion to the heroine; the country gentleman and his new wife (lifted – and cleaned up – from Wycherley's unplayably indecent *The Country Wife*); and the necessary figures of classic comedy, the heroine, her father, and the sophisticated bachelor who scorns her. What distinguishes Cowley's play from other attempts of the time to reinvent 'laughing comedy' is its emphasis on the experience of the female characters. Here, it is true, acknowledgement should be made to Goldsmith's wonderful writing for *She Stoops to Conquer*'s Kate Hardcastle, a character who also undertakes a 'stratagem' to win the man she fancies. Kate is a tough cookie: as she says to her father, 'Well, if he refuses, instead of breaking my heart at his indifference, I'll only break my glass for its flattery, set my cap to some newer fashion, and look out for some less difficult admirer' (Act I; a line echoed by Elizabeth apropos Wickham). We feel that she enjoys the game as much as – or even more than – she anticipates the happy-ever-after of the result. This is not the case with Cowley's Lettitia: she is a romantic, and she is looking for true love from Doricourt:

> LETTITIA. Ay, there's the sting; the blooming boy, who left his image in my young heart, improv'd in every grace that fix'd him there; it is the same face that my memory, and my dreams constantly painted to me, but its graces are finish'd, and every beauty heighten'd; how mortifying to feel myself at the same moment his slave, and an object of perfect indifference to him?
>
> (Act I)

The couple are already formally affianced by the wish of their families, but Lettitia concludes, 'I will touch his heart or never be his wife.' It is in pursuit of this ambition that she decides upon her stratagem: to pretend to be a foolish unsophisticated country girl so that he will take an active dislike to her (Figure 6) – while at the same time, under the protection of a mask at a ball, to flirt with him in witty banter strongly reminiscent of Congreve's Millamant or Shakespeare's Beatrice. The stratagem of course succeeds brilliantly: Doricourt falls in love with the masked charmer, who says she will reveal her identity to him at the moment when he least expects it. This comes about when he has reluctantly, but as a man of honour, married Lettitia the 'dull country girl'. On revealing herself she declares:

> You see, I can be any thing; chuse my character, your taste shall fix it; shall I be an English wife, or breaking at once from the bonds of nature, and education, step forth to the world in all the captivating glare of foreign manners?

6 *The Belle's Stratagem*, Act II; frontispiece to Elizabeth Inchbald (ed.), *The British Theatre*, London 1808, vol. XIX (By permission of the British Library, 1345.2.19)

To which Doricourt very properly and romantically replies:

> You shall be nothing but yourself; nothing can be captivating that you are not. I will not wrong your penetration, by pretending that you won my heart at the first interview; but have now my whole soul; your person, your face, your mind, I wou'd not exchange for that of any other woman breathing.
>
> (Act v)

Two points can be made about this exchange as the climax of *The Belle's Stratagem*. First, that it partakes of a persistent secondary discourse that circulates in the play: that of the contrast between 'Englishness' and 'Frenchness' that late eighteenth-century English culture was obsessed by, a contrast that attaches itself easily to the major discourse on sexuality.[4] Doricourt, as a young gentleman who has been completing his education on the Grand Tour of the Continent, has absorbed an idea of female sexuality that locates it in a recognisable theatricality:

> she should have spirit, fire, l'air en jour, that something – that nothing – which every body feels, and nobody can describe – in the resistless charms of France and Italy . . . English beauty, 'tis insipidity, it wants the zest; it wants poignancy, Frank; why I have known a french-woman, indebted to nature for no one thing but a pair of decent eyes, reckon in her suit, as many counts, marquisses, and petite-maitres as would satisfy three dozen of our first-rate toasts. I have known an Italian marquisina make ten conquests in stepping from her carriage, and carry her slaves from one city to another, whose real intrinsic beauty would have yielded to half the little grissets that pace your mall on a Sunday.
>
> (Act I)

The inclusion of Italian comparisons soon languishes; the next time this discourse is touched on, between Doricourt and Sir George Touchwood the country gentleman, the patriotic theme is clear:

DORICOURT. Oh, that the circle dans la place victoire, cou'd witness thy extravagance. I'll send thee off to St Evreux this night, drawn at full length, and colour'd after nature.

SIR GEORGE. Tell him then to add to the ridicule, that Touchwood glories in the name of husband; that he has found in one English woman, more beauty than Frenchmen ever saw; and more goodness than Frenchmen can conceive.

(Act II)

Lettitia's great achievement, therefore, in theatricalising her own sexual desire, is a victory for English women – they can flirt and put on airs if they need to. But she settles, of course, for openness, sincerity, and the modesty of an English wife (such as is exemplified in the secondary plot, the attempt to corrupt the country wife Lady Touchwood). The last words in the play are those of a reformed and truly educated Doricourt:

> My charming Lettitia, 'twas a strange perversion of taste that led me to consider the delicate timidity of your deportment as the mark of an unin-form'd mind, or inelegant manners. I feel now, it is to that innate modesty English husbands owe a felicity, the married men of other nations are strangers to; it is a secret veil to your charms; it is the surest bulwark to your husband's honour: and curs'd be the hour, shou'd it ever arrive, in which British ladies shall sacrifice to foreign graces – the grace of modesty.
>
> (Act v)

*The Belle's Stratagem*, in giving the principal actress a role in which she performs (almost simultaneously) the charms of French flirtatiousness *and* the deep and true feelings of an admirable young Englishwoman, at the same time deconstructs the essentialism of these political and gendered binaries. For it is all done by an actress, who in speaking the epilogue, reminds her audience of the 'masks' that constitute all social roles (see p. 23). As Beth Kowaleski Wallace argues in her analysis of this play, 'if human subjectivity is defined by constant role playing, then only on the stage do people really appear as what they are. The actor is the only truly sincere being, since his performativity is the explicit demonstration of ever shifting human nature.'[5] Wallace's formulation summarising the achievement of Hannah Cowley in this popular comedy may well contain the key to Austen's ambivalent fascination with theatricality.

In its telling of the story of the taming of the sophisticated and snobbish gentleman by the native wit and strong principles of a socially disadvan-taged young woman, Cowley's play approaches much more closely to *Pride and Prejudice* than does the lightweight oriental farce *The Sultan*. It is, of course, set in a theatrical version of contemporary England rather than a totally imagined Turkish court. But rather than arguing for a spe-cific influence of *The Belle's Stratagem* on *First Impressions* (Austen's 1790s version of *Pride and Prejudice*), I would suggest a confluence, a response to a perceived lack, in the strong need of these two women writers to imagine contemporary heroines who are complex, intelligent, witty, and virtuous, despite social disadvantages. (Cowley's dedication of *The Belle's Stratagem* to the Queen begins thus: 'In the following Comedy, my pur-pose was, to draw a FEMALE CHARACTER, which with the most lively Sensibility, fine Understanding, and elegant Accomplishments, should unite that beautiful Reserve and Delicacy which, whilst they veil those charms, render them still more interesting.') This model began with Shakespeare: *As You Like It*'s Rosalind, for example, who educates the heroic but naive Orlando. Socially closer to Austen's world are the ladies of *Love's Labour's Lost* who correct the men's proud certainty that all they do is right, that they are irresistible to the women when they choose to be: compare Rosaline's dismissal, 'We will not dance' (Act v, scene ii) with Elizabeth's promise to her mother '*never* to dance' with Mr Darcy (*P&P*, p. 20). Beatrice in *Much Ado about Nothing* is perhaps the strongest precursor of Elizabeth Bennet. As Juliet McMaster argues, 'Beatrice, "born in a merry hour" (II, i) is surely kin to Elizabeth, who "dearly love[s] a laugh" (50).'[6] And *Much Ado* has both the formal perfection and anteriority as a romantic comedy that allow it to stand as a model – it was, in fact, the most popular Shakespearean comedy performed in the eighteenth century. The structural and dramatic similarities between Austen's novel and Shakespeare's play can be tabulated in the following way.

Both begin with a patriarch and his daughters (or quasi-daughters) receiving news that unattached young men – active, worldly, all-conquering – are about to arrive in the area, their unconscious purpose to go courting. This sets up the basic situation for a romance (Mrs Bennet: 'A single man of large fortune; four or five thousand a year. What a fine thing for our girls!' (*P&P*, pp. 3–4)), but the comic impulse complicates the Mills & Boon model. Elizabeth, like Beatrice, is marked out as different from the other young women:

LEONATO. You must not, sir, mistake my niece: there is a kind of merry war betwixt Signor Benedick and her: they never meet but there's a skirmish of wit between them.

(*Much Ado about Nothing*, Act i, scene i)

'They have none of them much to recommend them,' replied [Mr Bennet]; 'they are all silly and ignorant like other girls; but Lizzy has something more of quickness than her sisters'. (*P&P*, p. 5)

The heroine is witty, intelligent, unconventional. Her potential partner disdains her at their first public meeting; his naive younger friend falls heavily for the rather insipid figure of the heroine's sister/cousin. 'As to Miss Bennet, he could not conceive an angel more beautiful' (*P&P*, p. 16) – the cliché announces a second-hand mode of thinking and experiencing, such as we also see in Claudio: 'Can the world buy such a jewel? . . . In mine eye she is the sweetest lady that ever I looked on'

(Act I, scene i). And just as Bingley is a type of Claudio, Jane is undoubtedly a variation on Shakespeare's Hero. Though she is older and wiser than Hero, she is no more outgoing in making her preference known, and is thus easily misread by the young men who are charmed by her beauty but unable to get to know her in any but a superficial manner. When she is apparently jilted by the young man whom everyone expects her to marry she does not of course 'die' – or disappear from society, as Hero does – but Elizabeth is worried by her lack of spirits despite her apparent acceptance of the situation. Jane does not behave like the tragedy heroine, Marianne, who makes immodest efforts to reclaim her lover. It is Elizabeth, like Beatrice, who speaks out to challenge the calumny against her sister (that she does not love Bingley). In due course, the man who loves her – Darcy, like Benedick – acts to rescue the honour of her family and is rewarded with her acknowledgement of love for him.

## PERFORMING THE MASKED DANCE OF COURTSHIP

Just as the unlikely Beatrice–Benedick love-story is played out in public, so Elizabeth and Darcy's unwilling attraction, and Elizabeth's flirtation with Wickham, attract the attention of onlookers – Caroline Bingley, Lady Catherine de Bourgh, Charlotte Lucas, the Gardiners. Very few scenes between these characters take place without this 'onstage audience' to remind us of the essentially theatrical quality of the daily life of the gentry. One of the most conscious examples is the early conversation between Elizabeth and Darcy at Netherfield (chapter 11). They continue their probing of each other's character, and Elizabeth asserts her delight in laughing at the 'follies and nonsense, whims and inconsistencies' of others while stressing that she 'never ridicule[s] what is wise or good' (*P&P*, p. 57). The dialogue, which has suffered occasional banal interruptions from the desperate Miss Bingley, concludes thus:

'There is, I believe, in every disposition a tendency to some particular evil – a natural defect, which not even the best education can overcome.'
'And *your* defect is a propensity to hate everybody.'
'And yours,' he replied, with a smile, 'is wilfully to misunderstand them.'
'Do let us have a little music,' cried Miss Bingley, tired of a conversation in which she had no share. (*P&P*, p. 58)

Miss Bingley's resentment subtly reminds us that the conversation she feels excluded from is indeed a performance – but a private and highly

sophisticated one in an unconscious courting dance between two complex and intelligent people. Miss Bingley's insistence on returning to
a conventional display of feminine accomplishments at least provides
Darcy with temporary relief from 'the danger of paying Elizabeth too
much attention'.

Other conversations between Elizabeth and Darcy almost obsessively
focus on the inescapable theatricality of social life. In each of these scenes
the term *perform(ance)* occurs, the author's choice of word establishing a
metatheatrical conspiracy with the reading audience. The first example
comes when Elizabeth and Jane are detained at Netherfield through
Jane's illness and her mother's plotting (or rather, stage-management).
This allows us to witness a full-scale performance of Miss Bingley's attempts to fascinate Darcy – a performance which fails to be effectual
because of the critical acuity of Darcy and Elizabeth, which in itself is
an unconscious demonstration of their compatibility and mutual attraction. The discussion, introduced by Miss Bingley concerning the absent
Georgiana Darcy's 'exquisite' performance on the pianoforte, turns on
the definition of an 'accomplished' woman (*P&P*, pp. 39–40). The scene
reads like a commentary on (and, ironically, dramatisation of) Hannah
More's famous strictures on the modern system of female education, in
which the training of a young lady to be 'merely ornamental' results in
a life which 'resembles that of an actress; the morning is all rehearsal,
and the evening is all performance'.[7] (The metaphor is drawn from close
observation: More herself, a sometime playwright, remained reluctantly
fascinated by the theatre all her life.) It also can be analysed in the same
way in which an actor will prepare a scene, with precise attention to
motivation, pace, and dynamics.

Darcy, cued by Charles Bingley, makes the opening speech in what
will become a debate:

> 'Your list of the common extent of accomplishments,' said Darcy, 'has too
> much truth. The word is applied to many a woman who deserves it no otherwise
> than by netting a purse or covering a screen. But I am very far from agreeing
> with you in your estimation of ladies in general. I cannot boast of knowing
> more than half-a-dozen, in the whole range of my acquaintance, that are really
> accomplished.'
> 'Nor I, I am sure,' said Miss Bingley[,]

who is only able to perform as chorus to this grand utterance.
Elizabeth, by contrast, counter-feints and dares him to expand on his
generalisation:

'Then,' observed Elizabeth, 'you must comprehend a great deal in your idea of an accomplished woman.'

'Yes, I do comprehend a great deal in it.'

Before he can continue, Miss Bingley seizes the opportunity – as she thinks – to demonstrate her intellectual and social grasp; as we see, to demonstrate the very opposite while unwittingly underlining the social expectations of femininity as performance:

'Oh! certainly,' cried his faithful assistant, 'no one can be really esteemed accomplished who does not greatly surpass what is usually met with. A woman must have a thorough knowledge of music, singing, drawing, dancing, and the modern languages, to deserve the word; and besides all this, she must possess a certain something in her air and manner of walking, the tone of her voice, her address and expressions, or the word will be but half-deserved.'

Darcy takes the flattering 'feed' without recognising its full implications:

'All this she must possess,' added Darcy, 'and to all this she must yet add something more substantial, in the improvement of her mind by extensive reading.'

Elizabeth swoops in for the kill:

'I am no longer surprised at your knowing *only* six accomplished women. I rather wonder now at your knowing *any*.'

Darcy attempts a recovery by taking the offensive:

'Are you so severe upon your own sex as to doubt the possibility of all this?'

But Elizabeth is unfazed, trusting her own observation and judgement rather than giving in to the superior social authority of a man:

'I never saw such a woman. I never saw such capacity, and taste, and application, and elegance, as you describe, united.'

Elizabeth 'soon afterwards left the room' since the enjoyable thrust and parry of their conversation is ended by the demands of more conventional members of the party. But there is a deliciously ironical postscript which rounds off and underlines the significance of the scene we have been watching:

'Eliza Bennet,' said Miss Bingley, when the door was closed on her, 'is one of those young ladies who seek to recommend themselves to the other sex by undervaluing their own; and with many men, I dare say, it succeeds. But, in my opinion, it is a paltry device, a very mean art.'

'Undoubtedly,' replied Darcy, to whom this remark was chiefly addressed, 'there is meanness in *all* the arts which ladies sometimes condescend to employ for captivation. Whatever bears affinity to cunning is despicable.'

Miss Bingley was not so entirely satisfied with this reply as to continue the subject. (*P&P*, p. 40)

When, in due course, Elizabeth finds herself, 'without knowing what she did' (*P&P*, p. 90), dancing with Darcy at the ball, she defends herself from her own instinctive attraction by aggressively turning on a performance about performance. This of course has the effect of strengthening their fascination with each other, since they patently speak the same language, and are critically aware of the behavioural conventions of their society. Elizabeth sets this game afoot:

'It is *your* turn to say something now, Mr. Darcy. – *I* talked about the dance, and *you* ought to make some kind of remark on the size of the room, or the number of couples.'

He smiled, and assured her that whatever she wished him to say should be said.

'Very well. That reply will do for the present. Perhaps by and by I may observe that private balls are much pleasanter than public ones. But *now* we may be silent.'

'Do you talk by rule, then, while you are dancing?'

'Sometimes. One must speak a little, you know. It would look odd to be entirely silent for half an hour together; and yet for the advantage of *some*, conversation ought to be so arranged, as that they may have the trouble of saying as little as possible.'

'Are you consulting your own feelings in the present case, or do you imagine that you are gratifying mine?'

'Both,' replied Elizabeth, archly; 'for I have always seen a great similarity in the turn of our minds. We are each of an unsocial, taciturn disposition, unwilling to speak, unless we expect to say something that will amaze the whole room, and be handed down to posterity with all the éclat of a proverb.'

'This is no very striking resemblance of your own character, I am sure,' said he. 'How near it may be to *mine*, I cannot pretend to say. *You* think it a faithful portrait undoubtedly.'

'I must not decide on my own performance.'

He made no answer . . . (*P&P*, p. 91)

Elizabeth's implications about Darcy's personality in the second half of this dialogue verge on rudeness, and there is something of the schoolmaster in Darcy's replies. In fact he takes up the challenge of her final remark (which emphasises her awareness of the theatricality of what has just passed) in the final part of their dancing conversation – a dialogue in which there is a much more equal mutual exploration of character. His tone remains, finally, somewhat censorious, although his opening gambit ('What think you of books?') is said 'smiling'. Despite this momentary willingness to engage in the game of social self-presentation, Darcy is not in fact comfortable with the obligation of public theatricality; he would rather remain an enigma to his peers (this is, of course, a type of pride):

> She shook her head, 'I do not get on at all. I hear such different accounts of you as puzzle me exceedingly.'
> 'I can readily believe,' answered he gravely, 'that reports may vary greatly with respect to me; and I could wish, Miss Bennet, that you were not to sketch my character at the present moment, as there is reason to fear that the *performance* would reflect no credit on either.' (*P&P*, pp. 93–4; my emphasis)

Elizabeth's almost wistful – certainly unexpected – reply, 'But if I do not take your likeness now, I may never have another opportunity', contains a realistic assessment of their relative social positions: Darcy is indeed lowering himself even to be seen at the Netherfield ball. But the novelist is the fairy godmother in this Cinderella story, and she precipitately removes Darcy and Bingley from the stage and introduces 'a new scene' with the arrival of Mr Collins (*P&P*, p. 104) – a comic parody of Mr Darcy's pomposity and self-importance, even to the extent of assuming he is irresistible to the heroine. Austen then arranges for the unlikely couple to meet again in social surroundings where Darcy is the one disadvantaged by his family, and Elizabeth is cool and distant. The climax of the novel's examination of the idea of public performance as a means of social interaction is the curious dialogue that takes place as Elizabeth plays the piano after dinner at Rosings.[8] It begins as a conventional enough instance of the social performance of femininity, in terms recognisable from the seminal discussion in chapter 8; but Elizabeth seizes the first opportunity to move the 'fair performer'/male observer relation onto ground where she has the advantage – witty and unconventional self-presentation:

> Lady Catherine listened to half a song, and then talked, as before, to her other nephew; till the latter walked away from her, and making with his usual deliberation towards the pianoforte, stationed himself so as to command a full view of the fair performer's countenance. Elizabeth saw what he was doing, and at the first convenient pause, turned to him with an arch smile, and said:
> 'You mean to frighten me, Mr. Darcy, by coming in all this state to hear me? But I will not be alarmed though your sister *does* play so well. There is a

stubbornness about me that never can bear to be frightened at the will of others. My courage always rises with every attempt to intimidate me.'

'I shall not say that you are mistaken,' he replied, 'because you could not really believe me to entertain any design of alarming you; and I have had the pleasure of your acquaintance long enough to know that you find great enjoyment in occasionally professing opinions which in fact are not your own.' (*P&P*, p. 174)

As the stakes rise, this badinage soon intensifies into Elizabeth's teasing critique of Darcy's failings in the performance of his social role – at Netherfield 'he danced only four dances, though gentlemen were scarce', to which Darcy replies with a defensive excuse:

'I certainly have not the talent which some people possess,' said Darcy, 'of conversing easily with those I have never seen before. I cannot catch their tone of conversation, or appear interested in their concerns, as I often see done.' (*P&P*, p. 175)

Elizabeth's response unexpectedly employs an elaborate metaphor, drawn from that very conventional situation in which, as a young woman, she has been placed. The effect is to heighten the reading audience's con-sciousness of the novel's meta-discourse of social theatricality:

'My fingers,' said Elizabeth, 'do not move over this instrument in the mas-terly manner which I see so many women's do. They have not the same force or rapidity, and do not produce the same expression. But then I have always supposed it to be my own fault – because I would not take the trouble of prac-tising. It is not that I do not believe *my* fingers as capable as any other woman's of superior execution.'

Nothing, however, can prepare us for Darcy's enigmatic answer to this challenge:

Darcy smiled and said, 'You are perfectly right. You have employed your time much better. No one admitted to the privilege of hearing you can think anything wanting. *We neither of us perform to strangers.*' (*P&P*, p. 146; my emphasis)

This claim can be read as Darcy's irrational love-induced desire to cre-ate an exclusive self-reflexive domain consisting solely of Elizabeth and himself. It is illogical because the very notion of performance, as the novel has consistently demonstrated up to this point, assumes a public audience, a social context. Also, it simply flies in the face of facts: the reader knows, though Darcy has apparently convinced himself other-wise, that Elizabeth certainly 'performs to strangers' – Wickham being the most striking example. In short, Elizabeth is neither a shrinking violet (like Jane) nor a proud recluse (like Darcy). She good-humouredly uses her talents – whether the 'feminine' accomplishment of piano-playing or her more individual wit and charm – in order to take her place on the stage of society in a smooth-running ensemble where most people know their parts (Mary Bennet, whether playing the piano to excess or uttering solemn platitudes, is in the novel to make the contrast clear). When she refuses to 'perform' socially it is because of a higher moral imperative, as the discussion in chapter 7 regarding her proposed visit to her sick sister at Netherfield demonstrates. Mrs Bennet cries, 'You will not be fit to be seen when you get there' – that is, you will be unable to play your proper role as a marriageable young woman – and Elizabeth replies, intransigently, 'I shall be very fit to see Jane – which is all I want' (*P&P*, p. 32). Here social performance is subordinated to the higher demands of a Christian and a sister's duty: privately, without display, to care for those in need.

Thus, it is Darcy's failure to understand the nature of Elizabeth's sense of herself as a societal being and performer of social roles which precipitates the ham-fisted disaster of his attempt to bring off a proposal scene. And it is Elizabeth's sense of moral outrage (on behalf of Jane and Wickham) which holds her back from any temptation to accept Darcy's extraordinary offer. The scene is in itself (for the benefit of the readers) a striking piece of drama, made all the more enjoyable by its echoes of Mr Collins's effort; but for the participants it marks the end of a concern with social performance and a move into more individually defined processes of self-reflection and moral growth.

## BEYOND THEATRICALITY

Darcy's proposal and his subsequent letter of self-justification come almost exactly halfway through the novel. Both Darcy and Elizabeth discount the importance of social performance after this crisis: they both, significantly, refer to their past behaviour as 'acting'. Darcy says in the letter, 'The part which I acted, is now to be explained' (*P&P*, p. 198); and Elizabeth, in response to it, 'How despicably have I acted! . . . Till this moment, I never knew myself' (*P&P*, p. 208). And the key term *perform(ance)* is used only three more times in the novel, contrasting with the sixteen uses of it in the first half. One is neutral of connotation: 'Their journey was performed without much conversation, or any alarm' (*P&P*, p. 217); the other two show that it is impossible entirely to throw off the demands of social performance, even though the narrative emphasis is now on the imperatives of new self-knowledge. 'She was confident of having performed her duty' (*P&P*, p. 232), Elizabeth reflects as she tries to persuade her father not to allow Lydia to go to Brighton; and, in similar acknowledgement of necessary conformity to the proper demands of society, Mr Gardiner writes to his brother-in-law, 'They are not married, nor can I find there was any intention of being so; but if you are willing to perform the engagements which I have ventured to make on your side, I hope it will not be long before they are' (*P&P*, p. 302).

When Darcy and Elizabeth meet unexpectedly at Pemberley, neither of them is at all comfortable on the social stage, though both do their best to recollect themselves to their social duty. Austen takes her hitherto very articulate hero and heroine into a world of minimal and instinctual communication through unconscious body-language – a technique which she was to use more extensively in her final novel *Persuasion*. The uncontrollable communication of face and body is the diametric opposite of the theatricality which is 'normal' behaviour for Austen's highly socialised characters – so that when the latter fails the reading audience is privileged to witness a very private moment. It is a kind of compliment to her readers that Austen represents the audience in this situation by the Gardiners – intelligent, sensible, and sensitive working people (note that they are accompanied by a real 'gardener') – who are observers rather than participants in the class-ridden world of social convention which is the habitus of the leisured gentry:

Their eyes instantly met, and the cheeks of each were overspread with the deepest blush. He absolutely started, and for a moment seemed immovable from surprise; but shortly recovering himself, advanced towards the party, and spoke to Elizabeth, if not in terms of perfect composure, at least of perfect civility.

She had instinctively turned away; but stopping on his approach, received his compliments with an embarrassment impossible to be overcome. Had his first appearance, or his resemblance to the picture they had just been examining, been insufficient to assure the other two that they now saw Mr. Darcy, the gardener's expression of surprise, on beholding his master, must immediately have told it. They stood a little aloof while he was talking to their niece, who, astonished and confused, scarcely dared lift her eyes to his face, and knew not what answer she returned to his civil inquiries after her family. Amazed at the alteration of his manner since they last parted, every sentence that he uttered was increasing her embarrassment; and every idea of the impropriety of her being found there recurring to her mind, the few minutes in which they continued together were some of the most uncomfortable of her life. Nor did he seem much more at ease: when he spoke, his accent had none of its usual sedateness; and he repeated his inquiries as to the time of her having left Longbourn, and of her stay in Derbyshire, so often, and in so hurried a way, as plainly spoke the distraction of his thoughts.

   At length every idea seemed to fail him; and, after standing a few moments without saying a word, he suddenly recollected himself, and took leave. (*P&P*, pp. 251–2)

Dramatic this scene certainly is, but it is not a scene which could have been performed in the huge theatres of Regency England (perhaps it had to await the intimate possibilities of television drama).[9] And the blush, which Austen relies on to betray the feelings of the body, is almost impossible for an actor to reproduce at will. What Austen is allowing her readers to see here is, as it were, the body stripped bare of its cover of social manners – and embarrassed by this. Darcy leaves the scene, but returns a few minutes later having recovered himself; and Elizabeth too has had time to recollect her manners:

With a glance, she saw that he had lost none of his recent civility; and, to imitate his politeness, she began as they met to admire the beauty of the place; but she had not got beyond the words 'delightful,' and 'charming,' when some unlucky recollections obtruded, and she fancied that praise of Pemberley from her might be mischievously construed. Her colour changed, and she said no more. (*P&P*, p. 254)

   He then asked her to walk into the house – but she declared herself not tired, and they stood together on the lawn. At such a time much might have been said, and silence was very awkward. She wanted to talk, but there seemed an embargo on every subject. At last she recollected that she had been travelling, and they talked of Matlock and Dove Dale with great perseverance. (*P&P*, p. 257)

   Darcy's introduction to her of his sister, the equally shy Georgiana, reinforces the reader's sense that Pemberley, though a glorious landscape and a fine building, is not a mere backdrop for the often tawdry theatricalities of social life, such as the Bingley sisters displayed at Netherfield. (In that sense it is something of a Utopia, or prelapsarian Eden, eliminating class barriers, as the novel's last paragraph reminds us by insisting on the Gardiners as 'the means of uniting them'.) We never hear Georgiana speak, but we are told that 'there was sense and good humour in her face, and her manners were perfectly unassuming and gentle' (*P&P*, p. 261).

   The novel offers one final full-blown theatrical scene, Lady Catherine's descent upon Longbourn House to bully Elizabeth out of any intention of marrying Darcy. Austen may have gained some clues for this scene from *The Sultan*: Roxalana prefigures Elizabeth in her ability to combine wit with a strong moral sense in debate with this quasi-omnipotent personage:

SULTAN. Why, won't you consider who I am, and who you are?

ROXALANA. Who I am, and who you are! Yes, sir, I do consider very well that you are the grand Sultan; I am your slave; but I am also a free-born woman, prouder of that than all the pomp and splendour eastern monarchs can bestow.

(Act I)

Compare Elizabeth: 'He is a gentleman; I am a gentleman's daughter; so far we are equal' (*P&P*, p. 356). The character of Lady Rusport, in Richard Cumberland's popular *The West Indian* (1771), may also have provided some inspiration for Lady Catherine's manner and tone. She attempts to bully the (rich) witty heroine Charlotte about her love for Lady Rusport's poor nephew Ensign Dudley:

LADY RUSPORT. ... because my sister chose to marry a beggar, am I bound to support him and his posterity?

CHARLOTTE. I think you are.

LADY RUSPORT. You think I am; and pray where do you find the law that tells you so?

CHARLOTTE. I am not proficient enugh to quote chapter and verse; but I take charity to be a main clause in the great statute of Christianity.

...

CHARLOTTE. A nephew of your ladyship's can never want for other recommendation with me; and, if my partiality for Charles Dudley is acquitted by the rest of the world, I hope Lady Rusport will not condemn me for it.

LADY RUSPORT. I condemn you! I thank heaven, Miss Rusport, I am no ways responsible for your conduct; nor is it any concern of mine how you dispose of yourself ...

(Act I, scene vi)

Lady Rusport's final exit line in the play matches Lady Catherine's indignation about the pollution of the shades of Pemberley: 'Am I become an object of your pity then? Insufferable! confusion light amongst you! marry and be wretched; let me never see you more.' But to my knowledge, there is no scene in the plays known to Austen that really matches the consummate dramatic technique Austen displays here, as Elizabeth skilfully and spiritedly parries every one of Lady Catherine's imperious diktats. Lady Catherine speaks from her sense of her role as an arbiter of social propriety; Elizabeth answers her not as the submissive young woman the *grande dame* expects, but as her own person, intelligent, articulate, polite, but completely unfazed by the artificial claims of

Lady Catherine's status. Lady Catherine, indeed, functions as the last obstacle in the classic structure of romantic comedy – the parental figure who refuses consent. That her dogmatic garrulity should be the proximate cause of Darcy's second proposal is, as Elizabeth later points out, a delicious irony, 'for she loves to be of use' (*P&P*, p. 381).

This comment comes in a postscript to the novel's dramatic structure which returns us more precisely to the world of *Much Ado about Nothing*. Two private scenes between Elizabeth and Darcy, to which only the reader is a privileged witness, allow them to look back over the course of their unwitting courtship, and articulate for themselves and for us its strange byways. The first is a serious discussion following the renewal and acceptance of Darcy's proposal – though even that is punctuated by Elizabeth's prevalent sense of irony: 'After abusing you so abominably to your face, I could have no scruple in abusing you to all your relations' (*P&P*, p. 367). The second begins with the narrator's comment, 'Elizabeth's spirits soon rising to playfulness again, she wanted Mr. Darcy to account for his having ever fallen in love with her' (*P&P*, p. 380). The line is a paraphrase of Benedick's 'I pray thee now tell me, for which of my bad parts didst thou first fall in love with me?' (Act v, scene ii), and the lighthearted conversation that follows in both cases is an important demonstration to the audience that the tensions and misunderstandings of the plot are now quite definitely resolved. Not even offstage villains – Don John, Lady Catherine – can now disturb the profound happiness of these lovers who have found each other despite all the signs that their prickly personalities would not allow it. But, importantly, the heroine does not, as Congreve's Millamant fears for herself, 'dwindle into a wife', nor is her mouth stopped with a masterful kiss as Beatrice's is: Elizabeth retains her 'lively, sportive, manner of talking to' Darcy – thereby providing the next female generation's representative, Georgiana, with an example of a world which perhaps not even Shakespeare imagined: 'By Elizabeth's instructions she began to comprehend that a woman may take liberties with her husband . . .' (*P&P*, pp. 387–8).

## THE LIMITATIONS OF SOCIAL PERFORMANCE

Early in Darcy's acquaintance with Elizabeth he finds himself having to redefine his notion of attractive femininity. Added to her face which has

hardly a good feature . . . [but is] rendered uncommonly intelligent by the beautiful expression of her dark eyes[,] . . . he had detected with a critical eye more than one failure of perfect symmetry in her form, [but] he was forced to acknowledge her figure to be light and pleasing; and in spite of his asserting that her manners were not those of the fashionable world, he was caught by their easy playfulness. (*P&P*, p. 23)

Like Roxalana in *The Sultan*, Elizabeth, low in social status as 'the fashionable world' judges it, nevertheless makes an impression on the most discriminating and sophisticated of men through her vitality, her 'easy playfulness'. A real-life analogy for this kind of cross-status attraction might be found in the various liaisons of the period between actresses and members of royalty. The figure of the beautiful Mrs Robinson ('Perdita', 1758–1800), mistress of the young Prince of Wales, and later a writer of novels and poems, springs to mind. Even more striking (though one would hardly call the lumpish Duke of Clarence a Darcy) are the Elizabeth-like qualities of Dora Jordan, Austen's contemporary (1761–1816), a great comic actress whose work we know Austen saw at least once, and whose most famous roles included the physically energetic and unconventional Priscilla Tomboy, Miss Hoyden, Little Pickle, Roxalana, and Rosalind. The stage's potential physical freedom for women is paralleled in this novel in the country, a space in which Elizabeth can 'run on in [a] wild manner' (*P&P*, p. 42) – both verbally and physically. She is the most energetic of Austen's heroines, as chapter 7's allegorisation of her approach to life emphasises – 'crossing field after field at a quick pace, jumping over stiles and springing over puddles with impatient activity' (*P&P*, p. 32), that activity producing not only unfeminine dirty stockings and petticoat but also a naturally brilliant and glowing (not painted) complexion.

It is the charismatic energy of the theatre's star that is attractive, not the often tawdry roles that she has to perform in order to make a living. Elizabeth is *not* a performer in this latter sense: 'I would really rather not sit down before those who must be in the habit of hearing the very best performers';[10] 'Her performance was pleasing, though by no means capital' (*P&P*, pp. 24–5). The novel's other young women, with the exception of Jane, *are* social performers – they perform the arts and roles that fashionable manners prescribe for femininity, those necessary to win a husband and thus a life-wage. Elizabeth's energy and 'playfulness' give her a charm that is much more organic than the mask of socially dictated femininity, and make her careless of the effect that she creates on those who subscribe to society's gender norms.

Femininity, masculinity, social status, and age are the major role-types performed by members of the society that Austen anatomises. Social status is the most easily observed: Darcy at the Meryton assembly refusing to dance with any of the local girls; Sir William Lucas's fawning on him and his disdainful response; the insulting doubts with which he bolsters his first proposal to Elizabeth: all these arise from Darcy's awareness of what is due to him as a man of high social status. Lydia's claiming precedence when she returns home a married woman is another example of the display that governs society's self-definition.

Jane Bennet, the eldest sister who should rightly – according to her status – have married first, in fact fails to conform to this social norm because her femininity is insufficiently theatrical. She does not sing or play the piano; her accomplishments are not such as attract notice in fashionable society. She doesn't even flirt, like Lydia or (more elegantly) Elizabeth. This point about a young woman's need for overt display is made early in the novel, before even the emphatic discussion of female accomplishments in chapter 8. Elizabeth is blinded by her love for her sister, believing that everyone must understand Jane as well as she does. Charlotte Lucas, however, sees things as they are:

'. . . it is sometimes a disadvantage to be so very guarded. If a woman conceals her affection with the same skill from the object of it, she may lose the opportunity of fixing him; and it will then be but poor consolation to believe the world equally in the dark. There is so much of gratitude or vanity in almost every attachment, that it is not safe to leave any to itself. We can all *begin* freely – a slight preference is natural enough: but there are very few of us who have heart enough to be really in love without encouragement. In nine cases out of ten a woman had better show *more* affection than she feels. Bingley likes your sister, undoubtedly; but he may never do more than like her, if she does not help him on.' (*P&P*, pp. 21–2)

Bingley himself is an indefinite young man, relying on his reputation for impetuosity as a substitute for adult masculinity and the responsibilities that (theoretically) go with the role. Darcy articulates this, using once again the key word *performance*:

'. . . The power of doing anything with quickness is always much prized by the possessor, and often without any attention to the imperfection of the performance. When you told Mrs. Bennet this morning, that if you ever resolved on quitting Netherfield you should be gone in five minutes, you meant it to be a sort of panegyric, of compliment to yourself – and yet what is there so very laudable in a precipitance which must leave very necessary business undone, and can be of no real advantage to yourself or anyone else?' (*P&P*, p. 49)

Bingley is dominated by Darcy, who makes decisions 'for the best' for him – in a way that marks the younger man as almost boyish, feminine (the onomatopoeia of his name suggests an unmasculine lightness). Like Claudio in *Much Ado*, he is barely ready for love – and quite content to accept the opinions of his elders as to the suitability or otherwise of his idealised lady, without, as Charlotte points out, having got to know her at all as an individual.

Charlotte, of course, takes her own advice as though it were medicine, in making clear her availability to Mr Collins. As she says to Elizabeth, 'I am not romantic you know. I never was. I ask only a comfortable home' (*P&P*, p. 125); and in performing enough of the submissive young lady to fill Mr Collins's bill, she in fact gains not only her own home and guaranteed support, but also control over the more offensive of Mr Collins's extravagant displays:

> Her ladyship, with great condescension, arose to receive them; and as Mrs. Collins had settled it with her husband that the office of introduction should be hers, it was *performed in a proper manner*, without any of those apologies and thanks which he would have thought necessary. (*P&P*, p. 161; my emphasis)

Mr Collins in fact matches Charlotte in his consciousness of the need to perform one's social role. It is just that he does it so badly, with such stupidity and overbearing punctiliousness that he is well-nigh unbearable to all but the equally stupid. For the reader, his exaggerated perception of the clergyman's role serves comically to underline the novel's abiding interest in society's problematic demands on the individual. Mr Collins is as interested in the word 'performance' as Darcy and Elizabeth are, but he does not have their ability to analyse the concept with critical sophistication. Who can forget his letter of self-introduction, with its hierarchy of good intentions: '. . . it shall be my earnest endeavour to demean myself with grateful respect towards her Ladyship, and be ever ready to perform those rites and ceremonies which are instituted by the Church of England' (*P&P*, p. 63). Likewise his ill-conceived determination 'to perform what I look on as a point of duty' in introducing himself at the Netherfield ball to Lady Catherine's nephew – his social superior (but for Mr Collins 'the clerical office [is] equal in point of dignity with the highest rank in the kingdom' (*P&P*, p. 97)). He further distinguishes himself there by an exhibition which adds to Elizabeth's embarrassment at the social performance of her family. Following Mary's display of her feeble musical accomplishments, and Mr Bennet's tactless – if acute – comment ('You have delighted us long enough. Let the other young ladies have time to exhibit'), he offers this absurdity as his contribution:

'If I,' said Mr. Collins, 'were so fortunate as to be able to sing, I should have great pleasure, I am sure, in obliging the company with an air; for I consider music as a very innocent diversion, and perfectly compatible with the profession of a clergyman . . .' (*P&P*, p. 101)

The 'bow to Mr. Darcy', with which 'he concluded his speech, which had been spoken so loud as to be heard by half the room', indicates how consciously Mr Collins is here performing what he considers to be a fine role, but

to Elizabeth it appeared, that had her family made an agreement to expose themselves as much as they could during the evening, it would have been impossible for them to *play their parts* with more spirit or finer success; and happy did she think it for Bingley and her sister that some of the *exhibition* had escaped his notice, and that his feelings were not of a sort to be much distressed by the folly which he must have witnessed. That his two sisters and Mr. Darcy, however, should have such an opportunity of ridiculing her relations, was bad enough, and she could not determine whether the silent contempt of the gentleman, or the insolent smiles of the ladies, were more intolerable. (*P&P*, pp. 101–2; my emphases)

Mr Collins's entire proposal to Elizabeth is a performance conned, one suspects, from the pages of those circulating-library novels which it is the clergyman's duty to condemn – as he does, 'protest[ing] that he never read novels' (*P&P*, p. 68), on his first night at Longbourn. Prurient private reading of these has taught him what to expect as the typical behaviour of 'elegant females' in the courtship situation:

'I am not now to learn,' replied Mr. Collins, with a formal wave of the hand, 'that it is usual with young ladies to reject the addresses of the man whom they secretly mean to accept, when he first applies for their favour; and that sometimes the refusal is repeated a second or even a third time. I am therefore by no means discouraged by what you have just said, and shall hope to lead you to the altar ere long.' (*P&P*, p. 107)

His egregious obtuseness allows him to show off his clerical rhetorical skills with repetition and elegant variation of the same point. Thus, unconsciously, he also serves Austen's aim of satirising the social construction of gender roles:

'When I do myself the honour of speaking to you next on the subject, I shall hope to receive a more favourable answer than you have now given me; though I am far from accusing you of cruelty at present, because I know it to be the established custom of your sex to reject a man on the first application, and perhaps you have even now said as much to encourage my suit as would be consistent with the true delicacy of the female character.' (*P&P*, p. 108)

And again: he *knows* how the rejected lover responds to this 'elegant' feminine performance:

'. . . As I must therefore conclude that you are not serious in your rejection of me, I shall choose to attribute it to your wish of increasing my love by suspense, according to the usual practice of elegant females.'

At least it can be said in Darcy's favour that in his first proposal to Elizabeth – which has so many echoes of this comic scene – he has the grace to accept her refusal and the intelligence not to contest it. His exit line is that of a true gentleman:

'You have said quite enough, madam. I perfectly comprehend your feelings, and have now only to be ashamed of what my own have been. Forgive me for having taken up so much of your time, and accept my best wishes for your health and happiness.'
And with these words he hastily left the room . . . (*P&P*, p. 193)

Difficult and even somewhat socially gauche Mr Darcy may be, but he emerges as the truly masculine man and hero of the novel. Austen was clearly fascinated by the contrasting figure of easy and attractive maleness: each of her novels presents as a major character one of those plausible actors whose charming performance is a genuine threat to the heroine's peace of mind. John Willoughby, George Wickham, Henry Crawford, Frank Churchill, William Walter Elliot, even Henry Tilney take cues for their behaviour from their immediate environment, in a way that will always show them to their best advantage. Chameleon-like in their ability to present an appropriate face (or mask) in every situation, these professional actors on the social stage are unfathomable to the right-thinking young women on whose experience of life the novels focus. Yet, the chief effect of their artful performance is to *appear* fathomable, to *act* as the epitome of 'normal' masculinity. In questioning this societal norm via a plot which shows them up ultimately as morally extremely dubious (with the exception of Henry Tilney, the fantastic combination of clergyman and charming man of the world), Austen engages in a radical and ongoing critique of her society's investment in surface appearance. But – like Henry Tilney – she also delights in it. She does not preach withdrawal, Darcy-like, from the little *theatrum mundi*, but rather observation, engagement, sympathy, and judgement – the characteristics of a good audience.

In this light, Elizabeth experiences her acquaintance with Wickham as an education in critical judgement of social performance (as do Jane and Charlotte to a lesser extent). His first appearance on the stage of Meryton is noted thus:

> the attention of every lady was soon caught by a young man, whom they had never seen before, of most gentlemanlike appearance . . . the young man wanted only regimentals to make him completely charming. His appearance was greatly in his favour; he had all the best part of beauty, a fine countenance, a good figure, and very pleasing address. The introduction was followed up on his side by a happy readiness of conversation – a readiness at the same time perfectly correct and unassuming. (*P&P*, p. 72)

It sounds like a description of a promising new young actor (who will look particularly good in a soldier's red coat). Within four pages, at their next meeting – and with very little by way of invitation – Wickham begins to perform for Elizabeth his self-scripted monodrama:

> Mr. Wickham was the happy man towards whom almost every female eye was turned, and Elizabeth was the happy woman by whom he finally seated himself; and the agreeable manner in which he immediately fell into conversation, though it was only on its being a wet night, and on the probability of a rainy season, made her feel that the commonest, dullest, most threadbare topic might be rendered interesting by the skill of the speaker. (*P&P*, p. 76)

In fact his performance, as it proceeds to cast Darcy as a villain, verges on the improper, as Elizabeth is later to recognise: after reading Darcy's letter, 'She was *now* struck with the impropriety of such communications to a stranger, and wondered it had escaped her before' (*P&P*, p. 207). What she had been seduced by was the world of theatre, where such scandalous revelations as Wickham's blackening of Darcy's character are the fascinating norm. She and Jane discuss the performance the next day, without yet being sophisticated enough in the ways of the world to recognise that it *is* a performance. For Jane, 'it was not in her nature to question the veracity of a young man of such amiable appearance as Wickham'. Elizabeth is impressed by his consummate naturalism:

> 'I can much more easily believe Mr. Bingley's being imposed on, than that Mr. Wickham should invent such a history of himself as he gave me last night; names, facts, everything mentioned without ceremony. If it be not so, let Mr. Darcy contradict it. Besides, there was truth in his looks.' (*P&P*, pp. 85–6)

Elizabeth anticipates 'seeing a confirmation of every thing in Mr. Darcy's looks and behaviour' at the Netherfield ball. But life fails to imitate art, and Darcy does not behave according to the script.

Wickham remains throughout the novel an actor, able to improvise a new mask in response to whatever reversals occur. His previous attempts to change his profession, narrated in Darcy's letter – clergyman, lawyer, or soldier, all simply roles on the public stage where he can earn both a living and admiration – underline our sense of his protean character. By the time of his departure for Brighton, Elizabeth 'had even learnt to detect, in the very gentleness which had first delighted her, an affectation and a sameness to disgust and weary' (*P&P*, p. 233). Wickham is not, finally, in the first rank of actors. And when he reappears, unabashed, at Longbourn, as a member of the family, the last dialogue between him and Elizabeth is one in which he barely survives as a performer, despite attempts to gain lost ground through a display of pathos:

'... One ought not to repine; but, to be sure, it would have been such a thing for me! The quiet, the retirement of such a life, would have answered all my ideas of happiness! But it was not to be ...' (*P&P*, p. 328)

It is Elizabeth who has the last word in the scene – indeed, she writes it, and directs her own performance so as to show up the shallowness of Wickham's:

unwilling for her sister's sake, to provoke him, she only said in reply, with a good-humoured smile:
    'Come, Mr. Wickham, we are brother and sister, you know. Do not let us quarrel about the past. In future, I hope we shall be always of one mind.'
    She held out her hand; he kissed it with affectionate gallantry, though he hardly knew how to look, and they entered the house. (*P&P*, p. 329)

In the course of the novel Elizabeth has learnt a lot, not only in the moral and emotional fields of self-knowledge, but as a critical observer of the whole range of social performance, and, when necessary, as a confident actor herself on that public stage. The occasional (and unavoidable) moments of ceremonial grandeur of Elizabeth's life at Pemberley will produce no stage-fright in this young woman. Like Roxalana, Lettitia, Beatrice, or Rosalind, she has gained respect, love, and status through her personal integrity combined with a charismatic vitality: 'sure, my lord, my mother cried, but then there was a star danced, and under that was I born'.[11]

# CHAPTER FIVE

# Mansfield Park: *Fanny's education in the theatre*

Julia Bertram may have missed out on the starring role she wanted in *Lovers' Vows*, but her author compensates her with the fine dramatic entry which brings down the curtain on volume I of *Mansfield Park*: 'the door of the room was thrown open, and Julia appearing at it, with a face all aghast, exclaimed, "My father is come! He is in the hall at this moment"' (*MP*, p. 172).[1]

Thus, in this most apparently anti-theatrical of her novels, Jane Austen employs the methods of the drama with brilliant panache. It is an audacious conclusion to an extraordinary series of chapters in the novel. In an earlier essay I argued that in *Mansfield Park* Austen is deliberately writing against the grain of her audience's expectations, after the success of *Pride and Prejudice*, that she should produce another 'light and bright and sparkling' romantic comedy.[2] Instead she placed issues such as sexual attraction, charm, and wit, and their relation to morality, in a different light, writing an anti-romance which can profitably be read as modelled in some ways on the late medieval English morality plays such as *Everyman*. Thus we are encouraged to think, at least on one level of our reading, of the Crawfords as the World (hence the narrator's insistent references to Henry's 'vanity'[3]), and the Bertram family as Pride (Sir Thomas), Sloth (Lady Bertram), Avarice (Mrs Norris, also Self Conceit), Lust (Maria), Envy (Julia, also Anger). (The minor character Dr Grant is the incarnation of the least heinous deadly sin, Gluttony.) Tom Bertram represents Dissipation, or the Prodigal Son. Against this set of allegorical figures are placed the hero and heroine of a Christian drama, Edmund or Everyman, who consciously tries to do good but is tempted and falls (significantly his home is named Man's-field), and Fanny, the steadfast virtuous woman – or, in biblical terms, the Pearl of Great *Price* (Matt.13:45–6). In this chapter I attempt to go beyond this schema and investigate the novel's recognition that theatricality, like the world, is always with us – and it cannot be harnessed uncomplicatedly to serve the cause of morality.

### HENRY CRAWFORD, THE VICE

Allegorical figures such as those from the medieval theatre mentioned above left their influence on Shakespeare and later dramatists. Cardinal Wolsey's famous speech from *Henry VIII*, 'Farewell, a long farewell to all my greatness' (Act III, scene ii), which Henry Crawford reads aloud to the Mansfield Park family (*MP*, p. 337), is a fine example of Shakespeare's use of this genre, Wolsey representing here the fall of Pride. But most strikingly, Shakespeare took over the character-type of the Vice for his own purposes. Characters like Richard III and Iago are clearly evil, but they are also witty, clever tricksters, who enlist the audience's complicity in their nefarious doings. Richard III is one of the characters that Henry Crawford says he would be happy to 'undertake', when the putting on of a play at Mansfield is first proposed (*MP*, p. 123). There is no doubt that he would play the role with relish: compare Richard's planned seduction of Lady Anne, which he announces gleefully to the audience in his opening scene, with this speech of Henry's to his sister and complicit audience, Mary:

'. . . I do not like to eat the bread of idleness.[4] No, my plan is to make Fanny Price in love with me.'

'Fanny Price! Nonsense! No, no. You ought to be satisfied with her two cousins.'

'But I cannot be satisfied without Fanny Price, without making a small hole in Fanny Price's heart . . .' (*MP*, p. 229)

The episode of the theatricals in *Mansfield Park*, by displaying Henry Crawford as an excellent and enthusiastic actor, emphasises his position as a star of the novel's morality play. As a performer he is quick, sensitive, and multi-talented:

'I really believe,' said he, 'I could be fool enough at this moment to undertake any character that was ever written, from Shylock or Richard III, down to the singing hero of a farce in his scarlet coat and cocked hat. I feel as if I could be any thing or every thing, as if I could rant and storm, or sigh, or cut capers in any tragedy or comedy in the English language.' (*MP*, p. 123)

This self-portrait is probably intended to recall the pre-eminent mid-eighteenth-century actor, David Garrick[5] – Richard III being one of his most famous roles. The actor was also noted for his versatility in both comedy and tragedy. Garrick retired from the stage in 1776, but his reputation as the greatest of naturalistic actors remained strong in Jane Austen's day. Sheridan's encomium is representative:

> The grace of Action – the adapted Mien
> Faithful as Nature to the varied Scene;
> Th'expressive Glance – whose subtle Comment draws
> Entranc'd Attention, and a mute Applause;
> Gesture that marks, with Force and Feeling fraught,
> A Sense in Silence, and a Will in Thought;
> Harmonious Speech, whose pure and liquid Tone
> Gives Verse a Music, scarce confess'd its own . . . [6]

To underline Henry Crawford's modelling on the consummate actor Garrick, Mr Rushworth is made to remark pointedly on Crawford's slight size: 'to see such an undersized, little, mean-looking man, set up for a fine actor, is very ridiculous in my opinion' (*MP*, p. 165). Garrick was only 5 feet 6 inches tall.[7] But for impressionable young women, Garrick was perfection. In Fanny Burney's *Evelina* (which Austen knew well), the heroine goes to Drury Lane Theatre early in her 'entrance into the world', where she sees Garrick as Ranger in Hoadly's *The Suspicious Husband*:

Such ease! such vivacity in his manner! such grace in his motions! such fire and meaning in his eyes! – I could hardly believe he had studied a written part, for every word seemed spoke from the impulse of the moment. His action – at once so graceful and so free! his voice – so wonderfully various in its tones – such animation! every look *speaks*![8]

The Bertram girls' private rhapsodies no doubt ran along the same lines. Henry progresses from being thought by the Bertram sisters 'absolutely plain' to 'not so very plain':

he had so much countenance, and his teeth were so good, and he was so well made, that one soon forgot he was plain; and after a third interview, after dining in company with him at the parsonage, he was no longer allowed to be called so by any body. (*MP*, p. 44)

Apart from the perception of his being 'well made' (like Garrick), this might almost be a transcription of Lady Anne's thought-process regarding Richard III. The man has a seductive charm that rewrites his audience's perceptions.

The *Encyclopédiste* Diderot, who was fascinated by Garrick's power and versatility, used him as an example of his *Paradoxe sur le comédien*, who needs

a great deal of judgement; he should be a cold and calm spectator; I require of him, consequently, penetration and *no sensibility*; the art of imitating everything, or, the same thing, an equal aptitude at all sorts of characters and roles.[9]

Henry Crawford is 'the best actor' at Mansfield Park because he possesses these basic prerequisites. On the other hand, as Jocelyn Harris has pointed out, 'changefulness' – the versatility exhibited in such Machiavellian villains as Richard III – was the most feared and reprehensible feature of theatricality in the eighteenth century: 'Lovelace [in *Clarissa*] himself is identified with the chameleon and the Proteus of Richard's speech, in *3 Henry VI* [Act III, scene ii].'[10] His versatility marks Henry Crawford even more specifically as the villain of the piece – in sum, the Vice.

Austen, like Shakespeare, ensures that we recognise the Vice's ancestry in the biblical figure of Satan and his avatars. Henry is a wanderer: 'To anything like a permanence of abode, or limitation of society, Henry Crawford had, unluckily, a great dislike' (*MP*, p. 41).[11] Like the medieval and Shakespearean Vice figures, Henry is an excellent impersonator and equally an accomplished card-player and gambler. Only Henry and his sister are fully at home in the game of Speculation: 'though it was impossible for Fanny not to feel herself mistress of the rules of the game in three minutes, he had yet to inspirit her play, sharpen her avarice, and harden her heart' (*MP*, p. 240). In the same episode the conversation turns to the alterations and 'improvements' to established houses that Henry proposes, first on the eventful trip to Sotherton ('what was done there is not to be told!' says Mary (*MP*, p. 244) – though it has in fact been told, by Jane Austen); and secondly at Edmund's parsonage at Thornton Lacey. Henry came upon this by chance in his wanderings – as he significantly comments, 'I never do wrong without gaining by it' (*MP*, p. 241). His plans for Edmund's parsonage propose another wholesale disruption of order:

'. . . You may raise it into a *place*. From being the mere gentleman's residence, it becomes, by judicious improvement, the residence of a man of education, taste, modern manners, good connections. All this may be stamped on it; and that house receive such an air as to make its owner be set down as the great landholder of the parish, by every creature travelling the road . . . ' (*MP*, p. 244)

Henry is imagining here a theatrical transformation, the production of an impressive but false 'scene' in which Edmund may pretend to be a grand landowner, rather than a gentleman and country parson. But Edmund is not tempted by the prospect of glamour: 'I must be satisfied with rather less ornament and beauty.'

Well after the episode of the theatricals, Henry's discussion with Edmund about the virtues of clerical eloquence turns on his seeing himself in the role of fashionable preacher:

'A thoroughly good sermon, thoroughly well delivered, is a capital gratification. I can never hear such a one without the greatest admiration and respect, and more than half a mind to take orders and preach myself . . . I never listened to a distinguished preacher in my life, without a sort of envy. But then, I must have a London audience. I could not preach, but to the educated; to those who were capable of estimating my composition. And, I do not know that I should be fond of preaching often; now and then, perhaps, once or twice in the spring, after being anxiously expected for half a dozen Sundays together; but not for a constancy; it would not do for a constancy.' (*MP*, p. 341)

There is nothing intrinsically wrong in using one's dramatic talents to woo an audience to spiritual improvement: Austen herself wrote of a preacher, 'I heard him [Mr Sherer] for the first time last Sunday, & he gave us an excellent Sermon – a little too eager sometimes in his delivery, but that is to *me* a better extreme than the want of animation, especially when it evidently comes from the heart as in him' (*Letters*, 25 September 1813). But *gratification, envy, audience* are words that point to Henry's true avocation; and it is only Fanny, of all his present audience, who has the courage to challenge him concerning his frivolous admission of a lack of 'constancy' in such serious matters. Ever eager for new roles, at another point Henry is momentarily taken with the idea of playing the heroic young sailor in emulation of William Price – but as the narrator comments, 'The wish was rather eager than lasting' (*MP*, p. 236).[12]

Henry Crawford, *reading* Shakespeare around the domestic hearth, is performing at his most admirable; he has turned his Garrick-like protean talents into the appearance of a gentleman's accomplishment:

in Mr. Crawford's reading there was a variety of excellence beyond what she had ever met with . . . whether it were dignity or pride, or tenderness or remorse, or whatever were to be expressed, he could do it with equal beauty. – It was truly dramatic. – His acting had first taught Fanny what pleasure a play might give, and his reading brought all his acting before her again . . . (*MP*, p. 337)

Shakespeare ('part of an Englishman's constitution', says Henry) escapes the taint of transgression that Mrs Inchbald's German-derived play produced. And Fanny recognises the 'pleasure' that the 'beauty' of true drama can give. Neither she nor her author is a puritanical prude regarding the place of legitimate theatre in their culture. 'For her own gratification she could have wished that something might be acted, for she had never even seen half a play, but every thing of higher consequence was against it' (*MP*, p. 131). The theatre's place in the education of a young woman cannot, however, be so easily dismissed.

Like his sister Mary, rootless and improperly parented (the Admiral who brought them up is specifically associated with vice through Mary's pointed and improper pun about '*Rears* and *Vices*', *MP*, p. 60), Henry is happiest when he has persuaded those around him to abandon their principles and plunge into the intoxicating world of make-believe, of acting, when anyone may be – or do – anything without reference to the normal restrictions on behaviour. Henry later refers to the theatricals with some nostalgia: 'There was such an interest, such an animation, such a spirit diffused! Every body felt it. *We were all alive.* There was employment, hope, solicitude, bustle, for every hour of the day' (*MP*, p. 225; my emphasis). That is, only while acting does Henry feel really alive and purposeful; he has no other 'employment'.

The 'bustle' of private theatricals had employed a great deal of the energy and money of the gentry and aristocracy in the period 1780–1805[13] (as we saw in chapter 1 above, even the Austen family indulged in thoroughly prepared home productions during several Christmas/New Year holidays). Anti-theatrical forces massed to the attack in the last years of the century: Thomas Gisborne's *Enquiry into the Duties of the Female Sex* (1797), which Austen read in 1805, had this to say:

> It is a custom liable to this objection among others; that it is almost certain to prove, in its effects, particularly injurious to the female performers . . . What is even then the tendency of such amusements? to encourage vanity; to excite a thirst of applause and admiration on account of attainments which, if they are to be thus exhibited, it would commonly have been far better for the individual not to possess; to destroy diffidence by the unrestrained familiarity with persons of the other sex, which inevitably results from being joined with them in the drama . . .[14]

By 1814, Marilyn Butler states, 'the increasingly strong Evangelical movement had sufficiently publicized the link between upper-class immorality and its rage for private theatricals',[15] so that even though the vogue was largely over when Austen was writing, she had recent cultural memory to draw on in pursuit of her larger agenda: not to attack the theatre, but through the first volume's focus on the theatricals, to alert the reader to the moral ambiguity pervading the highly theatricalised society that she anatomises.

Edmund's first response to the proposal of the theatricals is an objection on the grounds of its inappropriateness for 'gentlemen and ladies, who have all the disadvantages of education and decorum to struggle through' (*MP*, p. 124). Edmund's half-ironic comment here also indicates his awareness of the historic class difference between actors and their patrons: acting is a 'trade'. He is willing (even eager) to acknowledge the 'good hardened real' work of actors, who offer escapist fantasy in exchange for the audience's money, but he has been 'bred' to know that 'as *we* are circumstanced' it would be 'very wrong' (*MP*, p. 125): 'It would be taking liberties with my father's house in his absence which could not be justified' (*MP*, p. 127). In short, it would allow the sort of carnival disruption of hierarchised society that had been going on in France for the previous quarter of a century.

*Lovers' Vows*, the play that is finally (inevitably) chosen, was originally a German play by August von Kotzebue (1791), and therefore suffused with foreign radicalism, at least to English anti-Jacobin eyes. Cobbett, for example: 'It is the universal aim of German authors of the present day, to exhibit the brightest examples of virtues among the lower classes of society; while the higher orders, by their folly and profligacy, are held up to contempt and detestation.'[16] Wordsworth, Coleridge, and Hannah More were among the public intellectuals who inveighed against what Wordsworth in the Preface to *Lyrical Ballads* called 'sickly and stupid German tragedies'. *The Oracle* fulminated in the same year (1802) against the newest fashion in drama:

The most remarkable species of mental disease, which occasioned a temporary suspension of common sense in this capital, was imported in bundles of paper, inscribed with Teutonic characters which, when translated into English, communicated the contagion to the higher ranks of society with the rapidity of the electric fluid. The first symptoms were a strange admiration of ghosts, mouldering castles, sulphurous flames, bloody daggers, and other terrific images of a distempered imagination. In this stage of the disease it may be denominated the *Spectromania*; but on the introduction of a larger quantity of the infectious matter, the dangerous symptoms increased, and it assumed a formidable appearance under the name of *Kotzebue-mania*... The patients were afflicted with a childish passion for noise, faintings, the startings and ravings of others deeply affected with the same disease, and a strong abhorrence of common sense.[17]

As Inchbald remarked in her preface to the 1808 edition of *Lovers' Vows*: 'Plays, founded on German dramas, have long been a subject both of ridicule and of serious animadversion.' Even Hazlitt, in 1815, reviewing a revival of the play, felt it necessary to remark, 'The whole of this play, which is of German origin, carries the romantic in sentiment and story to the extreme verge of decency as well as probability.'[18] In the light of the deluge of melodramatic plays that was to characterise early nineteenth-century drama, giving voice to fallen women and working-class heroes, it is hard to see what was so objectionable about Kotzebue. But hindsight can be deceptive: Kotzebue's foreignness and his avowed enthusiasm for the ideas of Rousseau, during the political and philosophical turmoil that followed the French Revolution, made him an obvious whipping-boy for the anti-Jacobins.

Nevertheless *Lovers' Vows*, which premiered in Inchbald's adaptation in October 1798, was immensely popular both on the stage and as a reading drama. Published soon after its first performance at Covent Garden, it had gone into a twelfth edition by the following year. It was performed at the Bath theatre fifteen times during the years 1801–6 when the Austens lived there. Other plays based on Kotzebue were equally successful: Sheridan's spectacular patriotic drama *Pizarro* (1799), Thompson's tear-jerker *The Stranger* (1798).[19] As Margaret Kirkham first pointed out, Austen made use of another Kotzebue play, *Die Versöhnung* (done into English as *The Birth-Day*) in *Emma* (I discuss this play in chapter 6). English playwrights, that is to say, found Kotzebue extremely useful in providing new plots for an audience that had probably had their fill of Gothic sensationalism but still desired to indulge their emotions in the theatre.

The plot of *Lovers' Vows*, like that of many of the melodramas to come, criticises the immorality of Baron Wildenhaim, who years ago seduced and abandoned a lower-class woman, and who is now encouraging the marriage of his legitimate daughter Amelia with the rich but foolish Count Cassel. The happy dénouement defies class barriers as the Baron is persuaded by his conscience (and Anhalt the clergyman) to make an honest woman of Agatha and thus legitimise the hero Frederick (Figure 7). *Mansfield Park* approaches such radicalism in some elements of its plot: Sir Thomas is shown to be a weak father; Fanny the disregarded quasi-servant becomes a full member of the baronet's family.[20] On the other hand, one of the key inflammatory words of the French Revolution was the cry 'Liberty!' In the scene in *Lovers' Vows* in which Amelia/Mary and Anhalt/Edmund discuss the emotional bonds of marriage, 'Liberty!' is the one desire of the imagined couple in an unhappy marriage. Austen uses this idea with a conservative slant. Maria Bertram has locked herself into the cage of prudential marriage, and ' "cannot get out," as the starling said' (*MP*, p. 99). When she does, aided by Henry Crawford, she 'pass[es] around the edge of the gate' of morality; her 'liberty' finally

LOVERS VOWS

FREDERICK HA! MOTHER! FATHER

ACT V. SCENE.

7 *Lovers' Vows*, final tableau; frontispiece to Elizabeth Inchbald (ed.), *The British Theatre*, London, 1808, vol. XXIII (By permission of the British Library, 1345.2.23)

only leaves her in the purgatory of a remote private establishment with Mrs Norris.

As the critical literature demonstrates, Kotzebue's play, as adapted by Inchbald, can be used to support both a conservative and a radical reading of the novel. More to the point is that any play selected by the bored young people would have served for Austen's introduction of the theme of carnival disruption, the great house turned topsy-turvy; and for the theme of the unavoidable theatricality of adult social life, which makes up the novel's final two volumes. Inchbald's play is ultimately most useful to Austen, not for its questionably subversive politics, but because it provides two strong female parts in scenes which suit perfectly the development of plot, character, and theme in this novel. And Fanny's encounter with the theatre in this form offers a special educational experience to her – one might even call it sex education.

At the first opportunity after the decision to perform *Lovers' Vows* has been taken, Fanny eagerly reads the play:

> Her curiosity was all awake, and she ran through it with an eagerness which was suspended only by intervals of astonishment, that it could be chosen in the present instance – that it could be proposed and accepted in a private Theatre! Agatha and Amelia appeared to her in their different ways so totally improper for home representation – the situation of one, and the language of the other, so unfit to be expressed by any woman of modesty, that she could hardly suppose her cousins could be aware of what they were engaging in . . . (*MP*, p. 137)

Fanny knows about sex, knows what is 'immodest'; but the knowledge is theoretical. It has never yet been presented before her as an activity that real people – for example, her cousins – 'engage in'. Psychologically speaking, this is the perception of a child. Contrast Mary Crawford's easy double-entendre on the evening of the same day: 'What gentleman among you, am I to have the pleasure of making love to?' (*MP*, p. 143).

The East Room, where the rehearsal of Edmund and Mary's scene takes place, is the old school-room of the Bertram children and Fanny. Only she goes there now; it is her 'comfort' space: 'Her plants, her books – of which she had been a collector, from the very first hour of her commanding a shilling' (*MP*, p. 151). Edmund remarks on the books she is reading when he comes in to consult her about whether he should take part in the play – significantly, no plays or novels are mentioned. Mary's comment reinforces Austen's designation of this as a symbolic space, when she in her turn comes to rehearse:

'. . . We must have two chairs at hand for you to bring forward to the front of the stage.²¹ There – very good schoolroom chairs, not made for a theatre, I dare say; much more fitted for little girls to sit at and kick their feet against when they are learning a lesson. What would your governess and your uncle say to see them used for such a purpose? . . .' (*MP*, p. 169)

When Edmund arrives and 'propose[s], urge[s], entreat[s]' Mary to rehearse the scene with him the atmosphere is clearly as heady with desire as these verbs imply. And Fanny has to witness it: 'To prompt them must be enough for her; and it was sometimes *more* than enough; for she could not always pay attention to the book.' Here is theatre working at its most potent, in the terms of the contemporary critical theory I discussed in chapter 2:

she was inclined to believe their performance would, indeed, have such *nature and feeling* in it, as must ensure their credit, and make it a very *suffering exhibition* to herself. (*MP*, p. 170; my emphases)

Edmund has clearly contravened his role as preserver of decorum, not only in regard to his own behaviour but also in so far as he is violating Fanny's virginally pure imagination by playing out the scene with Mary. Within hours he is further transgressing in joining with the others to persuade Fanny to read Cottager's Wife in the public rehearsal.²² From this fate worse than death she is only saved by the fortuitous arrival of the true head of the household, Sir Thomas. Thus even Fanny is implicated, as 'victim' or melodrama heroine, in the novel's wide-ranging use of the discourse of theatre.

Notwithstanding her recruitment into the novel's metadrama, Fanny is unique as a heroine at this point in Jane Austen's oeuvre because she is *not* a public 'performer'. Her desperate declaration, 'I could not act any thing if you were to give me the world. No, indeed, I cannot act' (*MP*, p. 145), with its significant resonances of Christ's temptation on the mount (Luke 4:5–8), is also a statement about how she sees herself in the social world: unlike Elizabeth Bennet, she will not play its games. But in volume II of the novel Fanny is obliged, by the coercive power of the structure in which she lives, to enter upon the social stage. She is a young, marriageable woman: she cannot escape the role that her class and gender dictate.²³

Austen has prepared the reader for contemplation of the subtle but pervasive power of these structures by alerting us in volume I to the power of *acknowledged* theatricality. The play *Lovers' Vows* itself (and Austen clearly assumes that her contemporary readership is familiar with it) particularly emphasises the rules of the game of courtship, which are spectacularly transgressed by the role-reversals of the Amelia–Anhalt scene:

AMELIA. I will not marry.
ANHALT. You mean to say, you will not fall in love.
AMELIA. Oh no! [*Ashamed.*] I am in love.
ANHALT. Are in love! [*Starting.*] And with the Count?
AMELIA. I wish I was.
ANHALT. Why so?
AMELIA. Because *he* would, perhaps, love me again.
ANHALT. [*Warmly.*] Who is there that would not?
AMELIA. Would you?
ANHALT. I – I – me – I – I am out of the question.
AMELIA. No, you are the very person to whom I have put the question.
ANHALT. What do you mean?
AMELIA. I am glad you don't understand me. I was afraid I had spoken
    too plain. [*In confusion.*]
ANHALT. Understand you! – As to that – I am not dull.
AMELIA. I know you are not – And as you have for a long time instructed me,
    why should not I now begin to teach you?
ANHALT. Teach me what?
AMELIA. Whatever I know, and you don't.
ANHALT. There are some things, I would rather never know.
AMELIA. So you may remember I said, when you began to teach me
    mathematics. I said, I had rather not know it – But now I have learnt it,
    it gives me great deal of pleasure – and [*Hesitating.*] perhaps, who can tell,
    but that I might teach something as pleasant to you, as resolving a probem
    is to me.
ANHALT. Woman herself is a problem.
AMELIA. And I'll teach you to make her out.
ANHALT. You teach?
AMELIA. Why not? None but a woman can teach the science of herself: and
    though I own I am very young, a young woman may be as agreeable for
    a tutoress as an old one. – I am sure I always learnt faster from you than
    from the old clergyman, who taught me before you came.
ANHALT. This is nothing to the subject!
AMELIA. What is the subject?
ANHALT. – Love.
AMELIA. [*Going up to him.*] Come, then, teach it me as you taught me geography,
    languages, and other important things.
ANHALT. [*Turning from her.*] Pshaw!
AMELIA. Ah! you won't – you know you have already taught me that, and you
    won't begin again.

ANHALT. You misconstrue – you misconceive every thing, I say or do. The
     subject I came to you upon – was marriage.
AMELIA. A very proper subject for the man, who has taught me love, and I
     accept the proposal.

(Act III, scene ii)

In itself this is an extraordinary love scene for its period – I know of
nothing like it in contemporary drama – and one can imagine the delight
with which Austen seized upon it to add resonances to her own narrative.
Edmund and Mary are undoubtedly perfectly type-cast in these roles:
the idealistic and earnest young man, and the archly 'forward' young
woman, never slow to suggest a double-entendre (*pleasure* and the troping
of *teach* are her principal vehicles in this extract). But above all, what
is being performed here is a demonstration of the irresistible force of
sexual desire: it drives Amelia to extraordinary indecorums; and it places
Edmund and Mary in an electrically charged place apart – a 'stage' –
where more may be said and done than Edmund, at least, could imagine
in the normal world. And Fanny is the fascinated and suffering witness
of this private performance: 'she could not always pay attention to the
book. In watching them she forgot herself; and agitated by the increasing
spirit of Edmund's manner, had once closed the page and turned away
exactly as he wanted help' (*MP*, p. 170). Momentarily, one does wonder
exactly what kind of help Edmund might need – in some sense Fanny is
part of a threesome here.

David Marshall makes a strong case for this scene as one of the most
thematically crucial in the novel. Beginning with the incontrovertible
point that 'Fanny's insistence on being audience, auditor and spectator inscribes her in theatrical relations',[24] he argues that the complex
web of substitutions and impersonations that the scene suggests – 'a
love scene which takes place both alternatively and simultaneously between: Amelia and Anhalt, Mary and Edmund, Fanny and Edmund,
and Mary and Fanny' – foreshadows the next two volumes' 'challenge'
(via the Crawfords) of 'the distinction between genuine emotion and
the impersonation of feeling'. 'The crisis of meaning that the Crawfords
cause for Fanny is a crisis about theater: they force Fanny to confront
the possibility that theater might not signify nothing.' Marshall's reading
thus offers a further perspective on the education of Fanny Price – and
reinforces the response of generations of readers to the attractive and
vital Crawfords: they can never be simply dismissed as the villains of the
piece.

## MARY CRAWFORD'S DRAMATIC FORERUNNERS

'There, I will stake my last like a woman of spirit. No cold prudence for me. I am not born to sit still and do nothing. If I lose the game, it shall not be from not striving for it.' (*MP*, p. 243)

If Henry's dramatic ancestor is the ambivalent figure of the medieval and Shakespearean Vice, Mary has a more recent history as a dramatic type. A variant of the ingénue, clever, witty, worldly, flirtatious, she is developed from the Beatrices and Millamants of earlier English drama into a figure of more equivocal morality in eighteenth-century comedy. Foremost in this development is the work of the women dramatists Hannah Cowley and Elizabeth Inchbald.

Cowley, as I have already commented in relation to *The Belle's Stratagem*, wrote to fill a gap in the stage representation of contemporary femininity, to provide roles for actresses which let them do more interesting and varied things than the sentimental heroine is ever allowed. In her first play, *The Runaway* (1776), Cowley's first effort in this kind is Bella, whose love-interest does not appear in the play; his arrival is anticipated as the curtain falls. The tone anticipates that of Mary Crawford:

BELLA. Lord! you look so insulting with your happiness, and seem to think I make such an aukward figure amongst you – but here [*produces a letter*] – this informs me – that a certain person –
GEORGE [her cousin]. Of the name of – Belville –
BELLA. Be quiet – is landed at Dover, and posting here – with all the saucy confidence our engagements inspire him with.
MR. 2D. Say you so? – Then we'll have the three weddings celebrated on the same day.
BELLA. Oh mercy! – I won't hear of it – *Love*, one might manage that perhaps – but *honour*, *obey*, – 'tis strange the Ladies had never interest enough to get this ungallant form mended.

(Act v)

Although she is gently reprimanded by the moralising Lady Dinah as the play ends, like Mary Crawford or Emma or Elizabeth Bennet in such scenes, Bella has the last word, using the epilogue:

> Post-haste from Italy arrives my Lover!
> Shall I to you, good Friend, my fears discover?
> Should Foreign modes his Virtues mar, and mangle,
> And *Caro Sposo* prove – Sir *Dingle Dangle*;
> No sooner *join'd* than *separate* we go:
> Abroad – we never shall each other know,

At home – I mope *above* – he'll pick his teeth *below*.
In sweet domestic chat we ne'er shall mingle,
And, *wedded* tho' I am, shall still live *single*.

Cowley's *Which is the Man?* (1782), which Austen was familiar with from her early days, may have contributed considerably to the character of Mary Crawford. In Austen's lively juvenile 'The Three Sisters', the character of 'Mary', who sees herself as Cowley's Lady Bell Bloomer, is clearly a preliminary sketch for Miss Crawford:

He was going on but Mary interrupted him 'You must build me an elegant Greenhouse & stock it with plants. You must let me spend every Winter in Bath, every Spring in Town, every Summer in taking some Tour, & every Autumn at a Watering Place, and if we are at home the rest of the year . . . You must do nothing but give Balls & Masquerades. You must build a room on purpose & a Theatre to act Plays in. The first play we have shall be *Which is the Man*, and I will do Lady Bell Bloomer.'

'And pray Miss Stanhope (said Mr. Watts) What am I to expect from you in return for all this.'

'Expect? why you may expect to have me pleased.' (*MW*, p. 65)

Lady Bell Bloomer is a flower of heavily satirised London society. She is unable to decide between the rakish Lord Sparkle and her true love, the poor soldier Beauchamp. She teases the latter with her preference for the former almost until curtain fall, where she protests against her marriage to Beauchamp appearing as 'a prudent, sober business . . . I should lose the credit of having done a mad thing for the sake of the man – my heart prefers.' Despite her Millamant-like theatricality and wit, there are scenes in which she momentarily lets slip the facade. Just before their crucial meeting, she soliloquises:

I suppose he has at length vanquished his modesty, and is come to tell me that – that – Well, I vow I won't hear him. – Yes, I will. I long to know the stile in which these reserved men make love. – To what imprudence would my heart betray me? Yet I may surely indulge myself in hearing him *speak* of love; in hearing, probably for the first time, its genuine language . . . Now, how shall I receive him?

(Act IV)

And she nearly loses control during this scene: 'there is a man whom I sometime suspect not to be indifferent to me, – but 'tis not Lord Sparkle! Tell him so; and tell him that – that – tell him what you will.' Cowley allows this woman of 'beauty, wit, and spirit; but, above all, a *mind*' (Act I) to take the step that Mary Crawford cannot bring herself to:

LADY BELL. The hour of *trifling* is past, and surely it cannot appear extraordinary, that I prefer the internal worth of an uncorrupted heart, to the outward polish of a mind too feeble to support itself against vice, in the seductive forms of fashionable dissipation.

Cowley's vision is utopian here; for Austen, looking soberly at the same world thirty years on, the 'blunted delicacy and . . . corrupted, vitiated mind' of Mary Crawford (*MP*, p. 456) leads her to lose the uncorrupted heart of Edmund and exiles her from a potential Earthly Paradise:

Mary, though perfectly resolved against ever attaching herself to a younger brother again, was long in finding among the dashing representatives, or idle heir-apparents, who were at the command of her beauty, and her 20,000*l.*, anyone who could satisfy the better taste she had acquired at Mansfield, whose character and manners could authorise a hope of the domestic happiness she had there learned to estimate, or put Edmund Bertram sufficiently out of her head. (*MP*, p. 469)

In *Lovers' Vows* Elizabeth Inchbald took particular care in adapting the character of Amelia to the model that she believed acceptable to English audiences used to Cowley's unconventional but charmingly articulate young women:

the same situations which the author gave her, remain, but almost all the dialogue of the character I have changed: the forward and unequivocal manner, in which she announces her affection to her lover, in the original, would have been revolting to an English audience . . . Amelia's love, by Kotzebue, is indelicately blunt, and yet, void of mirth or sadness: I have endeavoured to attach the attention and sympathy of the audience, by whimsical insinuations, rather than coarse abruptness: she is still the same woman, I conceive, whom the author drew, with the self-same sentiments, but with manners conforming to the English rather than the German taste . . . [25]

Inchbald concludes by congratulating herself on the success of this character with audiences. 'Whimsical insinuations, rather than coarse abruptness' is the clue – it subsumes Amelia into the tradition of the witty and flirtatious English ingénue.[26]

For most people, falling in love begins with flirtation, which is often a consciously theatrical mode of social behaviour. Mary Crawford is certainly aware of this, and plays her role of fascinating woman to the hilt. Unfortunately Edmund refuses to play *his* part:

'. . . Come, do change your mind. It is not too late. Go into the law.'
   'Go into the law! with as much ease as I was told to go into this wilderness.'

'Now you are going to say something about law being the worst wilderness of the two, but I forestall you; remember I have forestalled you.'

'You need not hurry when the object is only to prevent my saying a bon-mot, for there is not the least wit in my nature. I am a very matter of fact, plain spoken being, and may blunder on the borders of a repartee for half an hour together without striking it out.'

A general silence succeeded. (*MP*, pp. 93–4)

It is only when Edmund is seduced into performing in *Lovers' Vows* that he finds a second-hand romantic language and situation that allow him to 'perform' the role of the reluctant lover: the character of Anhalt, who is unable to see that Amelia is virtually throwing herself at him, is wonderfully apt for Edmund. But what is the nature of this seduction? It is not directly Mary's work – she is more clever than that. Having seen her direct approach fail – '"If *any* part could tempt *you* to act, I suppose it would be Anhalt," observed the lady, archly . . . " – for he is a clergyman you know"' (*MP*, pp. 144–5) – she enrols the unwitting Fanny as 'straight man' in a performance for Edmund's benefit, so that *he* then speaks according to his role in the real world, that of preserver of the decorums of his father's house: 'Consider what it would be to act Amelia with a stranger' (*MP*, p. 154). But this performance as the representative of order and control is merely Edmund's cover for the disruptive drive of his desire to be in an intimate situation with Mary.

Mary is adept at improvising scenes which utilise her seductive powers. That in which she manipulates Fanny into accepting Henry's necklace is perhaps the subtlest and most triumphant display of her art. It begins, typically, with what seems to the reader and to Fanny a genuinely good impulse on Mary's part. Fanny has walked to the parsonage, anxious for advice as to what she should wear at the Mansfield ball:

Miss Crawford appeared gratified by the application, and after a moment's thought, urged Fanny's returning with her in a much more cordial manner than before, and proposed their going up into her room, where they might have a comfortable coze . . . (*MP*, p. 257)

'The dress being settled in all its grander parts', Miss Crawford moves onto the next stage of her scenario: '"But what shall you have by way of a necklace?" . . . And as she spoke she was undoing a small parcel, which Fanny had observed in her hand when they met.' The 'trinket-box' is put before Fanny, and although Fanny is the last person to be seduced by glittering trinkets, she is propelled into accepting by her good manners, that is, by her involvement in the social world. Fanny is given one actual speech in this scene: 'When I wear this necklace I shall always think of you, and feel how very kind you were' (*MP*, pp. 258–9). The rest of her reactions – although, considered realistically, they must have been verbalised – are recorded as 'modest reluctance', 'astonishment and confusion', 'deepest blushes', and so on. Miss Crawford is the eloquent persuader:

'You must think of somebody else too when you wear that necklace . . . You must think of Henry, for it was his choice in the first place. He gave it to me, and with the necklace I make over to you all the duty of remembering the original giver. It is to be a family remembrancer. The sister is not to be in your mind without bringing the brother too.'

. . . 'My dear child,' said she laughing, 'what are you afraid of? Do you think Henry will claim the necklace as mine, and fancy you did not come honestly by it? Or are you imagining he would be too much flattered by seeing round your lovely throat an ornament which his money purchased three years ago, before he knew there was such a throat in the world? Or perhaps' – looking archly – 'you suspect a confederacy between us, and that what I am now doing is with his knowledge and at his desire?'

. . . 'Well, then, . . . to convince me that you suspect no trick, and are as unsuspicious of compliment as I have always found you, take the necklace and say no more about it. . . . And as for this necklace, I do not suppose I have worn it six times; it is very pretty, but I never think of it; and though you would be most heartily welcome to any other in my trinket-box, you have happened to fix on the very one which, if I have a choice, I would rather part with and see in your possession than any other. Say no more against it, I entreat you. Such a trifle is not worth half so many words.' (*MP*, pp. 259–60)

This sequence of speeches is superbly crafted to lead Fanny (protest though she may) into recognition of her own body as an object of desire – metonymically signified by the doubly emphasised 'lovely throat'. Mary's almost prurient emphases insist that Fanny accept the necklace as a symbol for Henry's embrace of her body; she is in fact wooing Fanny for Henry here – 'the sister is not to be in your mind without bringing the brother too'. It is a sexually charged scene, and Austen supplies enough stage directions to help us see this: Mary 'putting the necklace round her and making her see how well it looked'; Fanny's 'consciousness' and 'deepest blushes'; Mary 'looking archly'. Mary's final speech effectively silences Fanny's protests by a superior display of urbane good manners. Fanny is now literally entrammelled by the world, by that which marks her body as displayable commodity, and leaves her 'reflecting and doubting, and feeling that the possession of what she had so much wished for, did not bring much satisfaction' (*MP*, p. 260).

Even before the ball proper, however, Mary is beginning to lose her finesse as an actress. Edmund's visit to the parsonage to ask Mary for the first two dances brings him back to confide in Fanny; he is successful but a little 'vexed': 'she does not *think* evil, but she speaks it – speaks it in playfulness – and though I know it to be playfulness, it grieves me to the soul' (*MP*, p. 269). What is also interesting about this scene is, once again, the stage directions, since for the first time Edmund is responding physically to Fanny: 'stopping her by taking her hand, and speaking low and seriously'; '"Dearest Fanny!" cried Edmund, pressing her hand to his lips, with almost as much warmth as if it had been Miss Crawford's . . . ' (*MP*, p. 269). As Austen remarks in the novel's final chapter, settling for what you *can* get by way of a partner is a 'quite natural' process, often unconsciously begun (*MP*, p. 470).

From this point in volume II on, as first Fanny and then Edmund remain obdurately steadfast in righteousness, Mary becomes more desperate in her efforts to make things go her way, and more coarse in her performances. She 'blunders' towards Fanny, misreading her, in her belief that Henry's courtship is welcome:

> She meant to be giving her little heart a happy flutter, and filling her with sensations of delightful self-consequence; and misinterpreting Fanny's blushes, still thought she must be doing so . . . (*MP*, p. 277)

Her failure to turn Edmund from his chosen path of ordination results in a lack of ease and naturalness in her social performances, demonstrated in the stagey quality of her gestures and speech when she revisits Fanny's East Room for the first time since the rehearsal with Edmund:

> 'Ha!' she cried, with instant animation, 'am I here again? The East Room! Once only was I in this room before'; and after stopping to look about her, and seemingly to retrace all that had then passed, she added, 'once only before. Do you remember it? I came to rehearse. Your cousin came too; and we had a rehearsal. You were our audience and prompter. A delightful rehearsal. I shall never forget it. Here we were, just in this part of the room; here was your cousin, here was I, here were the chairs. Oh! why will such things ever pass away?'
>     Happily for her companion, she wanted no answer. Her mind was entirely self-engrossed. She was in a reverie of sweet remembrances. (*MP*, pp. 357–8)

A significant part of those remembrances is to do with the *power* that theatre gives Mary:

'. . . If I had the power of recalling any one week of my existence, it should be that week, that acting week. Say what you would, Fanny, it should be *that*; for I never knew such exquisite happiness in any other. His sturdy spirit to bend as it did! Oh! it was sweet beyond expression.' (*MP*, p. 358)

There is an erotic feeling behind these words which anyone who has been involved in theatricals will recognise – putting on a play is emotionally and viscerally like falling in love. And the urge to carry that excitement back into the relationships of 'real life' is often irresistible. Ultimately Mary loses Edmund because she cannot distinguish between theatre (or social *appearance*) and a morally based life.

THE 'INFECTED' WORLD[27]

By the end of volume I Fanny has learnt, through the scopic seductiveness of theatre, about sexual desire. She has watched – often as the only spectator – the 'needlessly' frequent 'rehearsal of the first scene between [Maria] and Mr. Crawford' – for which Inchbald's stage directions are explicit regarding warm embraces:[28] when Sir Thomas's unexpected arrival home is announced by Julia, Fanny notices that 'Frederick [played by Crawford] was listening with looks of devotion to Agatha's narrative, and pressing her hand to his heart . . . in spite of the shock of her words, he still kept his station and retained her sister's hand' (*MP*, p. 175). She has been an unwilling voyeur of the erotically charged performance given by Edmund and Mary in her private space, her school-room. In being unable to keep away from the more public rehearsals she knows she is putting herself in danger ('she had known it her duty to keep away', *MP*, p. 172). She finds herself called upon to take a part, and cannot resist what her body desires, submission to Edmund's 'wish' and 'look of . . . fond dependence': she is 'left to the tremors of a most palpitating heart', to be rescued at the last minute by the arrival of the paternal figure who assumes his power of disposal over her.

By chapter 3 of volume II it is clear that Fanny cannot avoid the fate she most fears, of being 'looked at'. Her father-substitute, Sir Thomas, and the man she loves, Edmund, focalise the next event in Fanny's story: her becoming a desirable woman. Edmund observes to her,

'. . . the truth is, that your uncle never did admire you till now – and now he does. Your complexion is so improved! – and you have gained so much countenance! – and your figure – Nay, Fanny, do not turn away about it – it is but an uncle. If you cannot bear an uncle's admiration what is to become of you? You must really begin to harden yourself to the idea of being worth looking at.' (*MP*, pp. 197–8)

A 'distressing' comment, indeed, for Fanny, but more because of the person who says it than because of its content. In the same dialogue we learn that Fanny is beginning to 'perform' socially, at least in the safety of the family circle – 'I do talk to [Sir Thomas] more than I used. I am sure I do. Did you not hear me ask him about the slave trade last night?' But she soon loses confidence in her right to sustain a centre-stage role – 'while my cousins were sitting by without speaking a word, or seeming at all interested in the subject, I did not like – I thought it would appear as if I wanted to set myself off at their expense . . .' (*MP*, p. 198).

When Maria marries and Julia accompanies her on the wedding trip, Fanny, 'becoming as she then did, the only young woman in the drawing-room . . . it was impossible for her not to be more looked at, more thought of and attended to, than she had ever been before' (*MP*, p. 205). Henry Crawford comments at length to his sister on Fanny's attractiveness (*MP*, pp. 229–30), but he is nevertheless puzzled by her, because she does not play the familiar part of ingénue:

'I do not quite know what to make of Miss Fanny. I do not understand her . . . What is her character? – Is she solemn? – Is she queer? – Is she prudish? . . . I could hardly get her to speak. I never was so long in company with a girl in my life – trying to entertain her – and succeed so ill! Never met with a girl who looked so grave on me! . . .' (*MP*, p. 230)

Fanny never does play the role expected of her, despite Henry Crawford's most determined efforts: she proves herself a true Christian heroine by using the unavoidably public and performative nature of her courtship by Henry to bear witness to her own integrity. His complaint about her 'looking grave' relates to the 'speech' she made when he re-called the theatricals with such enthusiasm ('We were all alive', etc.):

'As far as *I* am concerned, sir, I would not have delayed his return for a day. My uncle disapproved it all so entirely when he did arrive, that in my opinion, every thing had gone quite far enough.'
    She had never spoken so much at once to him in her life before, and never so angrily to any one; and when her speech was over, she trembled and blushed at her own daring. (*MP*, p. 225)

This first 'speech' to Henry Crawford sets the tone for all her later intercourse with him. The irony is that Crawford's is such a vitiated mind that her moral fervour and capacity for feeling simply make her more attractive:

Fanny's attractions increased – increased two-fold – for the sensibility which beautified her complexion and illumined her countenance, was an attraction in itself. He was no longer in doubt of the capabilities of her heart. She had feeling, genuine feeling. It would be something to be loved by such a girl, to excite the first ardours of her young, unsophisticated mind! She interested him more than he had foreseen. A fortnight was not enough. His stay became indefinite. (*MP*, pp. 235–6)

Lovelace-like, Henry plans his campaign. Fanny is perfectly positioned to be his victim by the Mansfield ball, at which she is to 'make her first appearance' in society (*MP*, p. 266); the phrase is identical to that which announces a new actress in the theatre.[29] Austen is clear about what this sort of staging implies – commodification in 'the trade of *coming out*' (*MP*, p. 267). Fanny does not want to be 'looked at', or introduced to the guests, and is envious of William 'walk[ing] at his ease in the back ground of the scene' (*MP*, p. 273; Austen's natural application of theatrical metaphors to this situation is striking).

When Henry, to his and Mary's surprise, finds himself in love with Fanny and determined to marry her, theatrical language temporarily disappears. Instead the conversation between the siblings in chapter 30 turns on the 'good' that such a marriage will do Henry (and Fanny, in a less elevated sense). Momentarily they recognise Fanny's sterling moral qualities; and Henry, for quite some time, behaves better than the reader might expect from his showing in volume 1. Although disbelieving her negatives and persistent in his addresses, he behaves as a 'clever, pleasant man',[30] thoughtful towards Fanny and doing good as his rank and connections enable him. Uncharitably, one might say that this is just another act from Henry Crawford – and we are pointedly reminded of his theatrical propensities in the scene in which he reads from *Henry VIII* (albeit within a proper domestic context). But Henry's intentions are undoubtedly good here – even the narrator finally insists that 'would he have persevered, and uprightly, Fanny must have been his reward – and a reward very voluntarily bestowed – within a reasonable period from Edmund's marrying Mary' (*MP*, p. 467).

For much of this courtship period Fanny is also thrust onto the stage in a different drama – that of the daughter oppressed by a tyrannical father, a staple of the Victorian melodramas to come, but already to be seen on the eighteenth-century stage in, for example, Frances Sheridan's *The Discovery* (1763):

LOUISA. My Lord, I beg your permission to withdraw.

LORD MEDWAY. Stay where you are, madam. – When I condescend to talk with you, methinks you ought to know, 'tis your duty to attend to what I have to say. You know my mind already in regard to young Branville. – But observe what I say; I forbid you to think, but even to think, of Branville. That is the first, and perhaps the hardest part of my command. The next is, that you resolve immediately to accept of Sir Anthony for your husband. And now, miss, you may, if you please, retire to your chamber, and, in plaintive strains, either in verse or prose, bemoan your hard fate . . . [31]

Fanny's experience in the shabby house at Portsmouth with a vulgar drunken father and feckless mother further anticipates the tropes of Victorian melodrama. Potentially Dickensian these scenes may be, but Austen chooses not to write them in her usual quasi-dramatic mode. With the departure of the Crawfords and their vivacious dialogue from Mansfield, the last eleven chapters of volume III, telling of Fanny's visit to Portsmouth and her final return to Mansfield, are almost all third-person narrative, interspersed with several letters as the story draws to its climax. The only extended dialogues are between Fanny and Henry (chapter 42) and Fanny and Edmund (chapter 47). Austen uses the dramatic mode only in order to continue her presentation of Fanny's involvement in the social discourse of courtship – though Fanny, true to her nature and principles, re-writes the conventions.

With Henry she is merely polite, roused only to declare, 'We have all a better guide in ourselves, if we would attend to it, than any other person can be. Good bye; I wish you a pleasant journey to-morrow' (*MP*, p. 412) – an utterance typical of Fanny, mixing moral fervour and unfailing good manners. With Edmund there is one extraordinary moment in which she briefly takes centre stage as the romantic heroine. As he arrives at Portsmouth to take her home,

She was ready to sink as she entered the parlour. He was alone, and met her instantly; and she found herself pressed to his heart with only these words, just articulate, 'My Fanny – my only sister – my only comfort now!' She could say nothing; nor for some minutes could he say more. (*MP*, p. 444)

Fanny 'finds herself' in the embrace which Henry Crawford and Maria Bertram had so frequently rehearsed as she watched them, back in her days of innocence. Despite Edmund's fraternal language, the body's desires have asserted themselves, and Fanny is far from objecting. Nevertheless both participants prefer 'self-command'; and in the conversations that follow Fanny speaks principally to prompt Edmund in narrating his final dramatic interview with Mary. Austen thereby for the last time displays Mary as the stagey and worldly figure of the novel's morality play, framing her within Edmund's moralising re-telling of the event, which is itself framed by Fanny's loving and supportive role as listener.

'. . . She would have laughed if she could. It was a sort of laugh, as she answered, "A pretty good lecture upon my word. Was it part of your last sermon? At this rate, you will soon reform every body at Mansfield and Thornton Lacey; and when I hear of you next, it may be as a celebrated preacher in some great society of Methodists, or as a missionary into foreign parts." She tried to speak carelessly; but she was not so careless as she wanted to appear. I only said in reply, that from my heart I wished her well, and earnestly hoped that she might soon learn to think more justly, and not owe the most valuable knowledge we could any of us acquire – the knowledge of ourselves and of our duty, to the lessons of affliction – and immediately left the room. I had gone a few steps, Fanny, when I heard the door open behind me. "Mr. Bertram," said she. I looked back. "Mr. Bertram," said she with a smile – but it was a smile ill-suited to the conversation that had passed, a saucy playful smile, seeming to invite, in order to subdue me; at least, it appeared so to me. I resisted; it was the impulse of the moment to resist, and still walked on.' (*MP*, pp. 458–9)

'How have I been deceived! Equally in brother and sister deceived!' is Edmund's conclusion. It is a conclusion which reminds us, in the mouth of a clergyman just labelled 'Methodist' by the worldly Mary, of the old Puritan objection to acting which lurks at the back of many an English conscience: as it deceives and confuses us about the true nature of people and situations, it is a sign of the Arch-Deceiver himself. There is no avoiding role-playing in social life, however: Edmund is here playing the Christian hero. The scene as presented by Edmund (with excellent mimicry of Mary's performance) is at once superbly dramatic – the upright hero rejects the fascinating temptress – and deliberately distanced, first through its narrative mode (reported speech), and then through the intrusion of the narrator's voice to finish the chapter, ironising Edmund's great moment of renunciation as a tale to be indulged in, and repeated, in the comfort of domesticity:

such was Fanny's dependance on his words, that for five minutes she thought they *had* done. Then, however, it all came on again, or something very like it, and nothing less than Lady Bertram's rousing thoroughly up, could really close such a conversation. (*MP*, p. 459)

The foregrounding of the ironic narrator, and consequent de-emphasising of the narrative mode of dramatic realism, is most striking in the novel's final chapter, which immediately follows this conversation.

This is the point at which Austen disappoints her readers by refusing to provide even the truncated love scene which she concedes in *Pride and Prejudice*.

> I purposely abstain from dates on this occasion, that every one may be at liberty to fix their own, aware that the cure of unconquerable passions, and the transfer of unchanging attachments, must vary much as to time in different people. – I only intreat every body to believe that exactly at the time when it was quite natural that it should be so, and not a week earlier, Edmund did cease to care about Miss Crawford, and became as anxious to marry Fanny, as Fanny herself could desire. (*MP*, p. 470)

Our tendency to be seduced by theatricality, to consciously theatricalise our own personal history and actions, is here ironised; as is the audience's temptation to treat fiction (whether in the theatre or in novels) as reality. The novel's ending is deeply and deliberately undramatic; but it cannot negate the preceding 300 pages' exposition of the all-pervasive theatricality of Mansfield Park's *theatrum mundi*.

# CHAPTER SIX

# Emma: *private theatricals in Highbury*

The shadow of Kotzebue ambiguously haunts the novel that follows *Mansfield Park*, *Emma*. As Margaret Kirkham discovered several decades ago, the play that Austen first saw in Bath in 1799,[1] Thomas Dibdin's *The Birth-Day*, based on Kotzebue's *Die Versöhnung*, has some striking parallels with Austen's 1816 novel. The action takes place in a country village. The heroine is called Emma; she is motherless and her main occupation is looking after her sick father. Her lover is an altogether worthy and actively benevolent young man called Harry (as archetypal an English name as George). The old servant William (the name of Mr Knightley's rustic alter ego William Larkins) announces Emma's first entrance with the line, 'Here comes Miss Emma and the old gentleman. I do love the very sight of her.' As Mr Knightley says in an early chat with Mrs Weston about Emma, 'I love to look at her' (*E*, p. 39). Kirkham summarises the main points of comparison between *The Birth-Day* and *Emma* thus: 'both heroines believe that they cannot marry because of their duty to their invalid fathers. In both cases they are enabled to do so because they fall in love with a relation (in one case a cousin, in the other a brother-in-law) peculiarly acceptable in the invalid's house.'[2] Kirkham pursues further schematic parallels between play and novel, but the most extraordinary evidence of the persistence of the play in Jane Austen's imagination comes in these lines from early in the first act:

EMMA. Don't you think my father will live to be a very old man now?
HARRY. If he is careful not to exert himself too much.
EMMA. That shall be my care.
HARRY. And will you always remain with him?
EMMA. Always, always.
HARRY. But if other duties should call upon you?
EMMA. Other duties! What duties can be more sacred?
HARRY. The duties of a wife or a mother.
EMMA. No – I never intend to marry.

HARRY. Never marry?

EMMA. Not if I should be obliged to leave my father.

HARRY. Your husband would supply the place of a son.

EMMA. And the son would take the daughter from the father.

HARRY. But if a man could be found who would bestow on your father a quiet old age, free from every sorrow; who far from robbing the father of a good daughter would weave the garland of love round three hearts, who would live under his roof and multiply your joys.[3]

It is as though Kotzebue's simple tale provided Austen with the elegant solution to what, in the novel, is a very psychologically complex set of relationships. What Kotzebue and Dibdin – what the theatre of 1800 – could not supply is the ironic vision which Austen brings to the project of representing the lives of '3 or 4 families in a country village' (*Letters*, 9–18 September 1814). Whether conscious or not, these verbal and thematic parallels act as a sort of homage to the theatre of her young womanhood, and particularly to the changes brought about by the introduction of the 'German drama', which enabled feeling to be invested in simple characters and domestic situations rather than the distant and exotic worlds of mid-eighteenth-century tragedy. Dibdin wrote in his prefatory letter,

As it was last year the rage to applaud, it has now become the fashion to decry, the introduction of the German drama to our theatres. On this point I dare not presume to give any other opinion, than that a play which recommends peace, amity, and benevolence will be grateful to the feelings of an Englishman, whether the offspring of his own or of any other country.

The reviewer of the *Bath Herald* commented that Kotzebue had redeemed his reputation somewhat with this play:

If the German Author had justly drawn down censure for the immorality of his productions for the stage, this may be considered as expiatory – this may be accepted as his *amende honourable*; it is certainly throughout unexceptionable, calculated to promote the best interest of virtue, and the purest principles of benevolence . . . [4]

Austen surely would have agreed with this, and remembered with pleasure her visit to the Orchard Street Theatre to see *The Birth-Day*.[5]

In September 1813, on the same evening as she saw the pantomime *Don Juan*, Austen saw a musical farce by J.V. Millingen, *The Bee Hive* – 'rather less flat & trumpery' than *The Boarding House*, Austen commented (*Letters*, 15–16 September 1813). The play's star was the comedian Charles

Mathews (whom she had earlier liked in *The Hypocrite*), playing the innkeeper Mingle.[6] The voluble Mingle's style of speech anticipates the great comic flights of Miss Bates, or Mrs Elton's stream-of-consciousness at the strawberry-picking:

> Glorious day! lots of ships in our harbour – full of soldiers just come from abroad – decks red as a lobster – all coming on shore – success to trade! – All put up at the Bee-Hive – industry must prosper – no other inn. Soldiers fine fellows – fight hard – drink hard – long abroad – plenty of cash – long at sea – banyan day – salt pork – squeamish stomachs – eat any thing – stiff from abroad . . . [etc.] Poor souls! been fighting hard for us, and hope to meet good cheer and happiness at home.
>
> (Act I)

Like those of Miss Bates, Mingle's speeches, however they wander, always conclude in general benevolence. Here he is in more domestic mode, introducing the heroine to her accommodation:

> Here, Miss Emily – best in the house – Captain Cook's death on the curtain – Holland linen, well aired – blue ware – lots of pictures, amusing and instructive – dogs, flowers, horses – Faith, Hope, and Charity – pianoforte also, left by a debtor, who took leg bail – bad, good, or indifferent, don't know – no musician – but your sweet hands and voice would make lots of harmony of any thing.
>
> (Act I)

Emily, the fair musician and emotionally tried heroine, uses the alias 'Mrs Fairfax' as she attempts to test her lover Captain Merton, whom she's never met, but has corresponded with. He, of course, becomes aware of her masquerade, and sets up a counter-bluff, pretending that his friend Captain Rattan is the real Merton. Like Frank Churchill, Merton does like to tease, which distresses Emily, but in this fable she has her revenge, pretending in her turn to love Rattan. And her conclusion must have delighted Jane Austen: 'Well, well, I do forgive you, with all my heart; but never again try to outwit a woman' (Act II). The final chorus includes a duet for Emily and Cicely (her friend):

> In supporting woman's cause,
> We've reveng'd our sex;
> Ladies, having your applause,
> Critics we'll perplex.

It is easy to see why Austen would have enjoyed this little afterpiece, with its combination of fantastical comic characters and a heroine with both heart and brains – a musical young woman called Fairfax who disguises her real situation. It is clearly arguable that, as with *The Birth-Day*, some elements of this play may have been brewing in her subconscious as, four months later, she started writing *Emma*.

One other play may have contributed to *Emma* (apart from the possible traces of *A Midsummer Night's Dream*, as Jocelyn Harris has persuasively argued[7]). There are intersections between the psychological and emotional patterns of Elizabeth Inchbald's 1797 play *Wives as They Were, and Maids as They Are* and Austen's 1816 novel. We have no evidence that Austen knew this play, but the possibility that she at least read it must remain, given her use of *Lovers' Vows* in the immediately preceding novel, and given her known interest in the work of other contemporary women writers. Like Hannah Cowley, Inchbald was committed to writing that gave stronger and more complex roles to women.[8] And like Cowley, she was largely frustrated in this aim by the changes in theatre fashion of the new century.

Significantly, *Wives as They Were* is *not* a Kotzebue adaptation; it is an attempt on Inchbald's part to put on the stage issues that she had explored in her novel *A Simple Story* (1791) – particularly the tutelary relation between the heroine and her lover. But where the heroine of that novel is socially powerless, in *Wives as They Were* Miss Dorrillon is a vivacious London butterfly, intelligent and witty but with more heart than a Mary Crawford. Her father is absent; she has fallen into debt because there is no one to restrain her from doing as she likes. Her father returns from India in disguise and tries to reform her through criticising her; she dislikes this but feels some emotional tie to him. She is wooed by two men – a rake, Bronzely (who transfers his attentions to the quiet and virtuous Lady Priory), and the noble Sir George, whom she finally marries. But the important emotional dynamic is between Miss Dorrillon and her unrecognised father: in the play's most affecting scene, he rescues her from debtors' prison after she acknowledges her unconditional love for this supposedly absent figure. As Paula Backscheider aptly puts it, 'Their angry, witty sparring yields to affection and respect.'[9] It is a curious 'comedy', especially for a woman writer associated with Mary Wollstonecraft and the Godwin circle: despite the charm and articulacy of its heroine, it closes firmly with the view that a woman is grateful to have an authoritative man in her life. Miss Dorrillon finally has two – her father and her husband – and she brings down the curtain with the declaration, 'A maid of the present day shall become a wife like those – of former times.' Irony there is none, and the net effect of the play is to suggest a slightly depressing re-run of *The Taming of the Shrew*. And perhaps that socially realistic Shakespeare play is a more influential model for the emotional trajectory of *Emma* than the confused wanderings of the lovers in *A Midsummer Night's Dream*. There is no denying that Emma's relation to her lover-cum-father-substitute is that of pupil to teacher: 'I have blamed you, and lectured you, and you have borne it as no other woman in England would have borne it' (*E*, p. 430), Mr Knightley admits as he launches into his proposal of marriage. What Inchbald, for all her theatrical expertise, was unable (or unwilling) to bring off in exploring this emotional dynamic, was the deconstructive ironies with which Austen invests the conservative fable about the necessity of patriarchal control.

## WORLD AS STAGE

*Emma* is Jane Austen's most sustained performance, her most technically brilliant work, at once her most dramatic and her least obviously theatrical work. It assumes the centrality of watching, gazing, and judging in any community – and then it plays with this, in order to destabilise the notion that 'the structure of the gaze empowers the spectator over the spectacle'.[10] As Barbara Freedman remarks, 'the acts of framing and staging themselves depend upon the fiction of the objective observer, of the object itself, and of the boundary that separates the two'.[11] Throughout the novel Austen demonstrates her awareness of this, and indeed seems so delighted by its possibilities that she has *her* supposedly 'objective observer' meditating on it in a metafictional moment. When Mr Knightley in chapter 41 wonders if he is like Cowper, 'Myself creating what I saw' (*E*, p. 344), he points to the experience not only of several characters in the novel – Emma and Harriet particularly – but also of the reader, who largely shares Emma's point of view, but who may also pick up the clues offered almost subliminally by narrator and author: the signs of Emma and Mr Knightley's attraction to each other, the hidden drama of Frank Churchill and Jane Fairfax.

'I had always a part to act', says Jane, ashamed (*E*, p. 459). Both principal meanings of the word *act* are brought into play by this text: to perform theatrically and simply to do. Ultimately they are shown to be part of a continuum: all the world's a stage, and all the men and women more or less admirable in the roles they perform. And all are always both actors and audience.

The novel starts on the familiar ground already covered in Austen's earlier work: gender and class are performative. This is focused through Emma herself, Frank, Jane, Mr Knightley; and helped by the theatrical caricatures of behaviour offered by Mr and Mrs Elton, Miss Bates, Mr Woodhouse. Young ladies, in particular, as we know from the conversations at Netherfield and Rosings in *Pride and Prejudice*, must 'perform', must be on show with their accomplishments, presenting themselves theatrically in order to win entrance into the adult world of the audience, the gazers, via marriage. Several extended discussions of the relative virtues of the musical performances of Emma and Jane Fairfax emphasise this matter: Emma, in recognising her performance to be inferior to Jane's, feels herself shown up as wanting in true femininity, unworthy to be the 'first lady' of Highbury – a role which she had played with supreme confidence until doubly challenged by the arrival of two other performers, Jane Fairfax and Mrs Elton.[12]

On Jane's first public appearance in Highbury,

> They had music: Emma was obliged to play; and the thanks and praise which necessarily followed appeared to her an affectation of candour, an air of greatness, meaning only to show off in higher style [Jane's] own very superior performance. She was, besides, which was the worst of all, so cold, so cautious! There was no getting at her real opinion. Wrapped up in a cloak of politeness, she seemed determined to hazard nothing. She was disgustingly, was suspiciously reserved. (*E*, pp. 168–9)

Emma manages to disqualify Jane as a social equal who might outshine her in accomplishments by reading her personal manner as a suspicious mask. In allowing suspicion to rule her judgements, Emma is already behaving as an 'imaginist', herself creating what she sees. So Frank Churchill can use Emma's ambivalent consciousness of Jane's superior musical performance to build his own theatrical performance, asking Emma what she thinks of Jane's playing so that he can then introduce the false clue of her mysterious admirer:

> 'Ever hear her!' repeated Emma. 'You forget how much she belongs to Highbury. I have heard her every year of our lives since we both began. She plays charmingly.'
> 'You think so, do you? – I wanted the opinion of some one who could really judge. She appeared to me to play well, that is, with considerable taste, but I know nothing of the matter myself. – I am excessively fond of music, but without the smallest skill or right of judging of anybody's performance. – I have been used to hear her's admired; and I remember one proof of her being thought to play well: – a man, a very musical man, and in love with another woman . . .'
> (*E*, p. 201)

Thus Frank sets his trap, implying that he has been merely an ingenuous observer, never a performer. But he is, of course, acting the part of

Mr Unworldly (and evidence emerges at the Coles' dinner party that he does have musical skills, as he sings duets with Jane).

The overtly theatrical connotation of the word *act* in this novel is confined to variations of the phrase 'acting a part', and, as with 'perform', largely associated with the female characters (Jane, ashamed; Emma, self-consciously; Mrs Weston refusing to do it). 'Act', without specific theatrical connotations, is more commonly used in association with the behaviour of rational, sensible, adult people: an ideal represented in this society by the male. Proper masculinity is defined by the energetic enactment of the role of social and moral leader: to be truly adult is to conform to this masculine model – 'My Emma, does not every thing serve to prove more and more the beauty of truth and sincerity in all our dealings with each other?' (*E*, p. 446). This is a utopian ideal which the novel's recognition of the inescapable theatricality of social life critiques via narratorial and dramatic irony – even here, since Emma can't reveal Harriet's secret passion for Mr Knightley – while still at some level presenting it as an ideal.

As we have just seen, quasi-theatrical 'performance' is associated with femininity. In so far as they are actors, Frank Churchill and Mr Elton are effeminate, rather than admirable men.[13] Frank Churchill is liked 'in general' in Highbury because he is 'a handsome young man – one who smiled so often and bowed so well' (*E*, p. 206). The only other male in the novel who is seen to bow is Mr Elton. Mr Knightley dismisses the implications of this self-display: 'Elton may talk sentimentally, but he will *act* rationally', he says of the clergyman's marriage prospects (*E*, p. 66; my emphasis). But Mr Knightley is unaware of the bewitching nature of theatre. Elton is seduced by his own performance (of 'sentimental talk'); he is a narcissistically bad actor, and therefore does *not* 'act rationally', i.e. with a proper (masculine) sense of social decorum. Elton is clearly aware of the theatricality inherent in the social rituals of courtship, and enters confidently into this discourse as he attempts to gain the prize of Miss Woodhouse. In the climax to his performance we see him declaring his passion to Emma, using clichés of speech and movement drawn from the lexicon of sentimental drama (amusingly akin to his confrère Mr Collins's sentimental fiction-based proposal to Elizabeth): 'Charming Miss Woodhouse! allow me to interpret this interesting silence. It confesses that you have long understood me' (*E*, p. 131). His audience of one, Emma, thinks him drunk rather than inspired; and points out that she has been watching his earlier performance of the lover in a frame which includes Harriet as the recipient of his sighs and smiles. *He* has thought

Harriet his audience, Emma his partner in the sentimental drama. This confusion or deliberate obfuscation of frames marks the emotionally and morally immature members of the community – including Emma, for much of the novel.

Regarding the as yet unseen Frank Churchill, Mr Knightley once again has recourse to the paradigm of the performance of true manliness:

> 'There is one thing, Emma, which a man can always do, if he chuses, and that is, his duty; not by manoeuvring and finessing,[14] but by vigour and reso-lution . . . If he would say so to her at once in the tone of decision becoming a man, there would be no opposition made to his going.' (*E*, p. 146)

Emma deconstructs this expertly by pointing out the complex theatrical situation of such an imagined performance:

> '. . . Such language for a young man entirely dependent to use! Nobody but you, Mr. Knightley, would imagine it possible; but you have not an idea of what is requisite in situations directly opposite to your own. Mr. Frank Churchill to be making such a speech as that to the uncle and aunt who have brought him up, and are to provide for him! standing up in the middle of the room, I suppose, and speaking as loud as he could!' (*E*, p. 147)

Mr Knightley insists that his theoretical 'sensible man would find no difficulty in it. He would feel himself in the right; and the declaration, made, of course, as a man of sense would make it, in a proper manner' – but the 'man of sense' remains a Platonic idea, as Emma points out: Frank's character has been formed by a complex family and social situa-tion, which makes such a simple performance impossible: 'He may have as strong a sense of what would be right as you can have, without being so equal, under particular circumstances, to *act* up to it' (*E*, p. 148; my emphasis).

If George Knightley himself can be read as the ideal gentleman, a good landowner, a wise mentor, this too is framed by the novel as being inevitably a performance, simple and natural though it seems. He is typecast, as his name suggests, his circumstances making it easy to play his social role. Rescuing Harriet from Elton's petty humiliation at the Crown ball by dancing with her may be a 'kind action' rather than sexual display (though see below for Mr Knightley's entry into the public discourse of sexuality), but his demonstration of good manners and a kind heart is read by Harriet as an action of 'noble benevolence and generosity' (*E*, p. 407) – he becomes her knight in shining armour.

What makes Mr Knightley more interesting than this over-simplified reading is his awareness of the specular aspect of his position in the community, even though he tries to avoid his audience's gaze by behaving as a plain man whose best friend is his estate manager William Larkins. At the Coles' dinner party he has used his carriage to bring the Bates family; Emma observes to him, 'This is coming as you should do, ... like a gentleman. – I am quite glad to see you.' He responds drily,

> 'How lucky that we should arrive at the same moment; for, if we had met first in the drawing-room, I doubt whether you would have discerned me to be more of a gentleman than usual. – You might not have distinguished how I came, by my look or manner.' (*E*, p. 213)

He has a point – the common reading of a person's social role depends to a certain extent on stage sets and properties – but his claim that his plain-manliness is innate while gentility is a mask is simply evasive.

As for the heroine of the novel, one way of formulating her progress is to observe her movement from one who (over-)acts the part of the principal lady of Highbury to one who *acts rightly* in that role. Emma starts by playing the role of a queen who believes she knows best for her subjects, treating them as pawns in the games which save her from terminal boredom. The typical German drama ingénue Harriet – nameless and classless – is the chief victim of this behaviour, frequently being reduced to the touchingly sentimental spectacle of tears.

A fine example of Emma's manipulation of her little stage follows the visit to the poor cottagers, when Mr Elton is unexpectedly encountered in the lane. Emma contrives to allow Mr Elton and Harriet to go on ahead together, while she chats to a child of the cottage: 'To walk by the side of this child, and talk to and question her, was the most natural thing in the world, or would have been the most natural, had she been *acting* just then without design . . . ' (*E*, p. 88; my emphasis). Here the two meanings of 'act' are productively conflated by the narrator's representation of Emma's consciousness: she is doing what comes naturally, but she is also manipulating the situation by *consciously* acting the role of charitable lady.

Much later in the novel, this useful ambiguity is still at work to remind us of the complexities of Emma's situation: that she is, as Mr Knightley says in rebuking her over her insult to Miss Bates, a person whose public behaviour will be imitated by others of lesser status: 'I cannot see you acting wrong, without a remonstrance' (*E*, p. 374). In reflecting on her treatment of Harriet, Emma finally realises, 'How improperly had she been acting by Harriet! How inconsiderate, how indelicate, how irrational, how unfeeling, had been her conduct! What blindness, what madness had led her on!' (*E*, p. 408). It is perhaps not too fantastical to read the suggestion of a Dionysian frenzy in these last phrases: she has been 'led on' by the excitement of acting a part, convinced of her own priestess-like power to influence people's behaviour and emotions. A few pages later Austen returns to this theme:

> How to understand it all! How to understand the deceptions she had been thus practising on herself, and living under! The blunders, the blindness of her own head and heart! She sat still, she walked about, she tried her own room, she tried the shrubbery – in every place, every posture, she perceived that she had acted most weakly; that she had been imposed on by others in a most mortifying degree . . . (*E*, pp. 411–12)

No place is now a suitable stage for her, no action is appropriate to her inner emotions: she recognises that she has been a 'weak' actress, and that 'others' – Frank and Jane – have been stronger in their ability to influence the public's perceptions of reality.

But whereas Frank has positively revelled in 'acting a part' so supremely well that he is actually acting very badly by the community and ultimately by his fiancée ('his persisting to act in direct opposition to Jane Fairfax's sense of right' was behaving 'very shamefully', comments Mr Knightley (*E*, p. 446)), Jane is desperately ashamed that she has deceived her little world (Emma was after all right about Jane's appearance of 'reserve'). No doubt the private game in which she and Frank were engaged during the course of the novel had its pleasures, adding the erotic spice of secrecy to their affair; otherwise she would hardly have continued in it as long as she did. No doubt, also, there is a self-dramatising tendency in Jane's character that is attracted by the image of the tragedy queen: 'There are places in town – not quite for the sale of human flesh, but for the sale of human intellect' (*E*, p. 300) – thus she characterises her fate as a governess. Austen has earlier ironically represented Jane's tendency to see herself in the role of Gothic heroine: 'With the fortitude of a devoted noviciate, she had resolved at one-and-twenty to complete the sacrifice, and retire from all the pleasures of life, of rational intercourse, equal society, peace and hope, to penance and mortification for ever' (*E*, p. 165). Jane never entirely relinquishes this role: she gives way to 'severe headaches, and a nervous fever to a degree', refusing Emma's conciliatory offer of 'some arrow-root of very superior quality', and going on hunger-strike to impress her poor aunt and grandmother of the anguish of her soul (*E*, pp. 389–90). But notwithstanding this occasionally ironical treatment, Jane is ultimately a near-tragic figure haunting the edges of a comedy, and nowhere more truly so than in her remorse for her deceitful performance. Mrs Weston, as confidante, reports her performance on that other stage:

'Wrong! – No one, I believe, can blame her more than she is disposed to blame herself. "The consequence," said she, "has been a state of perpetual suffering to me; and so it ought. But after all the punishment that misconduct can bring, it is still not less misconduct. Pain is no expiation. I never can be blameless. I have been acting contrary to all my sense of right; and the fortunate turn that every thing has taken, and the kindness I am now receiving, is what my conscience tells me ought not to be...."' (*E*, p. 419)

## THE 'HARTFIELD EDITION' OF A COMEDY

Egging Harriet into a state of excitement over Mr Elton's charade, Emma has occasion to quote *A Midsummer Night's Dream*: '"The course of true love never did run smooth" – A Hartfield edition of Shakespeare would have a long note on that passage' (*E*, p. 75), she says. This, as Jocelyn Harris has argued,[15] can be read as Emma's (and *Emma*'s) signal to the audience to be aware of the resonances set up by intertextualities with Shakespeare's play. I want to use it more particularly as Austen's early signal, to a more sophisticated reader than Harriet, that this novel will make conscious use of theatrical analogies, both thematic and technical.

The narrative of *Emma*, more than any of the other novels (though closest to *Pride and Prejudice*) is a succession of 'scenes'. It begins with a domestic interior, with father and daughter about to settle to a quiet round of backgammon – until Mr Knightley refreshingly strides in, making the game 'unnecessary', substituting for it the bantering affectionate conversation of two who will obviously become lovers, though their course will not be smooth. Domestic comedy remains the mode, as the scene moves minimally outward, to the village, Randalls, the Bateses', the Coles', Donwell, and the dramatic climax in the most spectacular and distant setting, Box Hill. The basic situation of this comedy might be represented by a passage in chapter 27:

Emma went to the door [of Ford's emporium] for amusement. Much could not be hoped from the traffic of even the busiest part of Highbury: – Mr. Perry walking hastily by; Mr. William Cox letting himself in at the office-door; Mr. Cole's carriage horses returning from exercise; or a stray letter-boy on an obstinate mule, were the liveliest objects she could presume to expect; and when her eyes fell only on the butcher with his tray, a tidy old woman travelling homewards from shop with her full basket, two curs quarrelling over a dirty bone, and a string of dawdling children round the baker's little bow-window eyeing the ginger bread, she knew she had no reason to complain, and was amused enough; quite enough still to stand at the door. A mind lively and at ease can do with seeing nothing, and can see nothing that does not answer. (*E*, p. 233)

One can almost hear the theme-music. This is Emma's 'world' where she has 'lived nearly twenty-one years . . . with very little to distress or vex her' (*E*, p. 5). But it is a world which is here constituted as entertainment by the gaze of a viewer within it – and the danger of this is that she may begin to see connections and stories that are not really there – or not see what is really there, as the curiously ambiguous last comment suggests, with its hypnotic 'see . . . nothing'. The passage continues with an overtly theatrical metaphor: 'She looked down the Randalls road. The scene enlarged: – two persons appeared: Mrs. Weston and her son-in-law.' Miss Taylor's marriage has already 'enlarged' Emma's scene – safely, and, Emma believes, according to her plans; but the step-son who comes to Highbury apparently to pay his duty to his new mother is an unpredictable character, irrupting into the domestic comedy from not one place but several other parts of England – Yorkshire, London, Weymouth – the great world of money and intrigue. Once Frank arrives, Emma becomes the gullible audience rather than the complacent actress-manager of the theatre of everyday life in Highbury, though *she* believes herself to be a co-star with the brilliant performer Frank.[16]

On several other occasions Austen uses the word *scene* to remind us subtly of the novel's pervasive dramatic mode. At the beginning of the brilliant episode of the Coles' dinner party (which I examine in more detail below) the narrator remarks with apparent casualness, 'She meant to be very happy, in spite of the scene being laid at Mr. Cole's' (*E*, p. 213). By the end of this chapter, in which all the major characters have displayed themselves – or their masks – in a variety of performances, it has become obvious how strikingly apt the theatrical metaphor is for this examination of the lives of three or four families in a country village. To take another example, late in the novel when dramatic irony no longer rules the narrative events, we are allowed a glimpse of a 'scene' of pathos that would have been at home in a Kotzebue drama:

They had gone, in short; and very great had been the evident distress and confusion of the lady [Jane]. She had hardly been able to speak a word, and every look and action had shown how deeply she was suffering from consciousness. The quiet, heart-felt satisfaction of the old lady, and the rapturous delight of her daughter, who proved even too joyous to talk as usual, had been a gratifying, yet almost an affecting scene. (*E*, p. 418)

Unlike Kotzebue (in, for example, the last scene of *Lovers' Vows*), Austen chose not to indulge the audience in this moment with exclamatory dialogue. Yet she uses a kind of pantomime technique, describing the actors producing an 'affecting' picture solely through look and gesture, in order to convey the situation's emotional force, thus quietly giving heart to her characteristic comic mode.

The succession of dialogue-rich scenes that Austen does provide in this novel can be read as making up a three-act comedy. In volume I (chapters 1–18) we watch Emma as the unchallenged queen of Highbury, playing games with lesser members of the community, and beginning her unconscious rapprochement with the old friend who will become her lover, Mr Knightley. The arrival of new members of the community simply increases the obligation to perform with panache, to show off her superiority. Displaying her (largely unfinished) drawings before Harriet and Mr Elton, 'They were both in extasies . . . Miss Woodhouse's *performances* must be capital' (*E*, p. 45; my emphasis).

Mr Elton is of course the *jeune premier* of volume I; Emma's confusion is over who is playing the ingénue, Harriet or herself. Mr Elton turns in a spirited if provincial performance as the sentimental lover. His sighs and smiles and vacuous speeches, united with his charismatic status as the village rector, are guaranteed to produce a crush in the impressionable schoolgirl Harriet – 'Mr Elton being the adoration of all the teachers and great girls in the school' (*E*, p. 143). Unfortunately Emma, although protected by her rampant egoism from being impressed, has not seen enough of the world, or of good acting, to recognise the falseness of Mr Elton's posturing, though the reader is expected to. On her rare visits to London, Emma's theatrical experience has presumably been limited to Astley's (an equestrian circus to which the John Knightleys take Harriet and Robert Martin (*E*, p. 471)),[17] rather than pursuing the opportunity, as Jane Austen did, to see Edmund Kean or Sarah Siddons in Shakespeare.

Mr Elton's abortive proposal to Emma is the comic climax of volume I; absenting himself hastily after this humiliation, his place is taken, in general anticipation, by the much more glamorous figure of the promised visitor from the outside world, Frank Churchill. Chapter 18, the last in the volume, emphatically builds up Emma's and the reader's expectations that Frank will be the major star of the drama. It does so in a series of sophisticated observations about Frank as the object of a gaze; Frank is never, in Emma's imagination or experience, divorced from his theatricality.

Emma's impatience to see Frank Churchill is overtly an anticipation of theatrical pleasure. Frank is spoken of as a star, a charismatic figure, simply because of his exoticism:

> She was the first to announce it [his failure to come] to Mr. Knightley; and exclaimed quite as much as was necessary (or, being acting a part, perhaps rather more), at the conduct of the Churchills in keeping him away. She then proceeded to say a good deal more than she felt of the advantage of such an addition to their confined society in Surrey; the pleasure of looking at somebody new; the gala-day to Highbury entire, which the sight of him would have made . . . (*E*, p. 145)

Emma is 'acting a part' here because she is obliged to conceal her mortification over the Mr Elton affair; but it is significant that such acting requires her to invent speeches which further implicate her in the discourse of theatricality. She exaggerates, in order to create the effect of 'being her usual self', the pleasure that 'looking at' Frank will provide to the whole community, with herself of course the chief representative of it. The result is that Mr Knightley is misled from the very first about Emma's interest in Frank: he becomes audience to a romance that doesn't really exist.

It is following this performance of Emma's that the discussion occurs about Frank's questionable manliness, culminating in Mr Knightley's categorising him as 'amiable only in French, not in English. He may be very "aimable", have very good manners, and be very agreeable; but he can have no English delicacy towards the feelings of other people: nothing really amiable about him' (*E*, p. 149). This is the first indication in the novel of a political argument which will link the 'smooth, plausible' but ultimately disruptive Frank with England's enemy, the French (with whom his name is cognate, as well as being misleading: he is both 'French' and 'not frank'). Emma, at this stage in her education, is unable to appreciate the distinction Mr Knightley is making, and adds insult to injury by continuing to rave about Frank Churchill's star quality:

> 'Cannot you imagine, Mr. Knightley, what a *sensation* his coming will produce? There will be but one subject throughout the parishes of Donwell and Highbury; but one interest – one object of curiosity; it will be all Mr. Frank Churchill; we shall think and speak of nobody else . . . ' (*E*, pp. 149–50)

'Sensation', according to *OED*, is quasi-theatrical slang – as the italicising indicates – of the late eighteenth century.[18] Emma goes on to suggest that she will be a more discriminating fan, appreciating Frank's abilities as an actor:

'My idea of him is, that he can adapt his conversation to the taste of everybody, and has the power as well as the wish of being universally agreeable. To you, he will talk of farming; to me, of drawing or music; and so on to everybody, having that general information on all subjects which will enable him to follow the lead, or take the lead, just as propriety may require, and to speak extremely well on each; that is my idea of him.' (*E*, p. 150)

This fantasy of the protean performer is delivered without a hint of the irony which lurks in Emma's evocation of Frank the *sensation*-producer. Yet it suggests at the very least a type of Joseph Surface figure, ever ready with the right phrase in any social situation; and, at worst, a man without a character of his own – Diderot's actor of *nulle sensibilité* – interested only in being 'universally agreeable', and therefore special to nobody (contrast the prickliness of sexual jealousy that Mr Knightley displays in this very passage). The actual Frank Churchill, who arrives at last in Highbury hot on the heels of Jane Fairfax, is not only a more complex person but also a better actor than the theatrically naive Emma can imagine:

Emma watched, and decided that with such feelings as were now shown it could not be fairly supposed that he had been ever voluntarily absenting himself; that he had not been acting a part, or making a parade of insincere professions; and that Mr. Knightley certainly had not done him justice. (*E*, p. 197)

And so Highbury's most sophisticated private theatricals – before an unwitting audience – begin in volume ii as Frank plays the star and Jane uncomfortably follows his lead. Frank, as Emma later observes, undoubtedly has 'very great amusement in tricking [them] all' (*E*, p. 478), and in exercising the kind of brinkmanship that is evident in virtually all his public scenes with Jane. As Emma accurately remarks, it is a kind of narcissism: 'I am sure it was a source of high entertainment to you, to feel that you were taking us all in' (*E*, p. 478). He is practising a typically daring bluff in his first tête-à-tête with Emma (playing a 'son of Highbury' in the visit to Ford's) when he 'naturally' uses a theatrical metaphor to assert his own straightforwardness and inability to read below the surface of behaviour:

'There appeared such a perfectly good understanding among them all – ' he began rather quickly, but checking himself, added: 'However, it is impossible for me to say on what terms they really were – how it might all be *behind the scenes*. I can only say that there was smoothness outwardly. But you, who have known Miss Fairfax from a child, must be a better judge of her character, and of how she is likely to conduct herself in critical situations, than I can be.' (*E*, pp. 202–3; my emphasis)

The Coles' dinner party (chapter 26) – an occasion of particular significance for Emma, since the invitation confirms her status as first lady of Highbury – presents a scintillating demonstration of Frank's histrionic abilities. First, in the extended dialogue with Emma in which he blandly leads her to embroider her fantasy about Jane's illicit relation with Mr Dixon ('I, simple I, saw nothing but the fact . . .'), and then eloquently affirms its existence as reality: 'now I can see it in no other light than as an offering of love' (*E*, pp. 218–9). Garrick-like, his facial expression reinforces the words of his script: 'The conviction seemed real; he looked as if he felt it', Emma observes. A more sophisticated observer might note and suspect the narcissism at the base of Frank's character in his admission later that evening, 'I have no pleasure in seeing my friends, unless I can believe myself fit to be seen' (*E*, p. 222): he is too like Mr Elton here, careful of making the right impression, whether in physical appearance or in demeanour.

Second, Frank puts himself forward after dinner as a performer among the 'young-lady-performers' (*E*, p. 229), duetting unexpectedly with Emma and then singing confidently with Jane. Second-time readers can see that Frank sings with Emma so that he can naturally continue the role of duettist with Jane, celebrating and displaying their relationship while concealing it (Emma vaguely notices 'the sweet sounds of the united voices', *E*, p. 227), but first-time readers are more likely to share Mr Knightley's sense that 'That fellow . . . thinks of nothing but shewing off his own voice' (*E*, p. 229), an unmanly display of elegant accomplishment rather than action.

Finally, there is the impromptu dance which ends the party: 'Frank Churchill, coming up with most becoming gallantry to Emma, had secured her hand, and led her up to the top' (*E*, p. 229). Of course this consummate actor dances well, and in dancing with Emma he is publicly performing a specious sexual interest in her which furthers his secret agenda; but his concluding private performance for Emma's benefit is a sign to the alert reader of the malice accompanying his narcissism. At bottom Frank despises others – women, particularly, because of his easy sexual power over them; they are pawns in his game of self-aggrandisement. Both Emma and Jane are belittled here: '"Perhaps it is as well," said Frank Churchill, as he attended Emma to her carriage. "I must have asked Miss Fairfax, and her languid dancing would not have agreed with me, after your's"' (*E*, p. 230).

Reflecting on her 'condescension' in attending the Coles' dinner-party, Emma is ironically represented by the narrator as pleased with the stellar impression she has created with ease for these 'worthy people' – she has 'left a name behind her that would not soon die away' (*E*, p. 231). At the same time she has some doubts about her performance against the standards of her best self, worried first of all whether 'she had not transgressed the duty of woman by woman, in betraying her suspicions of Jane Fairfax's feelings to Frank Churchill.' And secondly, she recognises the superiority of Jane's performance of the accomplished young lady: 'She did unfeignedly and unequivocally regret the inferiority of her own playing and singing.' The point is reinforced by Emma's having to explain it to Harriet, who persists in her fan-worship of Emma. Narratologically, this dialogue frames the previous chapter's events as performances, since Harriet speaks as a conscious representative of the 'audience': 'Mr. Cole said how much taste you had; and Mr. Frank Churchill talked a great deal about your taste, and that he valued taste much more than execution' (*E*, p. 232). What neither of them comments on – because neither is aware of how they have been manipulated by it – is the subtly brilliant performance of Frank Churchill himself.

Emma is smart enough to be aware of Frank's general acting abilities: 'I am persuaded that you can be as insincere as your neighbours, when it is necessary' (*E*, p. 234); what she cannot do is see herself in the role of Frank's 'stooge', which is in fact how Frank has cast her. This role is continued in the following chapter (chapter 28), which further fetishises the piano as an erotic object, as the curtain rises on the more intimate scene of the Bateses' sitting-room:

> The appearance of the little sitting-room as they entered was tranquillity itself; Mrs. Bates, deprived of her usual employment, slumbering on one side of the fire, Frank Churchill, at a table, near her, most deedily occupied about her spectacles, and Jane Fairfax, standing with her back to them, intent on her pianoforte. (*E*, p. 240)

However, Emma is unaware that she is witnessing an erotically charged scene: the piano which Jane 'had not yet possessed . . . long enough to touch without emotion' stands for the body of Frank, unable to touch his lover in public. Frank's speeches – which are designed to tease both young women, one flirtatiously, the other erotically – produce in Emma a little consciousness of 'shame' (at her possible betrayal of Jane Fairfax), and in Jane, blushes, 'a smile of secret delight' (*E*, p. 243), which Emma misreads according to her own fantasised scenario.

Notwithstanding this unruly bodily evidence of the effects of real passion, Emma continues to fancy herself in love with Frank, which is the cue for her 'forming a thousand amusing schemes for the progress and close of their attachment, fancying interesting dialogues, and inventing elegant letters; [but] the conclusion of every imaginary declaration on his side was that she refused him' (*E*, p. 264). Frank, in Emma's naive dramatic imagination, is the rejected beau (Mr Elton's original role) – a role the very opposite of the one he is playing in real life, where he controls the plot through deployment of his sexual charisma.

Economic power he does not have, however; and with Frank's enforced absence from Highbury, the drama of erotic relationships goes on hold as Mrs Elton is introduced. She proceeds to behave in a way which parodies Emma's worst excesses in her self-assumed starring role as queen of Highbury society. Mrs Elton's vulgarity is an essential ingredient in the climactic series of dramatic scenes which make up volume III of the novel. Excess is the dominant note of these scenes, as Mrs Elton vies with Emma for top billing in the little *theatrum mundi* of Highbury, and Frank and Jane play out their intensifying private drama in coded public performances.

The Crown ball (chapter 38) is the first such scene. This presents the whole of Highbury's genteel society in theatrical mode. A public dance is a display of many codes: social status and hierarchy, sexual interests, wealth and taste, manners, decorum, social *nous*. Each member of the company at the ball is both performer and audience; as readers, we are in the position of lookers-on, gazers but not partakers in the glamorous activities of society. 'The whole party walked about, and looked, and praised again' (*E*, p. 320). Everyone looks at everyone else. Frank Churchill has 'a great curiosity to see Mrs. Elton', and 'Emma longed to know ... how he was affected by the studied elegance of her dress, and her smiles of graciousness'; her 'gestures and movements', as she attempts to take over Mrs Weston's role as hostess 'might be understood by any one who looked on like Emma' (*E*, p. 322). Mrs Elton explains to Jane that 'upon such an occasion as this, when everybody's eyes are so much upon me, and in compliment to the Westons, who I have no doubt are giving this ball chiefly to do me honour – I would not wish to be inferior to others; and I see very few pearls in the room except mine' (*E*, p. 324).

Mrs Elton's '*cara sposo*' takes the opportunity to insult Harriet publicly, and through her, Emma, by refusing to dance with her. 'Emma ... had leisure to look around, and by only turning her head a little she saw it all' (*E*, p. 327): hears the dialogue between Mrs Weston and Mr Elton, sees Harriet as silent victim of his malice, and the 'smiles of high glee [which] passed between him and his wife' (*E*, p. 328). But in another moment a happier sight caught her – Mr. Knightley leading Harriet to the set! Never had she been more surprised, seldom more delighted, than at that instant. She was all pleasure and gratitude, both for Harriet and herself, and longed to be thanking him; and though too distant for speech, her countenance said much, as soon as she could catch his eye again.

Emma mimes gratitude, momentarily using her status as performer in this melée of lookers and looked-at to convey a specific message to another on the social stage. For Mr Knightley by 'leading Harriet to the set' has given a *performance* of masculinity. The immediate and radical effect of this act of chivalry is to catapult him into the theatre of sexuality: dancing is courting display, whether intended or not by the performer. Emma, who has previously felt 'disturbed by Mr. Knightley's not dancing . . . so young as he looked!', registers his unconscious (if it is such) framing of himself as a figure of virility:

He could not have appeared to greater advantage perhaps anywhere, than where he had placed himself. His tall, firm, upright figure, among the bulky forms and stooping shoulders of the elderly men, was such as Emma felt must draw everybody's eyes; and, excepting her own partner, there was not one among the whole row of young men who could be compared with him. He moved a few steps nearer, and those few steps were enough to prove in how gentlemanlike a manner, with what natural grace, he must have danced, would he but take the trouble. (*E*, p. 326)

Of course, it is only Emma who is so fascinated by Mr Knightley's attractive maleness here, who sees him, that is, as a possible (sexual) partner; and by the end of the chapter, she has responded to his presentation of a new image, and a potential new social relation between them:

'I am ready,' said Emma, 'whenever I am wanted.'
'Whom are you going to dance with?' asked Mr. Knightley.
She hesitated a moment, and then replied, 'With you, if you will ask me.'
'Will you?' said he, offering his hand.
'Indeed I will. You have shown that you can dance, and you know we are not really so much brother and sister as to make it at all improper.'
'Brother and sister! no, indeed.' (*E*, p. 331)

And the curtain falls on the scene, closing the chapter.

While Emma, in the aftermath of Harriet's rescues at the ball and from the gypsies, is complacently misreading the romantic significance of these two examples of chivalrous masculinity, Mr Knightley is the subject of a rare narratorial focus as we are informed that he began to suspect [Frank] of some inclination to trifle with Jane Fairfax. He could not understand it; but there were symptoms of intelligence between them – he thought so at least – symptoms of admiration on his side, which, having once observed, he could not persuade himself to think entirely void of meaning, however he might wish to escape any of Emma's errors of imagination. (*E*, p. 343)

He has become the involuntary but fascinated audience of the true drama of Frank and Jane, as opposed to the public performance with which they are deceiving everyone else in Highbury. 'It was a child's play, chosen to conceal a deeper game on Frank Churchill's part' (*E*, p. 348), he concludes – with metaphoric resonance – of the letter game which enables Frank to signal *blunder* to Jane. Mr Knightley, older than the other protagonist by sixteen years, is a man of the world sophisticated enough to recognise the difference between child's play and adult drama.

'Child's *play*' might well describe the obvious and excessive theatricality of some of the behaviours narrated in the two climactic chapters (42 and 43), the Donwell strawberry-picking and the Box Hill picnic. Mrs Elton starts the thread, with her excited declaration:

'It is to be a morning scheme, you know, Knightley; quite a simple thing. I shall wear a large bonnet, and bring one of my little baskets hanging on my arm. Here – probably this basket with pink ribbon. Nothing can be more simple, you see. And Jane will have such another. There is to be no form or parade – a sort of gipsy party. – We are to walk about your gardens, and gather the strawberries ourselves, and sit under trees; and whatever else you may like to provide, it is to be all out of doors – a table spread in the shade, you know. Everything as natural and simple as possible . . . ' (*E*, p. 355)

Her fantasy role, complete with shepherdess's costume, is that of Marie Antoinette, playing with her maids at being peasants in the *Hameau* at Versailles. Of course Mrs Elton is too obtuse to see the irony of this fantasy (given what happened to Marie Antoinette); but Mr Knightley does see its implications, and gently rebukes her, insisting that her proper role is that of a member of the gentry, with all the decorous behaviour that that implies: 'The nature and the simplicity of gentlemen and ladies, with their servants and furniture, I think is best observed by meals within doors. When you are tired of eating strawberries in the garden, there shall be cold meat in the house.'

Donwell Abbey itself is a solid and untheatrical setting; unfashionable, unpicturesque, yet fertile, productive, and comforting: 'It was a sweet view – sweet to the eye and the mind. English verdure, English culture, English comfort, seen under a sun bright, without being oppressive'

(*E*, p. 360). In such an unpretentiously good place – the ideal to which Emma unknowingly aspires – Emma herself is at her best, and throughout this chapter we see her observing, walking, thinking – but not 'acting' nor attempting to control others' lives. We see, for example, one of her all too rare gestures of friendship towards the beleaguered Jane Fairfax: 'she saw it all; and entering into her feelings, promoted her quitting the house immediately, and watched her safely off with the zeal of a friend' (*E*, p. 363). Emma's conversation with the ill-tempered Frank at the end of the chapter is pleasant and cool, avoiding the theatrical flirtatiousness of their earlier encounters (and the one to come at Box Hill). It is Frank who is momentarily at a disadvantage here; 'out of humour' (*E*, p. 364) might be glossed as 'out of character', since he briefly lets the mask drop. As Emma percipiently comments next day, 'You had, somehow or other, broken bounds yesterday, and run away from your own management' (*E*, p. 369). What is revealed is Frank's unEnglishness: 'I am sick of England, and would leave it to-morrow if I could', he declares pettishly (*E*, p. 365). Frank, the 'double-dealer' (as Mr Knightley calls him, appropriately using the title of Congreve's play with its devious protagonist), is in the same camp as Mrs Elton, that of England's enemies: he is spiritually as 'French' as she, as his punning name implies: not frank, but *français*; and certainly not related to Churchill the English hero that his adopted name – his stage name? – suggests.[19]

The next day of high summer brings the expedition to Box Hill. Significantly, it is no common experience for Emma: she 'had never been to Box Hill; she wished to see what every body found so well worth seeing' (*E*, p. 352). Box Hill is thus conceptualised as a theatrical space, something special to look at. It is also a frivolous space, not in itself an ordered and productive place, like Donwell. It is somewhere to play; it both demands and encourages performers. Frank offers Emma her biggest part yet, co-starring with him in a comedy of flirtatious display which depends on the humiliation of lesser players. Readers and on-stage audience are treated to a three-page public performance of heartless banter, in which the linguistic register echoes that of eighteenth-century comedy at its most consciously artificial:

'You order me, whether you speak or not. And you can be always with me. You are always with me.'

'Dating from three o'clock yesterday. My perpetual influence could not begin earlier, or you would not have been so much out of humour before.'

'Three o'clock yesterday! That is your date. I thought I had seen you first in February.'

'Your gallantry is really unanswerable. But (lowering her voice) – nobody speaks except ourselves, and it is rather too much to be talking nonsense for the entertainment of seven silent people.'

'I say nothing of which I am ashamed,' replied he, with lively impudence. 'I saw you first in February. Let everybody on the Hill hear me if they can. Let my accent swell to Mickleham on one side, and Dorking on the other. I saw you first in February.' And then whispering – 'Our companions are excessively stupid. What shall we do to rouse them? Any nonsense will serve. They *shall* talk. Ladies and gentlemen, I am ordered by Miss Woodhouse (who, wherever she is, presides) to say, that she desires to know what you are all thinking of.' (*E*, p. 369)

Miss Bates, publicly insulted by Emma, is momentarily 'deceived by the mock ceremony of her manner' (*E*, p. 371); cheerful unthinking Mr Weston is drawn into the game-playing and offers with unconscious irony his feeble pun on 'M. and A.' as 'perfection'. And Frank continues to play out his secret drama with Jane, concluding with a sexual insult to her as he publicly requests Emma to choose him a wife: 'She must be very lively, and have hazel eyes. I care for nothing else. I shall go abroad for a couple of years – and when I return, I shall come to you for my wife. Remember' (*E*, p. 373). Jane's response to this coded insult is a quiet line which bespeaks her desperate situation, '"Now, ma'am," said Jane to her aunt, "shall we join Mrs. Elton?"' Jane is no willing performer in the heartless comedy of flirtation on Box Hill, but having had plenty of practice in communicating in code with Frank, she has already delivered her own message, and broken off the engagement: 'I *would be understood to mean*, that it can only be weak, irresolute characters . . . who will suffer an unfortunate acquaintance to be an inconvenience, an oppression for ever' (my emphasis).

When this public performance has ended, Mr Knightley, first 'look-[ing] around, as if to see that no one were near' (*E*, p. 374), rebukes Emma for her behaviour. The effect of his speech – a deliberately untheatrical and private performance of his role as her mentor – is that 'Emma felt the tears running down her cheeks almost all the way home, without being at any trouble to check them, extraordinary as they were' (*E*, p. 376). From this point on in the novel, Emma ceases to play the star of her self-directed show, and attempts instead to 'act' in a way which befits the role that she will properly take on in the real world, at Highbury and Donwell. She apologetically visits Miss Bates, attempts to show support and friendship to Jane, and in the remainder of the narrative events, finds that life has outwitted her plans to control it: Frank is engaged to Jane, Harriet is infatuated with Mr Knightley, and she herself realises that she has always loved Mr Knightley.

The last 'scene' which readers may well be expecting in this drama-tically structured novel is of course the love-scene. Austen's ambivalence about theatre is here at its most acute. Much in this climactic chapter (chapter 49) *is* theatrical: the setting, in the Hartfield garden refreshed by rain and sunshine; the mutual embarrassment of the two perform-ers, expressed in broken speeches, which contributes to several pages of tension-raising comedy. But when the moment of breakthrough comes, it is heralded by Mr Knightley's declaring, 'I cannot make speeches, Emma' (*E*, p. 430) – a refusal to enter into the theatrical discourse which heterosexual culture wants to force on him. It is unavoidably, however, just another kind of performance: in this speech Mr Knightley represents himself as sincere, untheatrical, and therefore a trustworthy alternative to the ambiguous masculinity of the Frank Churchills of this world. Emma's response, famously, is not recorded. Jane Austen draws the curtain on the privacy of the lovers, refusing readers the voyeurism of sentimental theatre: 'What did she say? – Just what she ought, of course. A lady always does' (*E*, p. 431). All that the narrator will allow us here is the ironical assurance that Emma finally acts like a lady.

Since this novel is more interested in ironical recognition of the com-plexities of social performance than in pictures of 'perfection', it is im-portant that in its last quasi-dramatic scene (chapter 54) we are reminded of the likeness between Emma and Frank Churchill. They are seen for the last time in now safely flirtatious dialogue, clearly enjoying the recog-nition of their mutual pleasure in performance. Says Emma, 'I think it [Frank's deception] might have been some amusement to myself in the same situation. I think there is a little likeness between us' (*E*, p. 478). But more important is the difference between the two now. Frank can-not disentangle himself from the discourse of theatricality; even now, as a publicly engaged man, his relation to Jane is that of a voyeur. His gaze theatricalises, dehumanises, and commodifies Jane:

'Did you ever see such a skin? – such smoothness! such delicacy! – and yet without being actually fair. – One cannot call her fair. It is a most uncommon complexion, with her dark eye-lashes and hair – a most distinguishing complexion! – So peculiarly the lady in it. – Just colour enough for beauty.'

'. . . She is a complete angel. Look at her. Is not she an angel in every gesture? Observe the turn of her throat. Observe her eyes, as she is looking up at my father. – You will be glad to hear (inclining his head, and whispering seriously) that my uncle means to give her all my aunt's jewels. They are to be new set. I am resolved to have some in an ornament for the head. Will not it be beautiful in her dark hair?' (*E*, pp. 478–9)

Though Jane may here unwittingly present a sentimental image of domestic submissiveness (the pose setting off her beauty), her fate is not,
perhaps, to be all that far removed from the slavery with which she
has associated her alternative future as a governess, much earlier in the
novel. She is first and last a decorative possession, a picture framed by
her husband's perception of her social role.

By contrast, despite our recognition that the novel has come to its
destined romantic ending, and that Emma's next role will be that of the
lady of the manor at Donwell, Austen refuses to commodify or theatricalise her heroine in similar terms to Jane Fairfax. Mrs Elton (who was
not present) has the task of explaining that the wedding was disappoint-
ingly untheatrical, 'Very little white satin, very few lace veils; a most
pitiful business! – Selina would stare when she heard of it' (*E*, p. 484).
There are witnesses, but they are described as 'the small band of true
friends'[20] – a non-hierarchised model of social grouping that eschews
theatricality. There is no final 'picture' of fathers, children, and lovers all
beatifically grouped, such as audiences expected in sentimental comedy
like *The Birth-Day* or *Lovers' Vows*. In the novel that follows, *Persuasion*, the
ideal of 'true friendship' plays an important part, but it has to struggle for its place in an imaginative world that insistently tends towards the
perspectives of the new romantic melodrama.

# CHAPTER SEVEN

# Persuasion *and melodrama*

When Jane Austen re-worked the scene of the private reconciliation between Anne and Wentworth into the extraordinarily dramatic public performance – of which the reader is the privileged audience – between a speaking Anne and a silent but impassioned Wentworth, she had no model for what her dramatic instincts told her to write. The original scene, in Admiral Croft's drawing-room, is the standard fare of sentimental drama, and of the sentimental novel. The woman is passive, an object of manipulation by the paternal Admiral Croft and of eloquent address by the lover Captain Wentworth. Anne, in this version, is virtually locked into a room with the suitor, in a scene which replays Henry Crawford's proposal to Fanny in *Mansfield Park*, stage-managed by Sir Thomas Bertram – though even Fanny is more articulate than the Anne depicted here.

Captain Wentworth does all the talking in this scene: the focus is on his emotional discomfort as, courteous, articulate, but deeply embarrassed, he delivers Admiral Croft's message. Two long paragraphs of this speech precede Anne's speaking 'a word or two, but they were unintelligible'; he interrupts, to speak again 'with a fortitude' of self-denial (expecting to hear that Anne is engaged to Mr Elliot). Anne's *only* speech in the scene is the minimal, '"No, Sir – said Anne – There is no message. – You are misin – the Adml is misinformed. – I do justice to the kindness of his Intentions, but he is quite mistaken. There is no Truth in any such report"' (*P*, p. 263).[1] Wentworth's response is once again to take the masculine initiative, in a 'silent . . . dialogue' in which Anne is passive and receptive:

he now sat down – drew [the chair] a little nearer to her – & looked, with an expression which had something more than penetration in it, something softer; – Her Countenance did not discourage. – It was a silent, but a very powerful Dialogue; – on his side, Supplication, on her's acceptance. – Still, a little nearer – and a hand taken and pressed – and 'Anne, my own dear

Anne!' – bursting forth in the fullness of exquisite feeling – and all Suspense & Indecision were over. (*P*, p. 263)

This is so extraordinarily different from the final much expanded version, two chapters climaxing in Anne's crescendo of eloquent and passionate speeches to Captain Harville, that the invitation to unpick the latter's structure is irresistible. The final version is patently more dramatic in its complexity, its affective power, and its use of performers and audience. It depends on the overhearing device (which Austen had already used in volume I, during the walk to Winthrop), which was a commonplace of last-act dénouements in eighteenth-century comedy. Austen's theatrical framing of the moment facilitates the display of extreme emotion which would normally be indecorous in Austen's fictional world. Anne is the principal vehicle, with an extraordinary series of speeches which publicly valorise women's emotional lives and culminate in the eloquently poetic 'All the privilege I claim for my own sex (it is not a very enviable one, you need not covet it), is that of loving longest, when existence or when hope is gone' (*P*, p. 235). The emotional truth of this performance leads to the momentary inability to speak that many actors have experienced: 'She could not immediately have uttered another sentence; her heart was too full, her breath too much oppressed.'

For Wentworth, now the passive-receptive (and seated) listener, the only intervention in this dramatic scene can be in the form of a letter, that literary form which most closely approximates the soliloquy in tenor (since its 'truth-telling' assumes an audience, but one that cannot immediately respond or interrupt). 'I can listen no longer in silence' – although that is literally what he does; – 'I must speak to you by such means as are within my reach.' The genre of the letter-soliloquy allows Wentworth to use heightened language: but it is not the fresh-minted poetry of Anne's speeches, rather the second-hand language that a man of the world grasps at when his own authoritative speech (such as we see in the original version) is finally inadequate:

'. . . You pierce my soul. I am half agony, half hope. Tell me not that I am too late, that such precious feelings are gone for ever. I offer myself to you again with a heart even more your own, than when you almost broke it eight years and a half ago. Dare not say that man forgets sooner than woman, that his love has an earlier death. I have loved none but you. Unjust I may have been, weak and resentful I have been, but never inconstant . . . I can hardly write. I am every instant hearing something which overpowers me. You sink your voice, but I can distinguish the tones of that voice, when they would be lost on others. – Too good, too excellent creature! You do us justice indeed. You do believe that there is true attachment and constancy among men.' (*P*, p. 237)

Wentworth, as a character in a fiction, is able to perform in this way – which is untypical of his presence elsewhere in Austen's novel – for two reasons, both to do with the emerging dramatic genre of melodrama. Most immediately, he is using what Peter Brooks has identified as melodramatic rhetoric,[2] that is, an inflated and hyperbolic 'unrealistic' language. Wentworth's vocabulary is almost embarrassingly extreme: *pierce my soul, agony, hope, precious feelings, heart, death*. Inversions of normal speech order heighten the style and give it something of the rhythm of verse: 'Tell me not'; 'Unjust I may have been, weak and resentful I have been'; 'For you alone I think and plan.' It is an exclamatory style, questioning self, other, and fate. Its origins can be traced to the climactic moments of eighteenth-century sentimental drama such as *The London Merchant* or *The Gamester*, and (once again) to Kotzebue's dramas of error and reconciliation – though there is nothing in the dramatic literature that at all closely foreshadows this extraordinary declaration. Brooks's analysis of the style is particularly helpful in identifying the effect of Wentworth's letter at this climactic point in a narrative which has offered a more intense accumulation of emotional tension than anything in the contemporary drama was able to do:

> melodramatic rhetoric, and the whole expressive enterprise of the genre, represents a victory over repression. We could conceive this repression as simultaneously social, psychological, historical, and conventional; what could not be said on an earlier stage, nor still on a 'nobler' stage, nor within the codes of society. The melodramatic utterance breaks through everything that constitutes the 'reality principle,' all its censorships, accommodations, tonings-down. Desire cries aloud its language in identification with full states of being.[3]

Wentworth responds to Anne's heartfelt utterances in the only way he can as a character subject to the 'reality principle'. His eloquent letter is a decorous substitute for the cry of longing he cannot express aloud; Wentworth is not, after all, an actor.

### HEARTS OF OAK

Secondly, however, Wentworth is able to 'speak' in this way because of what he represents in the national imagination; that is, he is also a figure beyond realism. Captain Wentworth belongs to a set of dramatic idealised figures which would have been immediately recognisable to Austen's first audience: he is the heroic yet sensitive British sailor (subset: the noble captain, rather than the worthy young midshipman or the salty 'tar'). From the moment of the British navy's first victory against Napoleon, the stages of London and provincial theatres were filled with naval spectacles and heroic sailors. Covent Garden, for example, saw Charles Dibdin's *Loyal Effusion* (1794), Franklin's *A Trip to the Nore* (1797, celebrating the victory of Camperdown), Thomas Dibdin's *The Mouth of the Nile*[4] (October 1798, following Nelson's victory there), *The Naval Pillar* (1799), *The English Fleet* (1803), and *Nelson's Glory* (1805). At Sadler's Wells in 1804 a water tank was installed on the stage, and the newly named Aquatic Theatre showed *The Siege of Gibraltar* (1804), *The Battle of Trafalgar* (1806), and *The Battle of the Nile* (1815).[5]

Terence Freeman's study *Britons, Strike Home*[6] demonstrates conclusively that the 'tar' in many permutations had a lively presence on the eighteenth-century stage. But the pressure of war with France produced a need for a more idealised figure, particularly once the series of naval victories against Napoleon got underway. Admiral Nelson and his peers filled the role to perfection.[7] Austen first touches on this theme in *Mansfield Park* in the figure of the manly but courteous William Price,[8] whose Christian name evokes the dozens of good-hearted sailor Williams who populated the drama of the preceding century. The most famous theatrical midshipman, William in Jerrold's *Black-Ey'd Susan*, did not make his debut until 1829, but he and Austen's character have a common origin, probably, in Leveridge's song 'Black-ey'd Susan' of 1731 (to words by John Gay), one of the most lastingly popular songs of the century:

> Though battle call me from thy arms,
> Let not my pretty Susan mourn;
> Though cannons roar, yet safe from harms,
> William shall to his dear return.

Performances of 'Black-ey'd Susan' were routinely inserted into naval spectacles. Sheridan's *The Glorious First of June* (1794), a hugely successful Drury Lane benefit for the widows and orphans of the sailors who died at Howe's naval victory, offered a naval spectacle[9] in the middle of a sentimental short play concerning a heroic midshipman, inevitably called William, his messmate Robin, an innocent young woman (Susan – again), and a villainous grasping lawyer, Endless. This piece predates the imported form of 'melodrama' – a play accompanied by atmospheric music – but in its naval and civilian stereotypes and its plot it is no different from the nautical melodramas later to be typified by the enormously popular *Black-Ey'd Susan*.[10] Ultimately it was the sentimental drama that survived as the stronger form, not the spectacle, which was always going

to be subject to the scepticism of observers who noticed the poor perspective and proportion, and the smoothness of the 'ocean', of even the
most technologically advanced of these shows.

By 1805, popular sentiment had changed, so that *Nelson's Glory* (1805),
a 'loyal musical impromptu' put together by Thomas Dibdin in response
to the victory of Trafalgar and Nelson's death, was considered by some
to be in poor taste. Gillian Russell argues that

the response to the dramatic treatments of Nelson's funeral interestingly suggests the influence of a Paineite discourse of theatricality, manifested by a desire
to efface the complications of theatre, the framing devices, the curtains, and
disguises, that might obscure the integrity of the event. Thus, in the view of the
*Monthly Mirror*, the problem of *Nelson's Glory* was that it could 'throw a sort of
ridicule upon events that, out of the theatre, we contemplate with mingled
gratitude, delight and admiration'.[11]

The libretto of this *pièce d'occasion* was by Thomas Dibdin, a popular
showman, who turned his hand to all the current theatrical genres (he
was the author-adaptor of *The Birth-Day*). However, he never achieved the
sentimental popularity of his father, the composer Charles Dibdin, who
generally wrote both the words and music of his songs, and performed
them in one-man shows called 'Table Entertainments'. The elder Dibdin
tapped into the sentimental vein of the British public (as opposed to its
desire for theatrical spectacle) and a number of his nautical songs became
popular evergreens. Charles Dibdin is represented by eight songs in Jane
Austen's collection of music, including 'The Soldier's Adieu' (1790) –
altered in Austen's hand to read *sailor's* in the opening verse:

> Adieu! adieu! my only life,
> My honour calls me from thee,
> Remember thou'rt a soldier's wife,
> Those tears but ill become thee;
> What tho' by duty I am call'd,
> Where thund'ring cannons rattle,
> Where valour's self might stand appall'd,
> When on the wings of thy dear love,
> To heav'n above thy fervent orisons are flown,
> The tender pray'r thou putt'st up there,
> Shall call a guardian angel down,
> To watch me in the battle.

Two more verses of the same sentiments follow. One imagines that
this piece is dear to Captain Harville's heart, on the evidence of his
speech to Anne in *Persuasion*'s chapter 23: 'Ah!... if I could but make you

comprehend what a man suffers when he takes a last look at his wife and children . . . ' (*P*, p. 235).

Perhaps Dibdin's most famous song (though it is not in Austen's collection) is 'Tom Bowling', a heartrending ballad written in memory of his brother, a naval captain, in 1789:

> Here, a sheer hulk, lies poor Tom Bowling,
> The darling of our crew;
> No more he'll hear the tempest howling,
> For death has broach'd him to.
> His form was of the manliest beauty,
> His heart was kind and soft;
> Faithful below, Tom did his duty,
> And now he's gone aloft.
>
> Tom never from his word departed,
> His virtues were so rare;
> His friends were many, and true-hearted,
> His Poll was kind and fair:
> And then he'd sing so blithe and jolly,
> Ah! Many's the time and oft;
> But mirth is turn'd to melancholy,
> For Tom is gone aloft.

It is against paragons like these in the popular imagination that *Persuasion*'s 'poor Dick Musgrove' is implicitly measured. Mrs Musgrove's 'large fat sighings' (*P*, p. 68) come from the same well of sentiment, but they have neither truth nor beauty to recommend them to the tart-tongued narrator.

In these popular songs[12] we find the heightened language (which modern readers tend to associate with the later melodrama) that is the idiom of the idealised British sailor as he faces death for his country. One final example, one of the most popular and dramatic songs of the early nineteenth century, is John Braham's 'Death of Nelson' (1811). The stirring refrain to this moment-by-moment account of Nelson's death at Trafalgar, is 'For England, home, and beauty', rhyming, inevitably, with Nelson's famous message to the Fleet: 'England expects that every man/ This day will do his duty.' The last stanza bears repeating:

> At last the fatal wound, [*a crashing piano chord*]
> Which spread dismay around,
> The hero's breast receiv'd.
> 'Heav'n fights upon our side!

The day's our own,' he cried!
'Now long enough I've liv'd!
In honour's cause my life was pass'd,
In honour's cause I fall at last,
For England, home, and beauty.'
Thus ending life as he began,
England confess'd that ev'ry man
That day had done his duty.[13]

Nelson's heroic death, sentimentalised in a thousand popular representations, provided the culture with the model of masculinity they had been seeking to counter the reality of the aristocracy's excesses and the corruption, frivolity, and sexual licence of the army (reflected in the military camp at Brighton where Lydia is seduced by Wickham in *Pride and Prejudice*). The preferred public performance of masculinity had developed into a more domestic, sensitive, genteel model, ready when the moment called for it to fight gallantly but also able to produce a heart-stirring speech which does not shy away from the language of sensibility. Wentworth, Harville, and the 'little knot of the navy' (*P*, p. 168) gathered around Admiral Croft in the street in conspicuously frivolous Bath are incarnations of this potent image. Margaret Kirkham comments that Admiral Croft

has many of the characteristics of 'the benevolent tar' who . . . became after 1800 the 'tar without reproach'. The Admiral's good heart and salty language belong to the stereotype but, since he must also be seen as Mrs Croft's respected partner in life, he must not be shown as exhibiting too much of the bluff insensitivity which also belongs to the stereotype. In the cancelled chapter of *Persuasion* he does; in the revised version this is avoided.[14]

Examples of this stereotype include Commodore Chace and Tom Oakum of *The Glorious First of June* and Captain Bertram of *The Birth-Day*. Admiral Cleveland of Joseph Richardson's *The Fugitive* (1792) is somewhat more novelistically articulate while still using the nautical idiom; he has a speech criticising Lord Dartford in terms that Admiral Croft might have used regarding Sir Walter Elliot:

I remember in my younger years, there were some few scattered remnants of such chaps as his lordship – some remains of your old school of beaux, who had been the insects of the former century, and which I had hoped were all extinct by this time; who, like him, were shewy and dangerous, fitter for manoeuvring than action, and more gaudy in their tackle, than sound in their bottom.[15]

These lines in a run-of-the-mill drama carry as critical an indictment of the effete old order as Admiral Croft's aspersions on Sir Walter's too numerous looking-glasses: 'I should think he must be rather a dressy man for his time of life' (*P*, p. 128).

MELODRAMA

By the time Jane Austen wrote *Persuasion*, the new form of melodrama was well established in the theatre; in most, the villain was a member of the aristocracy. This tendency to Jacobinism was already a characteristic of the Gothic theatre and the 'German drama'; what was more peculiar to melodrama was its focus on the powerless victim, in a 'mixture of dialogue and dumb show',[16] its affective power reinforced by the atmospheric music which underlies speeches and dumb-show alike. Whether or not Austen ever saw an example of this new genre is unknowable; though expressive movement accompanied by music was of course familiar to her in the form of pantomime (for example Delpini's *Don Juan* that she saw in 1813, discussed in chapter 1). But melodrama's recognition of the affective power of 'strong' scenes in a narrative in which speech and silence are equally fraught interestingly coincides with Austen's own artistic project in her last novel.

Simon Shepherd and Peter Womack argue that one of theatrical melo-drama's 'highly characteristic ploy[s]' is to 'put its audience in a position where it doesn't so much want to know what's happened as want to see expressed *what it already knows*... The plotting mechanics of frustration and release produce questions about what will happen next, how truth will be revealed.'[17] They point to a number of early nineteenth-century melodramas where the principal character is dumb: Holcroft's *Deaf and Dumb* (1801) and *A Tale of Mystery* (1802), Rayner's *The Dumb Man of Manchester* (1837). Austen has utilised this topos in *Persuasion* in the structure and organisation of the novel by making her heroine Anne virtually silent, because routinely not listened to, in her family: she 'was nobody with either father or sister: her word had no weight; her convenience was always to give way; – she was only Anne' (*P*, p. 5). Shepherd and Womack go on to argue that 'many narratives of early melodrama are organized to produce a climactic speaking out, the moment of the great line', and that this is characteristically the province of a disenfranchised figure. This aptly describes both the occasion and the spirit of Anne's great speech. Finally, 'melodrama's excitement may be said to relate to a fantasy of *agency*, the possibility of being able single-handedly to challenge authority and change it'.[18] In speaking out as she does to Captain Harville, Anne is challenging not only the gendered notion of decorum, but also patriarchal cultural authority: 'Men have had every advantage of us in telling their own story...I will not allow books to prove any thing' (*P*, p. 234).

Austen's narration takes the place of musical accompaniment in drawing our attention to the emotional weight of each moment in this climactic chapter; it is scattered with her typical 'stage directions', here emphasising the affective nature of the exchange: '(in a deep tone)', 'with a quivering lip', 'in a low feeling voice', '(with a faltering voice)', '(smiling at Anne)', '(lowering his voice)', 'in a tone of strong feeling', 'pressing his own [heart] with emotion' (*P*, pp. 232–5). Even less can we ignore her directions for dramatic movement in this scene: Captain Wentworth's dropping of his pen as he tries (Anne suspects) to catch what they are saying; his 'hurried, agitated' exit from the room and his dramatic re-entry a moment later –

instantly crossing the room to the writing table, and standing with his back towards Mrs. Musgrove, he drew out a letter from under the scattered paper, placed it before Anne with eyes of glowing entreaty fixed on her for a moment, and hastily collecting his gloves, was again out of the room... (*P*, p. 236)

This silent and very expressive mime continues with Anne's picking up the letter and 'sinking into the chair which he had occupied... her eyes devour[ing]' his words in a scene which was to become the staple of society melodramas of the later nineteenth century. We the readers are privileged to 'hear' Wentworth's fevered utterance through Anne's consciousness of it almost as though it is accompanied by music, in the way that Verdi, mid-century, was to make a heartbreaking moment out of Violetta's *reading* (not singing) of Germont's letter, 'Tenesse la promessa' in *La Traviata*.

Italian music of her own period – the *bel canto* style – held no affective power for Austen. Given the evidence of her own collection of favourite songs (overwhelmingly in English and therefore easily comprehensible to a domestic audience), it is arguable that the scene of the concert at the Upper Rooms, where Anne is so frustratingly 'applied to' by Mr Elliot for translation of the Italian songs being performed, subtly serves not only the story's emotional trajectory but also its patriotic agenda. Anne's comment – 'certainly the sense of an Italian love-song must not be talked of', backed up by Mr Elliot's 'You have... knowledge enough of the language, to translate at sight these inverted, transposed, curtailed Italian lines, into clear, comprehensive, elegant English' (*P*, p. 186) – suggests that showy music in a foreign tongue offers no genuine artistic pleasure (defined as affecting, heart-stirring).[19] By contrast, unfashionable domestic music-making of the simple songs and glees represented by Dibdin's topical English compositions has a heart (of oak, perhaps) and moves its audience to honest tears and cheers. Wentworth is instinctively right on both counts – the personal and the patriotic – when he leaves the concert, thinking himself ousted by Mr Elliot, with the comment, 'there is nothing worth my staying for' (*P*, p. 190).

The sexually threatening Mr Elliot, the interesting stranger encountered briefly at Lyme, turns out in volume II to be the villain of the piece in a classic melodrama plot of coincidences and secrets revealed. Mrs Smith's revelations of his nefarious doings are unproblematic within this genre, though they offend purists who see Austen as a writer only of the domestic realist novel. Like the villains of Victorian melodrama – in contrast to the murderers and perverts of the earlier Gothic drama – Mr Elliot's crimes are emotional and fiduciary, their victim a helpless widow. Mrs Smith uses the rhetoric of melodrama to describe the villain: 'Those whom he has been the chief cause of leading into ruin, he can neglect and desert without the smallest compunction. He is totally beyond the reach of any sentiment of justice or compassion. Oh! he is black at heart, hollow and black!' (*P*, p. 199). Anne's intuitive dislike of Mr Elliot has already focused on her distrust of his smooth exterior, his performance of the character of 'an agreeable man' (*P*, p. 160): 'She felt that she could so much more depend upon the sincerity of those who sometimes looked or said a careless or a hasty thing, than of those whose presence of mind never varied, whose tongue never slipped' (*P*, p. 161). (She similarly sees through the less accomplished performer Mrs Clay – 'Anne admired the good acting of the friend, in being able to shew such pleasure as she did' (*P*, p. 213).) Even before Mrs Smith's revelations, Anne's emotionally overwrought mind lights on the word 'evil' to describe the pernicious effects of Mr Elliot's attentions at the concert (*P*, p. 191). The next morning, at Mrs Smith's unfashionable lodgings, she learns the unvarnished truth about the smooth interloper.

It is Captain Wentworth who eventually rights the wrongs revealed by Mrs Smith, thereby showing that he is able to act as a true hero in peace as well as in war, not through the exercise of military ability, but through 'writing for her, *acting* for her, and seeing her through all the petty difficulties of the case, with the activity and exertion of a fearless man and a determined friend' (*P*, p. 251; my emphasis). In short, he proves himself a model of true masculinity, here made even more admirable by his association with the idealised sailor of contemporary myth-making.

## EXPANDING THE GENRE OF REALISM

Although the novel's earlier scenes can be read as preparing the ground for the appearance of the melodrama hero – in the cutting satire of the barren and superficial upper-class behaviour of Anne's father and sisters contrasted with the ignored heroine and her agitated inner life – Austen's writing seems only to recognisably invoke the stage when Wentworth is first required to 'perform' his role as idealised patriotic sailor devoted to his ship; a slightly eccentric seaman on shore leave and come a-courting: 'Ah! she was a dear old Asp to me. She did all that I wanted. I knew she would. – I knew that we should either go to the bottom together, or that she would be the making of me; and I never had two days of foul weather all the time I was at sea in her . . . ' (*P*, pp. 65–6).

If the modern reader is able to psychoanalyse Wentworth's fetishisation of his ship as a substitute for his frustrated desire to possess and control Anne, it is only because Austen has provided the context which cues us: 'It was a great object with me, at that time, to be at sea, – a very great object. I wanted to be doing something' (*P*, p. 65). To this one could add the evidence from the surprising metaphor that Wentworth employs to explain his feelings to the Musgrove girls,

'I knew pretty well what she was, before that day . . . I had no more discoveries to make, than you would have as to the fashion and strength of any old pelisse, which you had seen lent about among half your acquaintance, ever since you could remember, and which at last, on some very wet day, is lent to yourself.' (*P*, p. 65)

It is in touches of psychological realism such as these (used, indeed, ever since Henry Tilney showed that he was no ordinary young man by discoursing learnedly about muslins) that Austen rounds out her portrait of the idealised sailor and, while utilising the popular language of stage stereotypes, embeds the character in a rich earth of unpredictable naturalness. Many scenes throughout the novel use Austen's tried and true technique of domestic comedy shading into satire – but these, finally, are not what we remember *Persuasion* for; rather for its almost unbearable emotional intensity. Here melodrama's characteristic use of silence and gesture, of affect made visible rather than audible, can be recognised. In the pages that follow I am not arguing for an 'influence' of the new

dramatic form on Jane Austen (as might be argued in the case of the popular figure of the idealised sailor) but rather for a confluence of creative
intentions: the aim is to affect the audience/reader with the significance
of a single epiphanic moment, typically *embodied* rather than a product
of thought. Two striking examples, unique in their genre in Austen's
fiction, are the miniature episodes in chapters 9 and 10: Wentworth's
silent rescuing of Anne from the tormenting behaviour of young Walter
Musgrove, and his helping her into the Crofts' carriage at the end of the
walk to Winthrop.

It is easy, and very satisfying, to read each of these episodes symboli-
cally. In the first, Wentworth is the deliverer of Anne from the oppression
of her family; in the second, he enables her to rise into the new and amiable society of his brother officers. But for generations of readers they
have held a pleasure and fascination which is less easy to decode, because of what I have called their generic uniqueness. I want to suggest
that in writing so explicitly of Anne's bodily sensations, and her inability
to separate her physical feelings from her emotional and intellectual response, Austen is drawing on a character/audience relationship that is
most commonly to be found in the drama. In short, as audience to this
moment we are voyeurs of sexual intimacy. (And Austen knows whereof
she speaks: when she saw Eliza O'Neill in *Isabella* in 1814, she remarked,
'She is an elegant creature however & hugs Mr Younge delightfully',
*Letters*, 29 November 1814.) Although in her preceding novels Austen
was reticent about indicating physical contact between lovers (if suggesting enough for readers to make their own inferences), in this last novel
she developed silent dramatic vignettes between Anne and Wentworth
which depend upon each character's consciousness of the body of the
other. These moments replace the sexually charged speech with which
the earlier lovers conduct their unconscious courtships. Both Anne and
Wentworth are silenced by the decorums of the social class in which they
live. While they were once intimate, acknowledged lovers conducting a
normal courtship through conversation and social events such as dancing, Anne and Wentworth must now to all appearances be 'nothing' to
each other.

In both episodes we witness taboo-breaking physical contact – such as
audiences might see at any point in theatre history from a daring actor
who wanted to stretch the boundaries of dramatic representation. But
as readers we are privileged to see these moments empathetically rather
than as simple voyeurs: it is as though 'Anne Elliot' is being performed by
a great actress, who allows us to see and share her succession of feelings.

Austen's recording of them reads like a combination of stage directions and the performer's notes to herself:

> Her sensations on the discovery made her perfectly speechless. She could not even thank him. She could only hang over little Charles, with most disordered feelings. His kindness in stepping forward to her relief – the manner – the silence in which it had passed – the little particulars of the circumstance – with the conviction soon forced on her by the noise he was studiously making with the child, that he meant to avoid hearing her thanks . . . produced such a confusion of varying, but very painful agitation, as she could not recover from, till enabled by the entrance of Mary and the Miss Musgroves to make over her little patient to their cares, and leave the room. (*P*, p. 80)

In both episodes the focus of Anne's perception is that Captain Wentworth 'had done it'. The sexual connotations of 'done' in the context of Anne's febrile responses cannot be ignored. His body has been in close contact with hers, unfastening Walter's 'little sturdy hands . . . from around her neck'. In the carriage episode a few pages later Anne's thought processes move swiftly from an almost shocked registration of the quasi-sexual nature of Wentworth's act to an attempt consciously to rationalise and thus censor the event:

> Yes, – he had done it. She was in the carriage, and felt that he had placed her there, that *his will and his hands had done it*, that she owed it to his perception of her fatigue, and his resolution to give her rest. She was very much affected by the view of his disposition towards her which all these things made apparent. This little circumstance seemed the completion of all that had gone before. She understood him. He could not forgive her, – but he could not be unfeeling. Though condemning her for the past, and considering it with high and unjust resentment, though perfectly careless of her, and though becoming attached to another, still he could not see her suffer, without the desire of giving her relief. It was a remainder of former sentiment; it was an impulse of pure, though unacknowledged friendship; it was proof of his own warm and amiable heart, which she could not contemplate without emotions so compounded of pleasure and pain, that she knew not which prevailed. (*P*, p. 91; my emphasis)

It is particularly satisfying for the reader who has been following these indications of physical intimacy to observe that after Louisa's disastrous leap from the Cobb (which I discuss below as a fine example of 'sensation' drama), Captain Wentworth 'place[s] himself between' Anne and Henrietta in the carriage for the anxious ride to Uppercross with the news (*P*, p. 116). The lovers' bodies move ever consciously closer: how frustrating, then, for Anne and the reader, when Mr Elliot disrupts

Anne's plan that Wentworth should take the vacant seat on the bench beside her at the concert in Bath; and what a consummation is enacted in the mind's eye when at last Anne 'sink[s] into the chair which he had occupied, succeeding to the very spot where he had leaned and written' the passionate letter in which he finally declares his love (*P*, p. 237).

Austen's awareness and enjoyment of the inescapable embodiment of drama was useful, I suggest, to her own imaginative processes as she explored new affective techniques in *Persuasion*. That she was indeed conscious of developments in the new century's drama and its tendency to slip too easily into sensationalism is indicated in her treatment of the epiphanic moment of Louisa's fall on the Cobb. As the climax of volume 1, and a necessary development in the plot (freeing Louisa from Captain Wentworth by changing her character via a convenient bump on the head), the episode is both sensational and at the same time ironically comic – an effect which the drama rarely aimed for, but which is the hallmark of Austen's writerly presence.

'In all their walks, he had had to jump her from the stiles; the sensation was delightful to her' (*P*, p. 109). Louisa has hitherto enjoyed the life of the body within the limits (just) of female decorum. She is now demanding an excess of pleasure; 'sensation', being a bodily (uncontrollable) exper-ience, can too easily tip over into dangerous ground, become an addiction, as Austen's narration of Louisa's habit suggests. Indulgence in sensation can lead to *sensation* in the newspaper or theatrical sense – which is exactly where the story takes us, complete with exclamatory captions:

he put out his hands; she was too precipitate by half a second, she fell on the pavement on the Lower Cobb, and was taken up lifeless!

There was no wound, no blood, no visible bruise; but her eyes were closed, she breathed not, her face was like death. – The horror of that moment to all who stood around! (*P*, p. 109)

What we have here is an affective *appearance* of death, a performance of it to an audience who read the impressive signs correctly (note also the absence of blood and wounds, theatrically difficult to produce on cue). Mary responds as a naive audience member might do (like the hysterical ladies watching *The Castle Spectre*): ' "She is dead! she is dead!" screamed Mary, catching hold of her husband' (*P*, p. 109) – and immediately the scene begins to pick up an edge of comedy to offset the profounder distress of the more admirable characters. As the participants make their way offstage, the ironising narrator reminds us of its genre as theatrical sensation – not an event about whose outcome we need to worry, but rather a momentary thrill before we return to the prosaic demands of domestic realism:

> By this time the report of the accident had spread among the workmen and boatmen about the Cobb, and many were collected near them, to be useful if wanted, at any rate, to enjoy the sight of a dead young lady, nay, two dead young ladies, for it proved twice as fine as the first report. (*P*, p. 111)

Even Wentworth, in retrospect, thinks of this overwrought episode and its sequence in theatrical terms: 'the scenes on the Cobb, and at Captain Harville's, had fixed [Anne's] superiority' (*P*, p. 242). At Lyme he is at last able to see her as the heroine she really is – no longer an ingénue (Louisa's role in the current comedy), but an adult woman able to act decisively: 'no one so proper, so capable as Anne!' (*P*, p. 114).

Act One of *Persuasion*'s structural melodrama is set in the country, and there are plenty of Austen's characteristic scenes of domestic comedy to interlard the story of Anne's painful forced silence. Act Two takes the audience to Bath, that most theatrical of English environments (as we saw in chapter 3). And here, as I have already remarked, William Walter Elliot enters into play as the insidious villain of the piece. Various episodes that take place against the backdrop of Bath's streets emphasise the theatricality of the performative social life in which Anne is now inescapably involved; thus the ground is prepared for her great performance in chapter 23.

One function of the caricatured figure of Sir Walter is to emphasise this pervasive theatricality. On Anne's first evening in Camden Place his longest speech concerns the parade of fashion in the streets of Bath:

> '. . . The worst of Bath was, the number of its plain women. He did not mean to say there were no pretty women, but the number of the plain were out of all proportion. He had frequently observed, as he walked, that one handsome face would be followed by thirty, or five and thirty frights; and once, as he had stood in a shop in Bond-street he had counted eighty-seven women go by, one after another, without there being a tolerable face among them.' (*P*, pp. 141–2)

He is delighted to be able to insert himself as a star in this parade:

> 'It was evident how little the women were used to the sight of any thing tolerable, by the effect which a man of decent appearance produced. He had never walked any where arm in arm with Colonel Wallis, (who was a fine military figure, though sandy-haired) without observing that every woman's eye was upon him; every woman's eye was sure to be upon Colonel Wallis.' (*P*, p. 142)

Modest Sir Walter! as the narrator ironically comments. (We note in passing that of course Sir Walter associates himself with the flashy-looking army man, rather than the weather-beaten heroes of the navy.) But in such a thoroughly theatricalised environment, the viewer is spoiled for choice: the streets offer the experience of a carnival procession rather than the contained structure of a five-act drama.[20]

Austen encourages us to recognise this omnipresent but subjectively received theatricality in the ironic little episode of Lady Russell and the curtains. As Anne and Lady Russell return from a morning expedition, Anne notices, on the wide expanse of Pulteney-street, Captain Wentworth approaching on the opposite pavement. Convinced that Lady Russell must see him, and indeed be admiring his manly grace as she herself is, she is astonished to hear Lady Russell utter this banal observation:

'You will wonder,' said she, 'what has been fixing my eye so long; but I was looking after some window-curtains, which Lady Alicia and Mrs. Frankland were telling me of last night. They described the drawing-room window-curtains of one of the houses on this side of the way, and this part of the street, as being the handsomest and best hung of any in Bath, but could not recollect the exact number, and I have been trying to find out which it could be; but I confess I can see no curtains hereabouts that answer their description.' (*P*, p. 179)

The theatrical streets of Bath provide many objects for the gaze, feeding indiscriminately the desires of all who walk there: for Sir Walter, a mirror to prove that he is still a handsome man; for Lady Russell, the decorative commodities of an affluent lifestyle (for her, curtains are more important than what is behind them); for Anne, a glimpse of the man she loves but cannot approach. We are reminded that she too, like everyone in Bath, is a potential object of another's gaze: 'The part which provoked her most, was that in all this waste of foresight and caution, she should have lost the right moment for seeing whether he saw them' (*P*, p. 179).

Chapter 20, the concert at the Upper Rooms, is a masterful example of the set-piece which Austen had long made her own: the gathering together of many of the major characters in the novel during a social event which allows them to interact, change partners, exchange glances, have private conversations amidst 'all the various noises of the room, . . . and ceaseless buzz of persons walking through' (*P*, p. 183). Austen's liberal stage directions regarding characters' movements towards and away from each other (the chapter starts with Anne 'making yet a little advance' towards Captain Wentworth, arriving solo (*P*, p. 181)), glances, blushes, averted eyes, offer the sort of detail which only in the twentieth century was it possible to represent theatrically, in the realistic formats and observant lenses of film and television. But the mode of melodrama can still be called on when needed to underline a point in the larger dramatic structure: Wentworth has recourse to the exclamatory language of sensibility when his feelings insist on being uttered, albeit indirectly: 'A man like him [Benwick], in his situation! With a heart pierced, wounded, almost broken! . . . A man does not recover from such a devotion of the heart to such a woman! – he ought not – he does not' (*P*, p. 183).

Chapters 22 and 23, the late revisions, offer another brilliant deployment of private performances within a public social event – this time, within the more sympathetic confines of the Musgroves' hotel sitting-room. Anne and Wentworth's increasingly eloquent communication of their feelings for one another is private in chapter 22 – climaxing with '"I am not yet so much changed," cried Anne' (*P*, p. 225) – and semi-public in chapter 23. Anne's debate with Harville, as I have already suggested, is a performance; it has a secret audience, Wentworth, who cannot resist the urge to become an actor in the drama. With the hidden letter, the return to the room with 'eyes of glowing entreaty' directed to Anne (*P*, p. 236), his performance becomes an intensely dramatic mime, to which the remainder of the possible audience in Mrs Musgrove's hotel sitting-room is oblivious.

Christine Gledhill argues that melodrama's 'aesthetics of the visible' insist that 'at the climax of an English melodrama, all should see and be seen'.[21] It is significant that Austen plays both with and against this prescription: we, the readers, have been the privileged audience of Anne's speech and Wentworth's response (though the Musgroves have not). But the curtain is drawn over what follows, the private reconciliation between Anne and Wentworth: after another silent exchange of looks in the public street (with Charles as unwitting audience, again), 'soon words enough had passed between them to decide their direction towards the comparatively quiet and retired gravel-walk, where the power of conversation would make the present hour a blessing indeed' (*P*, p. 240). This conversation's topics are reported by the narrator, but the reader is no longer a member of an audience: we see and hear nothing directly for some minutes of reading-time. By the time we resume our privilege of overhearing, Wentworth is well launched into his narrative of explanation of his behaviour; the highly affecting first moments of rapture have remained private. Roger Michell's 1995 film of *Persuasion* bows to that genre's 'aesthetics of the visible' by showing us Anne and Wentworth kissing in the midst of a busy street, and the film's melodramatic methods are again displayed in Wentworth's arrival at the Elliots' evening party with the loud public declaration, 'Sir Walter, I have come on business...My proposal of marriage has been accepted by your daughter Anne, and I respectfully request permission to fix a date.'[22] Austen, however, once again insists on her characters' privacy, in allowing the as yet unacknowledged lovers to meet only briefly at the party while 'apparently occupied in admiring a fine display of green-house plants' (*P*, p. 246). The point of this scene is to provide the privileged audience of her readers with the characters' final reflections on their story. The emphasis is on the rational rather than the affective; the 'moral' of the preceding drama. For Anne, 'I must believe that I was right, much as I suffered from it, that I was perfectly right in being guided by the friend whom you will love better than you do now' (*P*, p. 246); for Wentworth, 'I must learn to brook being happier than I deserve' (*P*, p. 247).

Like the eighteenth-century novels and sentimental drama which preceded it, melodrama usually concludes with the application of poetic justice: the good end happily, the bad unhappily. But Austen's endings have always had a significant dose of the irony that recognises the complexity of the real life which her texts imitate. So the melodramatically villainous William Walter Elliot exits from the novel not with a snarl of defiance or a deathbed repentance, but rather he sneaks offstage, watched only by Mary Musgrove and a reluctant Anne from the window in the Musgroves' sitting-room: 'he disappeared on one side, as Mrs. Clay walked quickly off on the other...' (*P*, p. 222). The colonnade under which the conspirators have been standing is strikingly like an eighteenth-century stage set (it is unchanged today), and separate, opposite exits for plotters were of course a standard convention. Mary has been watching the goings-on in the street theatre of Bath from the equivalent of a front box in the White Hart hotel; Anne cannot refuse to join in when called upon, though she is conscious that at the same time she is the object of Captain Wentworth's gaze: 'she felt that Captain Wentworth was looking at her' (*P*, p. 222). Catherine Morland, we remember, at the Orchard Street Theatre, desperately wanted Henry Tilney to look at her rather than at the stage; Wentworth, here, is emotionally mature enough to recognise where the real drama is happening.

The theatrical resonances of this moment are reinforced by the very next narrative unit, Charles Musgrove's proposal that this group of good-hearted people should spend the following evening at the theatre:

'Well, mother, I have done something for you that you will like. I have been to the theatre, and secured a box for to-morrow night. A'n't I a good boy? I know you love a play; and there is room for us all. It holds nine. I have engaged Captain Wentworth. Anne will not be sorry to join us, I am sure. We all like a play. Have I not done well, mother?' (*P*, p. 223)

Of course it is the snobbish Mary Musgrove who protests, reminding them that they are engaged to appear at the Elliots' evening party, with its sprinkling of minor aristocrats and 'family connections'. If it were still necessary to argue against the view that Jane Austen was anti-theatrical, here, surely, is final evidence. Her modest and virtuous heroine has 'no pleasure in the sort of meeting [i.e. the party], and should be happy to change it for a play' (*P*, pp. 224–5) in the more congenial company proposed. This deliberate deployment of the theatrical trope in chapters 22 and 23 has no parallel in the original version of Anne and Wentworth's reconciliation; it is clearly a rich resource for Austen's imagination as she negotiates the novel's final play with the ideas of goodness, agency, and identity.

If William Walter Elliot is something of a cardboard villain who ultimately does not demand our full attention (hence the minor exit), he certainly does not merit a place in the novel's conclusion, which reverts to the familiar mode of romance, a resolution based on the removing of obstacles between lovers. But in so far as Wentworth, the alternative suitor, is also an actor in the nation's heroic dramatisation of the navy, the lovers' future cannot be guaranteed the happy-ever-after of the romantic comedies *Pride and Prejudice* and *Emma*. Anne's 'dread of a future war [is] all that could dim her sunshine. She gloried in being a sailor's wife, but she must pay the tax of quick alarm for belonging to that profession which is, if possible, more distinguished in its virtues than in its national importance.' The novel's last note is that of the scores of patriotic melodramas that filled the theatres of Regency England.

# Epilogue

'It is not the fashion to see the lady the epilogue', declares Shakespeare's Rosalind as she cheekily steps out from the last act's conventional picture of a joyful wedding-dance. For a gleeful extra minute or so of theatre time she plays with the audience's expectations of conventional gender behaviour, and invites applause for her – and her company's – performance. In so doing she both ironises the apparent closure of the story that the audience has just enjoyed, and leads the audience to appreciation of an even more sophisticated pleasure: recognition of the creative energy of the author and the actors.

Rosalind was one of the favourite roles of the late eighteenth century's two premier comediennes, Dorothy Jordan and Frances Abington: they must have spoken these teasing, disconcerting yet pleasurable lines many times in their careers, as well as the witty and topical epilogues given them by contemporary playwrights such as Cowley. Indeed, by the late eighteenth century it was almost invariably the fashion to see 'the lady' – the principal comedienne – speak the epilogue, taking a position that was hers by right, as the centre of the play's energy and emotional interest.

Jane Austen, I suggest, takes a similar position on the stage of her own creations, her novels, as they come to an end, putting on with a flourish the mask of 'author', and speaking with affectionate irony of the story that we have all – author, actors, and audience – been involved in:

> The anxiety, which in this state of their attachment, must be the portion of Henry and Catherine, and of all who loved either, as to its final event, can hardly extend, I fear, to the bosom of my readers, who will see in the tell-tale compression of the pages before them, that we are all hastening together to perfect felicity.
> . . . I leave it to be settled by whomsoever it may concern, whether the tendency of this work be altogether to recommend parental tyranny, or reward filial disobedience. (*NA*, pp. 250, 252)

Let other pens dwell on guilt and misery. I leave such odious subjects as soon as I can, impatient to restore every body, not greatly in fault themselves, to tolerable comfort, and to have done with all the rest. (*MP*, p. 461)

Who can be in doubt of what followed? When any two young people take it into their heads to marry, they are pretty sure by perseverance to carry their point, be they ever so poor, or ever so imprudent, or ever so little to be likely to each other's ultimate comfort. This may be bad morality to conclude with, but I believe it to be truth . . . (*P*, p. 248)

Austen, like the principal actress, is both inside and outside the novel as it ends: both authoritatively knowledgeable about her fictional world and ironically dismissive of its reality.

The cover of this book shows Frances Abington in another favourite role – that of Roxalana, the clever, witty and unconventional Englishwoman in *The Sultan*, a character whom Austen first encountered in the Steventon home theatricals of 1789. She looks out smilingly from behind a half-pulled curtain: she seems to be both actress and author of the comic fable. She engages us in a delightful complicity. The image seems an appropriate emblem for my argument in the foregoing chapters. Jane Austen looks out at us from around the curtain of her novels' pages, inviting us to recognise our inevitable involvement – and pleasure – in theatricality.

# Notes

## 1 JANE AUSTEN'S EXPERIENCE OF THEATRE

1 Claire Tomalin, *Jane Austen: A Life* (London: Viking, 1997), p. 42. The school developed a strong reputation for teaching through drama; it moved in the 1790s to London (Hans Place, where Austen visited it), and finally to Paris. Mary Russell Mitford and Fanny Kemble were among the later pupils. (Thanks to Christina de Bellaigue for this information.)

2 It would be pleasant to think that Austen was making an intertextual joke here about Prince Hoare's popular musical farce *My Grandmother*, which is the subject of Tom Bertram's theatrical pun in *Mansfield Park* (p. 123). The play premiered in December 1793 and was published in 1794 (Chapman dates 'The Visit' at 1793).

3 John Quick, a 'low comedian' who was the first Tony Lumpkin in Goldsmith's *She Stoops to Conquer*, and William Lewis, a noted performer of 'mannered comedy', were the two top-salaried comedians at Covent Garden in the 1790s. Quick was said to be George III's favourite actor.

4 Brian Southam (ed.), *Jane Austen's 'Sir Charles Grandison'* (Oxford: Clarendon Press, 1980), Introduction, p. 21.

5 Ibid., p. 12.

6 George Holbert Tucker, *Jane Austen the Woman: Some Biographical Insights* (London: Robert Hale, 1994), pp. 87–92, gives details of this family tradition of performance. Tucker speculates that their cousin Eliza de Feuillide's flirtations with two of Jane's brothers during their performance of Centlivre's *The Wonder* in 1787 may have provided Austen with material for the situation in *Mansfield Park*.

7 Philadelphia Walter to James Walter (19 September 1787), in R.A. Austen-Leigh (ed.), *Austen Papers, 1704–1856* (London: privately printed, 1942), p. 126.

8 *The Selected Writings of William Hazlitt*, Duncan Wu (ed.), vol. III, *A View of the English Stage* (London: Pickering & Chatto, 1998), p. 164.

9 Betty Askwith, 'Jane Austen and the Theatre', in The Jane Austen Society, *Report for the Year 1983* (Overton: The Jane Austen Society), p. 272.

10 Also evident in many theatrical prologues and epilogues, as Mary E. Knapp demonstrates in *Prologues and Epilogues of the Eighteenth Century* (New Haven: Yale University Press, 1961), chapter 5, 'The Patriotic Prologue'.

11 Tucker points out that this was either Fielding's satirical original or 'Kane O'Hara's later adaptation and condensation' of 1780 (*Jane Austen the Woman*, p. 92). Since O'Hara's burletta has many songs, it is more probable that Fielding's original was performed. (For 'burletta' see note 32 below.)

12 Roxalana, like Mozart's Blonde, is 'an English girl who puts down the harem system single-handed by a combination of courage and outrageous cheek'. Claire Tomalin, *Mrs Jordan's Profession* (London: Viking, 1995), p. 334.

13 Tucker, *Jane Austen the Woman*, pp. 152, 154.

14 For a detailed description of Colman's expensive production at Covent Garden, see Joseph Donohue, 'The London Theatre at the End of the Eighteenth Century', in Robert D. Hume (ed.), *The London Theatre World, 1660–1800* (London and Amsterdam: Southern Illinois University Press, 1980), pp. 363–4. Review in the *Bath Herald and Reporter*, cited in Tucker, *Jane Austen the Woman*, p. 96.

15 Margaret Kirkham, *Jane Austen, Feminism and Fiction*, 2nd edn (London: Athlone Press, 1997), pp. 121–7.

16 Arnold Hare (ed.), *Theatre Royal, Bath: A Calendar of Performances at the Orchard Street Theatre 1750–1805* (Bath: Kingsmead Press, 1977), pp. vii–viii.

17 'The legitimate came to connote the stock dramatic repertoire, thus encompassing dramatists such as Shakespeare, Otway and Massinger as well as those contemporary playwrights (notably Sheridan and George Colman the Younger) whose work was perceived to conform to dramatic tradition.' Jane Moody, *Illegitimate Theatre in London, 1770–1840* (Cambridge University Press, 2000), p. 51.

18 Reminiscences of John Bernard (an actor in the company), quoted in Hare, *Bath Calendar*, p. vi.

19 David Thomas and Arnold Hare (compilers), *Restoration and Georgian England, 1660–1788*, Theatre in Europe: a Documentary History (Cambridge University Press, 1989), p. 394. Betsy Bolton in *Women, Nationalism and the Romantic Stage* (Cambridge University Press, 2001), p. 13, remarks, however, that contemporary commentators (e.g. in prologues and epilogues) 'often replaced contemporary reality with stylized portraits of audience members . . . by reiterating older views of class distribution throughout the playhouse audience'. Figure 1 also shows some women occupying the pit benches, an accepted practice by the 1780s – see, for example, Frances Burney's *Cecilia*, Book II, chapter 4.

20 Hare's *Bath Calendar* shows that *The Gamester* had been performed at the theatre before 1801.

21 Kirkham, *Feminism and Fiction*, Appendix.

22 *Nelson's Glory* is discussed in chapter 7 as an example of nautical drama.

23 Robert D. Hume, drawing on Hogan's *London Stage* listings, charts what he calls the decline of the 'mainpiece comedy' from its dominance in the earlier part of the eighteenth century:

Of the twelve most frequently staged mainpieces in the years 1776–1800 four were Shakespeare plays (*Hamlet, Macbeth, The Merchant of Venice,* and *Romeo and Juliet*). Only two were contemporary legitimate comedies: Sheridan's *The School for Scandal,* and Hannah Cowley's *The Belle's Stratagem* (1780). The other six (in descending order of popularity) were all musical comedies of one sort or another: *The Beggar's Opera,* Bickerstaff's *Love in a Village* (1762), Sheridan's *The Duenna* (1775), the younger Colman's *Inkle and Yarico* (1787), the elder Colman's *The Spanish Barber* (1777), and Cobb's *The Haunted Tower* (1789). Caught between the delights of musical comedy and the continuing appeal of farcical afterpieces, traditional mainpiece comedy stagnated.

Robert D. Hume, 'The Multifarious Forms of Eighteenth-Century Comedy', in G.W. Stone (ed.), *The Stage and the Page: London's 'Whole Show' in the Eighteenth-Century Theatre* (Berkeley: University of California Press, 1981), p. 24. (See also Mrs Inchbald's comments on the decline of comedy quoted on p. 15 above.)

24 Hume points out the popularity of plays for reading: '*Lovers' Vows* achieved eleven [editions] in 1798. Older plays were steadily reprinted, and the popularity of Bell's British Theatre and other such collections is solid evidence of the enormous demand for reading texts' ('Eighteenth-Century Comedy', p. 27).

25 Cited in Deirdre Le Faye, *Jane Austen: A Family Record* (London: The British Library, 1989), p. 133.

26 *The Spoilt Child* (1789) was an immensely popular vehicle for Dora Jordan, who played the breeches role of Little Pickle.

27 Cited in Le Faye, *Family Record*, p. 163.

28 Cited in Tucker, *Jane Austen the Woman*, p. 89.

29 Tomalin, *Jane Austen*, p. 203. The play in fact is more critical of the loose morals of the foppish men than of the behaviour of the women; the friendship of the two principal female characters – a neglected wife and a woman of the world – is the unusual central topos of the play.

30 James Winston's 'View' of the Southampton theatre's facade (*The Theatrical Tourist*, London, 1805) is reproduced in *Persuasions*, 12 (1990), p. 67, in a note by Mary Belle Swingle. The still-surviving 1820 theatre in Bury St Edmunds is typical of the shape and size of these smaller provincial theatres.

31 Tucker, *Jane Austen the Woman*, p. 98. He infers from the letter of 20 November 1808 that Austen 'had taken a dislike to the French Street Theater either because of its dirtiness or the poor quality of its performances'.

32 Burletta: a species of theatrical performance given entirely to musical accompaniment (anything from harpsichord continuo to full orchestral support) – nominally without use of the spoken word (Donohue, 'The London Theatre', p. 345). George Colman the younger defined burletta as '*a drama in rhyme,* and which is *entirely musical;* a short comick piece, consisting of *recitative* and *singing,* wholly accompanied, more or less, by the orchestra' (Colman's *Random Records* [1830], cited in Donohue, 'The London Theatre', p. 353). *Midas* (first produced in England 1764) is considered to be typical (p. 350).

Its plot is based on Ovid – Midas's faulty judgement in the singing contest between Pan and Apollo; but the characterisation is in the English comic mode: 'Midas, the rural English Justice of the Peace; Damaetas, his dull-witted clerk; Silenus, the kindly shepherd, and Pol, the brash and handsome bucolic depiction of Apollo, are closer to the English humorous pastoral tradition . . . than to the characters of the Italian burletta, who were essentially derived from the *Commedia dell'Arte* tradition . . . Moreover, O'Hara's choice of music for *Midas* was also distinctively English. He included airs that had been used in popular plays and pantomimes, well-known tunes and contemporary songs that had become popular at the minor theatres and public gardens . . . *Midas* was destined to become one of the favourite afterpieces on the English stage and was performed 226 times [in London] by the end of the century' (Phyllis T. Dircks, 'Garrick's Fail-Safe Musical Venture', in G.W.H. Stone (ed.), *The Stage and the Page: London's 'Whole Show' in the Eighteenth-Century Theatre* (Berkeley: University of California Press, 1981), pp. 142–3).

33 Jane Moody argues that 'The emergence of the term "legitimate" as a category of dramatic classification during the late 1790s reflects [a] feverish desire to distinguish between authentic and spurious dramas and between loyal and seditious performances.' Austen's tastes in drama are clearly conservative and resist what Moody calls the 'exciting collision of traditions (sentimental, Gothic, humanitarian) at the heart of dramatic innovation during the late 1790s' (*Illegitimate Theatre*, p. 51). However, she responded enthusiastically to Kean's acting (see below, pp. 17–19), which Moody reads as 'revolutionary': 'the work of an iconoclastic actor who defined himself in opposition to the traditions of legitimate performance' (p. 230).

34 Johanna Schopenhauer, journal of a visit to London, 1803–5, translated in Russell Jackson, 'Johanna Schopenhauer's Journal: A German View of the London Theatre Scene, 1803–5', *Theatre Notebook*, 52, 3 (1998), p. 146.

35 Ibid., pp. 147–8.

36 Austen was familiar with Siddons's work, whether or not she had actually seen her. She makes a knowing comparison between Siddons's grand style and the tragedy acting of the new favourite Eliza O'Neill: 'That puss Cassy [a niece] . . . does not shine in the tender feelings. She will never be a Miss O'neal [sic]; – more in the Mrs Siddons line' (*Letters*, 30 November 1814). I discuss Sarah Siddons's style and favourite roles in chapter 2.

37 William Dowton and Charles Mathews were popular comedians of the London stage. Dowton's Hypocrite, according to Leigh Hunt, was 'one of the few perfect pieces of acting on the stage; and after that long exhibition of smoothness and affected humility of which everybody has spoken in praise, nothing can shew the greatness of this actor more . . . than his foregoing the temptation to rant in the concluding scene, and braving the scorn of those who have detected him, not with the ordinary outcry of stage desperation, but with a rage too deep for violence, and a black, inward-breathing, quivering malignity'. Lawrence Huston Houtchens and Carolyn Washburn Houtchens (eds.), *Leigh Hunt's Dramatic Criticism*

*1808–1831* (New York: Columbia University Press, 1949), p. 97. Austen had presumably seen Elizabeth Edwin during her Bath seasons, 1797–8 and 1803–4; her roles, which were overwhelmingly in comedy 'in the Jordan line', included Emma in *The Birth-Day*.

38 Richard Cumberland, *Memoirs* (London, 1806), in A.M. Nagler, *A Source Book in Theatrical History* (New York: Dover, 1959), p. 408. Cf. Leigh Hunt (1811), 'such large theatres are not fit for a delicate and just representation of the drama . . . they inevitably lead to the substitution of shew for sense' (*Dramatic Criticism*, p. 50).

39 Sir Walter Scott, 'Essay on the Drama', in *The Prose Works of Sir Walter Scott, Bart.*, 28 vols. (Edinburgh: Robert Cadell, 1849), vol. VI, pp. 389–90. He goes on to comment on the encouragement to licentiousness of these huge venues: 'In the present theatres of London, the best part of the house is openly and avowedly set off for [prostitutes'] reception; and no part of it which is open to the public at large is free from their intrusion, or at least from the open display of the disgusting improprieties to which their neighbourhood gives rise. And these houses, raised at an immense public expense, are so ingeniously misconstructed, that, in the private boxes, you see too little of the play, and, in the public boxes, greatly too much of a certain description of the company. No man of delicacy would wish the female part of his family to be exposed to such scenes . . .' (p. 392). Austen does not comment on this social problem associated with theatre-going; but it may be implicit in the expressed need for a male escort on a theatre visit.

Scott's survey essay, from the Greeks to 'the present', was originally written for the *Encyclopedia Britannica*, 1819.

Joanna Baillie, author of *Plays on the Passions*, a popular series with readers though unsuccessful on the stage, also wrote in detail about the disadvantages of the new large theatres, particularly in forcing actors to perform without subtlety, exaggerating voice, facial expression, and gesture. She comments astutely on the inappropriateness of the modern large stage to 'comedy, and all plays on domestic subjects', where 'the diminutive appearance of individual figures, and the straggling poverty of grouping . . . is very injurious to general effect' ('To the Reader', in *Plays on the Passions*, series 3 (London, 1812), p. xvi).

40 Hume, 'Eighteenth-Century Comedy', p. 7. Cf. Hazlitt, on an 1815 production of *The School for Scandal* at Covent Garden, 'Genteel comedy cannot be acted at present' because of the 'vulgarity' of the acting style (*View*, p. 82).

41 Elizabeth Inchbald, prefatory Remarks to *To Marry or Not to Marry*, in Inchbald (ed.), *The British Theatre* (London, 1808), vol. XXIII.

42 Donald C. Mullin, 'Theatre Structure and its Effect on Production', in G.W. Stone (ed.), *The Stage and the Page: London's 'Whole Show' in the Eighteenth-Century Theatre* (Berkeley: University of California Press, 1981), p. 84.

43 'With the clarity and perception of Hogarth, [the prologues and epilogues] set before us generations of theatre-goers – the alert and hostile critics, the self-centered beaux, the ladies adorning the boxs, the sailors . . . in the

upper gallery. But they have an additional liveliness in their constant appeals, admonitions, denunciations, and cajolery. This auditory quality gives the pieces their unique value in recreating the audience in its relationship to the playwright and actor.' Knapp, *Prologues and Epilogues*, pp. 176–7. Knapp's chapter on 'The Audience as It Is Reflected in the Prologues and Epilogues' gives a particularly rich array of examples.

44 'Low partitions separate each box from its neighbour. Lit as bright as day, filled with spectators, they make a charming sight.' Johanna Schopenhauer, in Jackson, 'Journal', p. 147.

45 The Lyceum theatre was built in 1765 as a concert hall and converted to a small theatre in 1794; it is still on the same spot in the Strand, though rebuilt in 1834, 1904, and 1996.

46 It is extremely misleading of theatre historians and Austen biographers to describe this piece, which the mime artist Delpini (who played Scaramouche) devised in 1787, as based on Shadwell's Restoration five-act drama *The Libertine* (1676). Shadwell's play was far too indecent for public representation, and had not been performed since 1740 (the playbill then claimed 'not acted these twelve years', so it was unfashionable even in 1740); nor was it reprinted after 1705. Molière's *Dom Juan* and Tirso de Molina's *Il Burlador de Sevilla* were the fairly distant ancestors of both Shadwell's play and the scenarios for Gluck's ballet and Delpini's pantomime.

47 C. Delpini, 'Address', in *Don Juan; or, The Libertine Destroy'd*, A Tragic Pantomimical Entertainment, in Two Acts; as performed at the Royalty-Theatre, Well-Street, Goodman's Fields (London: Printed for Mr. Delpini, n.d. [1789?]). Gluck and Angiolini's ballet-pantomime, on which this was based, is generally considered to be 'the first complete drama in dance since Antiquity'. Bruce Alan Brown, *Gluck and the French Theatre in Vienna* (Oxford: Clarendon Press, 1991), p. 1.

48 Mozart's *Don Giovanni* (1787) was not performed in London until April 1817, three months before Austen's death.

49 A combination of prudence and modesty obliges Fanny and Lovewell to keep their marriage secret, despite the fact that the secretly pregnant Fanny is still living at home with her father; various other eligible men complicate matters by courting her. Austen had been familiar with this play since her childhood: in *Love and Friendship* she spoofs its sentimental hero and heroine:

> I need not I imagine inform you that their union had been contrary to the inclinations of their Cruel & Mercenary Parents; who had vainly endeavoured with obstinate Perseverance to force them into a Marriage with those whom they had ever abhorred, but with an Heroic Fortitude worthy to be related & Admired, they had both, constantly refused to submit to such despotic Power.
> After having so nobly disentangled themselves from the Shackles of Parental Authority, by a Clandestine Marriage . . . (*MW*, p. 87)

50 *The Morning Chronicle*, 27 January 1814. Hazlitt, *View*, pp. 1–4. Of Miss Smith's Portia, Hazlitt remarked, 'It would be an equivocal compliment

to say . . . that her acting often reminds us of Mrs. Siddons' (though he later found her 'more animated').

51 Ibid., pp. 3–4.

52 One of Kean's biographers, Raymond Fitzsimmons, relates that he 'rag[ed] like a lion in the dialogue with Tubal'. Cited in Askwith, 'Jane Austen and the Theatre', p. 280.

53 The plot of the exotic entertainment *Illusion* was based on a novella by Frances Sheridan, whose play *The Discovery* I discuss in chapter 2.

54 This tragedian, considered the successor to John Philip Kemble, was 'noted for his dignity, good looks, and strong melodious voice' (notes to *Letters*, p. 589).

55 Hazlitt was an enraptured admirer of Mrs Jordan's Nell in *The Devil to Pay*. In a retrospective comment on her career, he wrote, 'Her face, her tones, her manner were irresistible. Her smile had the effect of sunshine, and her laugh did one good to hear it. . . . She was all gaiety, openness, and good-nature. She rioted in her fine animal spirits, and gave more pleasure than any other actress, because she had the greatest spirit of enjoyment in herself' (*View*, p. 83).

56 Hazlitt, *View*, pp. 115–16.

57 Elin Diamond, 'The Violence of "We": Politicizing Identification', in Janelle G. Reinelt and Joseph R. Roach (eds.), *Critical Theory and Performance* (Ann Arbor: University of Michigan Press, 1992), p. 394.

58 Judith Butler, 'Performative Acts and Gender Constitution: An Essay in Phenomenology and Feminist Theory', in Katie Conboy, Nadia Medina, and Sarah Stanbury (eds.), *Writing on the Body: Female Embodiment and Feminist Theory* (New York: University of Columbia Press, 1997), pp. 402, 404; original emphases.

59 Ibid., p. 410.

60 Diamond, 'Violence of "We"', p. 396; original emphasis.

61 Terry Castle's work on 'The carnivalesque in eighteenth-century English culture and fiction', in *Masquerade and Civilization* (Stanford University Press, 1986), argues finally that 'the impulses embodied in the carnivalesque, for one reason or another, are increasingly internalized in fiction of the late eighteenth and nineteenth centuries. The scene of transformation moves inward, in both a literal and a figurative sense, and transgression is figured in more psychological ways' (p. 341). She understands Austen as a case in point.

## 2 *SENSE AND SENSIBILITY*: COMIC AND TRAGIC DRAMA

1 'An Essay on the Theatre; or, a Comparison between Laughing and Senti-mental Comedy', Arthur Friedman (ed.), *Collected Works of Oliver Goldsmith*, vol. III (Oxford: Clarendon Press, 1966), pp. 211–13.

2 Richard Bevis, *The Laughing Tradition: Stage Comedy in Garrick's Day* (Athens, OH: University of Georgia Press, 1980).

3 William B. Worthen has some helpful pages on the relation between mid-eighteenth-century acting theory and sensibility in his chapter '*Realize the feelings of his Character*: Gesture, Feeling, and Community in the Sentimental Theater': 'By harmonizing feeling and form [through a codified 'language of gesture'], acting theory transcends the restricted problem of the actor's emotional engagement . . . In the widest sense, neoclassical acting theory defines the actor by defining how his acting creates and communicates meaning.' *The Idea of the Actor: Drama and the Ethics of Performance* (Princeton University Press, 1984), p. 73.

4 *She Stoops to Conquer* in Goldsmith, *Collected Works*, vol. v, p. 129 (Act ii).

5 Edward's engagement to Lucy was 'the consequence of ignorance of the world – and want of employment . . . I had seen so little of other women, that I could make no comparisons, and see no defects' (*S&S*, p. 362). From the evidence in the novel of Lucy's acting abilities, it is easy enough to imagine the scenes in which she overcame his shyness at the Longstaple tutorial establishment.

6 'I loves to hear him sing, bekeays he never gives us nothing that's *low*.' 'O damn anything that's *low*, I cannot bear it!' cry Tony Lumpkin's drinking mates in Act i. The only other time that Austen uses the phrase 'low company' is in Sir Walter Elliot's snobbish condemnation of Anne's visits to Mrs Smith.

7 *The Rivals*, in *The Dramatic Works of Richard Brinsley Sheridan*, Cecil Price (ed.) (Oxford: Clarendon Press, 1973), vol. i, p. 135 (Act v, scene i). Lydia's enthusiasm for an elopement may well have prompted the naming of *Pride and Prejudice*'s Lydia Bennet. In terms of *Sense and Sensibility*, Lydia's affectation is more strongly echoed by the self-dramatising 'heroine' Lucy Steele: 'for my own part, I could give up every prospect of more [fortune] without a sigh. I have always been used to a very small income, and could struggle with any poverty for him' (*S&S*, p. 147).

8 Interestingly, Austen writes of Elinor and Lucy as 'rivals' for Edward (*S&S*, p. 145); other references are in chapters 10, 23, 26, 45. Colonel Brandon and Willoughby are also 'rivals' for Marianne (*S&S*, p. 162). The word is used in *Sense and Sensibility* considerably more than in any other of Austen's mature novels – as though some part of Austen's imagination were under Sheridan's influence.

9 Goldsmith, 'Essay', in *Collected Works*, vol. iii, p. 213.

10 Hazlitt, *View*, p. 59.

11 Reynolds's painting is in the Huntington Library Collections, San Marino, California.

12 Hazlitt, *View*, p. 145. For further details of Siddons's acting of Lady Macbeth, see the notes on *Macbeth* Act ii, scene ii made by G.J. Bell in 1809 and published in *The Nineteenth Century* (February 1878); reprinted in Gamini Salgado, *Eyewitnesses of Shakespeare* (London: Sussex University Press, 1975), pp. 303–5.

13 Quoted in Michael R. Booth, 'Sarah Siddons', in M.R. Booth, J. Stokes, S. Bassnett, *Three Tragic Actresses: Siddons, Rachel, Ristori* (Cambridge University Press, 1996), p. 49.

14 Sheridan's *The Critic* has fun with this convention:

> TILBURINA. The wind whistles – the moon rises – see
> They have kill'd my squirrel in his cage!
> Is this a grasshopper! – ha! no, it is my
> Whiskerandos – [etc.]

'And pray what becomes of her?' asks Sneer. Puff, the proud writer: 'She is gone to throw herself into the sea to be sure.' Sheridan, *Works*, vol. II, pp. 548–9.

Austen's youthful spoof *Love and Friendship* is an even funnier parody of the tragedienne's mad scene, possibly inspired by Sheridan: 'Talk not to me of Phaetons (said I, raving in a frantic, incoherent manner) – Give me a violin – I'll play to him & sooth him in his melancholy Hours – Beware ye gentle Nymphs of Cupid's Thunderbolts, avoid the piercing Shafts of Jupiter – Look at the Grove of Firs – I see a Leg of Mutton – They told me Edward was not Dead; but they deceived me – they took him for a Cucumber –' (*MW*, p. 100).

15 Booth, 'Siddons', p. 32.

16 *The Public Advertiser*, 15 November 1782, quoted in Charles Beecher Hogan (ed.), *The London Stage, Part 5: 1776–1800* (Carbondale, IL: Southern Illinois University Press, 1968), vol. III, p. 569.

17 W.C. Macready, *Reminiscences*, Sir Frederick Pollock (ed.) (New York: Macmillan Co., 1875), p. 42.

18 Booth, 'Siddons', p. 65.

19 This eighteenth-century theatrical term is frequently used by Austen in *Sense and Sensibility* (I quote most examples in the course of this chapter). Sarah's son Henry Siddons's *Practical Illustrations of Rhetorical Gesture and Action* (1807) represents an attempt to codify the practice. Emma Hamilton's famous after-dinner entertainments in which she imitated statues from the antique were known as her 'Attitudes'. Other examples from the period include '*Puts himself in an attitude*' (stage direction in *The Rivals*, Act V, scene iii). The word is used ironically by Keats in the last stanza of the 'Ode on a Grecian Urn' (1819): 'O Attic shape! Fair attitude . . .'.

20 Leigh Hunt, *Dramatic Essays*, in Thomas and Hare, *Restoration and Georgian England*, pp. 347–8.

21 Judith Warner Fisher in 'All the "Write" Moves: or, Theatrical Gesture in *Sense and Sensibility*' (*Persuasions*, 9, 1987, pp. 17–23) briefly but usefully explores eighteenth-century theories of gesture in acting to explicate the workings of sensibility. She points out that 'Apart from *Love and Freindship* with its obvious histrionics, *Sense and Sensibility* is the most theatrical of all Jane Austen's novels. Not even in the rehearsals of *Mansfield Park* do we find gestures – the universal language of the emotions – so much aligned with conventional theatrical gesture, as observed on the contemporary stages and discussed so extensively in the acting theories of the late eighteenth and early nineteenth centuries . . . The gestures of Jane Austen's "players" in *Sense and*

*Sensibility* . . . are so well defined that the "truth of their action" delineates the emotions of her characters, even when words often conceal the truth of their feelings.' Fisher notes the coincidence of the major characters' movements and gestures with contemporary acting theories; I argue, however, that it is more likely that Austen is responding directly to the affective power of those actors whose work she saw, and using it for her own purposes.

22 Hannah More, *Memoirs and Correspondence* (1834), quoted in Salgado, *Eyewitnesses of Shakespeare*, p. 240. For further discussion of Garrick as the quintessential eighteenth-century actor, see chapter 5.

23 Worthen, *Idea of the Actor*, p. 95.

24 Austen does not use the word *star* in this sense, but it is possible that she knew it: *OED* cites the *Edinburgh Weekly Journal* in 1827: 'He had hitherto been speaking of what, in theatrical language, was called *stars*.'

25 Goethe's 1774 novel had been translated into verse and prose fiction, and made into a stage play; the latter by Frederick Reynolds, in 1786. 'That *Werther*, Frederick Reynolds's first play, did reach Covent Garden in 1786 despite obvious weaknesses is also significant. More an evocation of Goethe's mood than a rendering of his novel, *Werther* offers three short acts of *Sturm und Drang* . . . A new Zeitgeist announces itself, between sobs, and settles down for a long stay.' Richard W. Bevis, *English Drama: Restoration and Eighteenth Century, 1660–1789* (London and New York: Longman, 1990), p. 248.

26 It is probably no coincidence that the recipient of the lurid tale of sensibility that Laura tells here is named Marianne.

27
      LOTHARIO. . . . two Nights since,
        By message urg'd, and frequent Importunity,
        Again I saw her. Strait with Tears and Sighs,
        With swelling Breasts, with Swooning, with Distraction,
        With all the Subtleties, and pow'rful Arts
        Of wilful Woman lab'ring for her purpose,
        Again she told the same dull nauseous Tale.
        Unmov'd, I beg'd her spare th'ungrateful Subject. . . .
             (Nicholas Rowe, *The Fair Penitent*, Act 1)

The role of Calista (set in a vaguely sketched sixteenth-century Italy) remained playable by Siddons and other tragediennes because she is shown as in the *penitent* rather than passionate phase of her relationship with Lothario. Lothario is of course a role that has survived the play and become a byword for a charming cad (*à la* Willoughby): 'Lothario, with gaiety which cannot be hated, and bravery which cannot be despised, retains too much of the spectator's kindness', said Dr Johnson ('Life of Rowe', quoted in Jocelyn Harris, *Jane Austen's Art of Memory*, Cambridge University Press, 1989, p. 42). Significantly, it was one of Garrick's best roles. In showing Marianne's encounter with Willoughby, Austen is expanding the fictive possibilities of drama into the contemporary public world.

28 Juliet McMaster writes illuminatingly and amusingly of Austen's principal butt in 'From *Laura and Augustus* to *Love and Freindship*', *Thalia: Studies in Literary Humor*, 16, 1&2 (1996), pp. 16–26. Austen doubles the number of protagonists and rapidly accelerates the action in comparison with the lachrymose anonymous novel of 1784: 'Each heroine acts and postures one against the other, and they mutually reinforce each other's absurdities. The sensibility joke gains immensely from being performed as a *pas de deux*' (p. 18).

29 Margaret Anne Doody writes 'For his primary inspiration, Richardson was indebted to the drama'; she cites Richardson's letter to Aaron Hill: 'it is of the Tragic Kind'. She points out that the episode in which Lovelace takes Clarissa to see *Venice Preserv'd* 'assumes that his readers will remember the play and see the point' (p. 115). Later, 'Clarissa, in her incoherent communications during her temporary derangement after the rape, recalls snatches of the play she has seen a few weeks ago' (p. 116); before the rape, 'Her desire for death rather than dishonour is typical of all the victim-heroines' (p. 119). Margaret Anne Doody, *A Natural Passion: A Study of the Novels of Samuel Richardson* (Oxford: Clarendon Press, 1974). See also Jocelyn Harris, Introduction, *Samuel Richardson's Published Commentary on Clarissa 1747–65* (London: Pickering & Chatto, 1998), '*Clarissa* and the Theatre' (pp. xxiv–lxxxvi), and passim.

30 Hannah More, quoted in Sheridan, *Works*, vol. I, p. 51.

31 Robert Hogan and Jerry C. Beasley (eds.), *The Plays of Frances Sheridan* (London and Toronto: Associated University Presses, 1984), *The Discovery*, pp. 91–2 (Act IV, scene ii).

32 Prologue (by Mrs Sheridan), *The Discovery*, in *Plays*, pp. 41–2. The 'sister's art' referred to here is not, of course, the novel, but tragedy.

33 *The Discovery*, in *Plays*, pp. 70–71 (Act III, scene i).

34 The closest parallel, in fact, as Jocelyn Harris demonstrates in *Jane Austen's Art of Memory*, is in Richardson's *Clarissa*: 'a virtual word-by-word reworking of the equally extraordinary scene at the ball where Anna meets Lovelace, the man who drugged her friend and raped her. Anna is forced to hear him out, only to find herself won by the appearance and personality of the rake (VI. letter lxxiv)', p. 64. For comments on Richardson's acknowledged debt to the theatre, see note 29 above. Ang Lee's 1995 film of *Sense and Sensibility* famously omitted this 'wonderful scene in the novel which unfortunately interfered too much with the Brandon love story' – i.e. it was too intrinsically dramatic. Emma Thompson (screenwriter), *Sense and Sensibility: The Screenplay and Diaries* (London: Bloomsbury, 1995), p. 272.

35 Barbara M. Benedict, in *Framing Feeling: Sentiment and Style in English Prose Fiction 1745–1800* (New York: AMS Press, 1994), has an interesting commentary on this and subsequent scenes in relation to 'the stylistic patterns of literary sensibility': 'As her "passion" turns to action, Elinor has changed from witness to participant, from a disinterested judge to a sentimental heroine . . . a detached observation distinguishes a right view, yet sensation also allows a kind of truth. In *Sense and Sensibility*, Austen turns emotion into spectacle'

(pp. 204–5). It is interesting to observe how unavoidable theatrical metaphors are in writing about sensibility.

## 3 *NORTHANGER ABBEY*: CATHERINE'S ADVENTURES IN THE GOTHIC THEATRE

1 Gothic theatre was at its height 1790–1810, as Ranger's list of premieres indicates: 12 significant premieres in the 1770s, 15 in the 1780s, 33 in the 1790s, 29 in 1800–9. Paul Ranger, *'Terror and Pity reign in every Breast': Gothic Drama in the London Patent Theatres, 1750–1820* (London: Society for Theatre Research, 1991), Appendix One.

2 Ranger, *'Terror and Pity'*, p. 145.

3 M.G. Lewis's prologue to *The Castle Spectre* and epilogue to Holcroft's *Knave or Not* (1798).

4 Notwithstanding this observation (based on Hare's lists of plays performed), a local historian of Bath claims that 'at the height of [the theatre's] reputation . . . the scene-painter Thomas French ranked among the most ingenious in the country – pantomime and the new popular genre of gothick melodrama giving him great scope for spectacle and special effects'. Trevor Fawcett, *Bath Entertain'd: Amusements, Recreations and Gambling at the 18th-Century Spa* (Bath: Ruton, 1998), p. 82.

5 Kelly was also the composer of *Blue Beard*; and, incidentally, of music for *The Castle Spectre*.

6 Betsy Bolton reads this play (designed by its author George Colman as a Christmas pantomime) as an 'emphatic restaging' of 'the threat of violence against women': 'As Abomelique forbids Fatima the knowledge inscribed within the Blue Chamber, so Colman's comic spectacle distracts its audience from the violent implications of this mode of sentiment: spectators learn the dangers of transgression, but without profiting more fully from the vision for which Fatima nearly pays with her life.' *Women, Nationalism and the Romantic Stage*, pp. 68–9. We do not know what Jane Austen thought of this play when she saw it in Bath in December 1799; her usual ironical view of sensationalism and the piece's predominantly comic mode probably protected her from the serious consideration that the historian affords it, while perhaps its motifs contributed to her concurrent imagining of Catherine's Gothic adventures.

7 James Boaden, *Memoirs of the Life of John Philip Kemble*, 2 vols. (London, 1825); *Mrs Siddons* followed in 1827, *Mrs Jordan* in 1831, and *Mrs Inchbald* in 1833.

8 An interesting example of the 'crossover' between Gothic novel and theatre occurs in *The Italian*, vol. III, chapter 1, as the guilty Schedoni, travelling with the heroine Ellena who he believes to be his daughter – whom he was on the point of murdering – is profoundly affected by a company of travelling actors: 'The people above were acting what seemed to have been intended for a tragedy, but what their strange gestures, uncouth recitation, and incongruous countenances, had transformed into a comedy.' The 'peasant' accompanying them is transfixed by the drama, calling out to Schedoni,

'"Look! Signor, see! Signor, what a scoundrel! what a villain! See! he has murdered his own daughter!" At these terrible words, [Schedoni] turned his eyes upon the stage, and perceived that the actors were performing the story of Virginia. It was at the moment when she was dying in the arms of her father, who was holding up the poniard, with which he had stabbed her. The feelings of Schedoni, at this instant, inflicted a punishment almost worthy of the crime he had meditated.' Ann Radcliffe, *The Italian* (Oxford University Press, 1981), pp. 274–5. In this passage Radcliffe seems to be both signalling her contempt for the vulgarity of theatre and indicating her acknowledgement of its power to move; perhaps also, signalling to Boaden or another playwright that this novel, like *The Romance of the Forest*, had dramatic potential. Radcliffe returns to this point two chapters later, when she writes that Schedoni 'seemed to experience again the horror of that moment, when, with an uplifted poniard in his grasp, he had discovered Ellena for his daughter' (p. 294).

9  Boaden, *Memoirs*, vol. II, pp. 96–7.
10  Ibid., p. 98.
11  Ibid., p. 119.
12  *Fontainville Forest*, a Play in Five Acts (Founded on the Romance of the Forest,) as performed at the Theatre-Royal Covent-Garden, by James Boaden, of the Honourable Society of the Middle Temple. London. Printed for Hookham and Carpenter, New Bond Street, 1794.
13  The final chorus in Siddons's *Sicilian Romance* (1794) similarly concludes with the patriotic stanza: 'May our Monarch's glory still afar / Bear the thunders of his war . . .'
14  Ranger interestingly argues that 'the gothic reflected the subconscious aspirations and fears of some members of the audience. The Industrial and the French Revolutions brought respectively unrest and horror in their wake and this was reflected in the turbulence of gothic dramas; the constant travels of the stage characters were a mirroring of the ingress of the artisan class to urban areas and the rootlessness which inadequate living conditions induced.' *'Terror and Pity'*, pp. 145–6.
15  Ann Radcliffe, *The Romance of the Forest* (Oxford University Press, 1986), p. 261.
16  Ibid., p. 363.
17  Boaden, *Memoirs*, vol. II, p. 97; my emphasis. The apparition as a real stage presence was later deliberately imitated by 'Monk' Lewis in the even more popular *Castle Spectre*. John Genest, for one critic, thought such stage tricks 'contemptible'. *Some Account of the English Stage*, 10 vols. (Bath: 1832), vol. VII, p. 163.
18  For theatrical 'sensations' see Emma's comment on the anticipated arrival of Frank Churchill in Highbury (*E*, p. 124).
19  Radcliffe, *Romance*, p. 163.
20  Radcliffe cannot bring herself to name the putative incest: 'when [La Motte] knew that Adeline was the daughter of the Marquis, and remembered the

crime to which he had once devoted her, his frame thrilled with horror' (*Romance*, p. 334).

21 Douglas Murray, 'Jane Austen's *Northanger Abbey*: "a neighbourhood of voluntary spies"', paper delivered at the Jane Austen Society of North America AGM, October 1998, Quebec; quoted by kind permission of the author.

22 For further discussion of Austen's crucial distinction between 'acting' with the intention to deceive or impress and 'acting' one's proper, adult social role, see chapter 6 on *Emma*, passim.

23 De Loutherbourg, brought to England by David Garrick to improve scenic effects at Drury Lane in 1771, 'transferred to the stage the influence of Salvator Rosa and Gaspard Poussin. In contrast to the quiet pastoralism of his predecessors, he depicted, both in his pictures and in his scenery, mountain grandeur and wild torrents under dramatic and even lurid light, to create effects of the sublime and the picturesque.' Sybil Rosenfeld, 'Landscape in English Scenery in the Eighteenth Century', in Kenneth Richards and Peter Thomson (eds.), *The Eighteenth-Century English Stage* (London: Methuen, 1972), p. 174.

24 For example: Joanna Baillie's *De Monfort* (1798), Act v, scene i, stage direction: 'The inside of a convent chapel, of old Gothic architecture, almost dark: two torches only are seen at a distance, burning over a newly covered grave. Lightning is seen flashing through the windows, and thunder heard, with the sound of wind beating upon the building.' Lewis's *The Castle Spectre* contains numerous directions for torches, moonlight, 'lights from above' into a dungeon, etc. Henry Siddons's less successful Radcliffe adaptation is perhaps most faithful to the original in this stage direction: 'Ferrand muffled in a red cloak, with a dark lanthorn in one hand, and a sword in the other, stalks along the back part of the rock, unlocks and enters the tower' (*The Sicilian Romance*, Act i).

## 4 *PRIDE AND PREJUDICE*: THE COMEDIENNE AS HEROINE

1 Eliza de Feuillide to Philadelphia Walter, from Paris, 11 February 1789. Miss Cooper was an Austen cousin. Austen-Leigh, *Austen Papers*, p. 138.

2 'You must do nothing but give Balls & Masquerades. You must build a room on purpose & a Theatre to act Plays in. The first Play we have shall be *Which is the Man*, and I will do Lady Bell Bloomer' ('The Three Sisters', *MW*, p. 65). Cf. *Letters*, 16–17 December 1816: 'tell him what you will' (in thanks for some pickled cucumbers), a quotation from the heroine's last-act admission of love. I discuss this play in relation to the character of Mary Crawford in chapter 5.

3 Hogan, *The London Stage*, vol. i, pp. clxxi–clxxii.

4 I look at Austen's use of 'Frenchness' in my discussion of the character of Frank Churchill in chapter 6. Cf. also *The Sultan*, where the heroine's

Englishness is emphasised and contrasted to the unreformed 'Turkish' manners of the Sultan whom she wins over. Betsy Bolton (*Women, Nationalism and the Romantic Stage*, p. 170) comments on *The Belle's Stratagem* that 'it makes visible the impossibility of mimicking feminine identity without simultaneously engaging issues of class and national identity'.

5 Beth Kowaleski Wallace, 'Affirming Performativity in *The Belle's Stratagem*', a paper presented at the January 2001 conference of the British Society for Eighteenth-Century Studies; quoted with kind permission of the author. The paper goes on to argue that 'Cowley's ideas about the nature of theatrical character bear directly on broader questions about English character', particularly the 'naturalness' of English feminine decorum, seen in this play to be performable by the same actress who plays the cosmopolitan flirt. This position is implicit in my argument in chapter 5 about Fanny the 'anti-actress' in *Mansfield Park*.

6 Juliet McMaster, *Jane Austen the Novelist* (London: Macmillan, 1996), p. 156. McMaster points out a number of other parallels in a note, including 'the making and breaking of the Hero/Claudio and Jane/Bingley matches'; and 'when Beatrice brings herself to love Benedick, she might be Elizabeth soliloquizing after talking to the housekeeper at Pemberley' (p. 172).

7 Hannah More, *Strictures on the Modern System of Female Education*, 2 vols. (New York and London: Garland, 1974), vol. i, p. 105 (facsimile of 1st edn, London, 1799).

8 The Rosings episode also contains the novel's Don Pedro figure (from *Much Ado*) in Colonel Fitzwilliam – an admirer of the heroine and friend of the prickly hero; amiable, but ultimately not available for marriage.

9 In the popular 1995 BBC TV series, Darcy's appearance in this scene wet and dripping in his shirt-sleeves from his dive into the pond is a crass and unnecessary visual metaphor given the abilities of the principal actors, Jennifer Ehle and Colin Firth, to convey the subtleties of this scene as written by Austen.

10 We learn in chapter 27 that Elizabeth enjoys her evening 'at one of the theatres' (*P&P*, p. 152) during her stopover in London – where, like Austen, she has clearly honed her discriminatory powers so that she is well aware of the difference between amateur (gentry) performers and real professionals.

11 *Much Ado about Nothing*, Act ii, scene i.

## 5 *MANSFIELD PARK*: FANNY'S EDUCATION IN THE THEATRE

1 I would like here again to acknowledge Margaret Kirkham's pioneering work in regard to Austen and the theatre, in particular her observation that 'In *Mansfield Park* allusion to plays and the theatre takes the place of allusion to fiction, and the novel itself is constructed in a quasi-theatrical way' (*Feminism and Fiction*, p. 107). I cannot, however, agree with Kirkham that Kotzebue is necessarily 'the target of [Austen's] scorn' because of his sentimentality and

sensationalism, which is surely no greater than that of the popular tragedy of the day (see chapter 2). For further discussion of Kotzebue and *Lovers' Vows*, see above, pp. 104–10.

2 Penelope Gay, 'Theatricals and Theatricality in *Mansfield Park*', *Sydney Studies in English*, 13 (1987–8), pp. 61–73.

3 Nine of the novel's fourteen narratorial uses of *vanity* directly describe Henry Crawford; two apply to Mary.

4 Cf. 'I am determined to prove a villain / And hate the idle pleasures of these days. Plots have I laid . . .' *Richard III*, Act 1, scene i.

5 It is also perhaps worth noting that Crawford was a theatrical name of considerable fame in the late eighteenth century. Mrs Ann Crawford (1734–1801) was preferred by many to Mrs Siddons – a passionate tragedienne, she was also a fine comedienne, particularly in witty parts. Her husband Thomas Crawford, although possessed of a fine person and a good voice, was not so successful.

Mr Yates is, presumably, ironically named after the comic actor Richard Yates (1706?–96). He played the heavy father in George Colman the Elder's *Polly Honeycombe* (1760), one of the first plays to feature an ingénue addicted to sentimental novels; but he was *not* famous in 'ranting' parts. Austen's Mr Yates was originally to have played Count Cassel at Lord Ravenshaw's theatricals – a part to which he was undoubtedly better suited.

6 Sheridan, 'Verses to the Memory of Garrick' (1779), ll. 63–70, in *Works*, vol. ii, p. 461.

7 Cf. a contemporary German visitor's description of Garrick: 'His stature is rather low than of middle height, and his body thickset. His limbs are in the most pleasing proportion, and the whole man is put together most charmingly.' Most strikingly, 'When he steps onto the boards, even when not expressing fear, hope, suspicion, or any other passion, the eyes of all are immediately drawn to him alone; he moves to and fro among other players like a man among marionettes.' Georg Christoph Lichtenberg, in Nagler, *Source Book*, p. 364.

8 Frances Burney, *Evelina* (Harmondsworth: Penguin, 1994), p. 28 (Letter x).

9 'Paradoxe sur le comédien' (my translation, original emphasis), in F.C. Green (ed.), *Diderot's Writings on the Theatre* (Cambridge University Press, 1936), pp. 253–4.

10 Harris, Introduction to *Samuel Richardson*, p. xl.

11 An Elizabethan edict made all actors 'vagabonds' unless they formally belonged to an aristocrat's company, like Shakespeare's company the King's Men. The trope of wandering was still associated with actors in the eighteenth century: a 1772 writer commented, 'The life of a player that is not marked with *peregrination*, *vice* or *distress*, abounds very little with these kinds of incidents and adventures that please the million' (quoted in Kristina Straub, *Sexual Suspects: Eighteenth-Century Players and Sexual Identity*, (Princeton University Press, 1992), p. 110). Straub cites a number of complaints from eighteenth-century actors about their legal status as vagabonds, pp. 159–61.

12 Roger Sales points out that Henry, who has 'play[ed] the part of a soldier [in *Lovers' Vows*] for his own enjoyment at a time when others had to fight against the Napoleonic armies', continues this practice during his visit to Portsmouth: 'Locations such as the dockyard and the Garrison Chapel, which were inextricably linked with the war effort . . . become theatrical sets against which he stages a play to try to convince Fanny to accept his marriage proposal.' *Jane Austen and Representations of Regency England* (London and New York: Routledge, 1994), pp. 90–1.

13 Sybil Rosenfeld's research indicates that the fashion was widespread: 'There were apprentices' theatricals, military and naval theatricals, children's and school theatricals and small theatres in which amateurs could try out their histrionic abilities for a small fee.' But by the time Austen was writing *Mansfield Park* 'private theatricals were no longer the vogue in country houses'. 'Jane Austen and Private Theatricals', *Essays and Studies*, n.s., 15 (1962), p. 42.

14 Thomas Gisborne, *Enquiry into the Duties of the Female Sex* (1797), chapter IX, excerpted in Claudia L. Johnson (ed.), *Mansfield Park*, Norton Critical Edition (New York and London: W.W. Norton, 1998), p. 401. Rosenfeld further comments on the 'smouldering opposition' to the amateur theatricals of the Pic Nic Society which 'burst into a flame of hysteria which scorched the newspapers with vituperative paragraphs and lampoons. It was one of the greatest storms in a teacup of the day and one that Jane Austen must have well remembered.' 'Private Theatricals', p. 43. For another description of such aristocratic entertainments, see Venetia Murray, *High Society in the Regency Period 1788–1830* (Harmondsworth: Penguin, 1999), pp. 229–32.

15 Marilyn Butler, *Jane Austen and the War of Ideas* (Oxford: Clarendon Press, 1975), p. 231.

16 William Cobbett, *The Porcupine and Anti-Gallican Monitor*, 7 September 1801, quoted in Kirkham, *Feminism and Fiction*, p. 94.

17 Quoted in Price's introduction to *Pizarro*, in Sheridan, *Works*, vol. II, pp. 635–6. Syndy McMillen Conger has calculated that 'out of 301 references to dramas in the periodicals in 1798, 181 were to Kotzebue's . . . The anti-Jacobins renew their attacks on Kotzebue repeatedly until 1805.' 'Reading *Lovers' Vows*: Jane Austen's Reflections on English Sense and German Sensibility', *Studies in Philology*, 85 (1988), pp. 101–2. The Chadwyck-Healey *English Drama* database has fifty entries for Kotzebue translations in the short period 1796–1801.

18 Hazlitt, 'Lovers' Vows', in *View*, p. 80. Edmund draws ironically on this anxious xenophobia as he attempts to forestall the theatricals: 'Let us do nothing by halves. If we are to act, let it be in a theatre completely fitted up with pit, box, and gallery, and let us have a play entire from beginning to end; so as it be a German play, no matter what . . .' (*MP*, p. 124).

19 *The Stranger*, a vehicle for Siddons and Kemble, has an entire cast of benevolent people: the thin plot turns on the reconciliation of the embittered husband with his errant and repentant wife. Benjamin Thompson published

a six-volume set of *The German Theatre* in 1801; it included at least nine plays by Kotzebue.

20 Further to the argument that the novel has a radical aspect, Austen ensures that the 'infection' of theatricals is brought in from an aristocratic household, Lord Ravenshaw's seat at Ecclesford in Cornwall; Mr Yates is 'the younger son of a lord' (*MP*, p. 121). The extravagance of Yates's plans for the Mansfield theatre is indicative of the gentry's disapproval of this sort of excess: 'only just a side wing or two run up, doors in flat, and three or four scenes to be let down' (*MP*, p. 123).

Susan C. Greenfield formulates the play's and novel's shared radicalism thus: 'Because she proves to have the best character, Fanny's class position (illegitimate status as it were) is disregarded, and Sir Thomas welcomes her into the family. In both play and novel, the ailing household is reconstituted around a child who comes inside from the outside by demonstrating that traditional standards of status and kinship are less important than just behavior and deserts.' 'Fanny's Misreading and the Misreading of Fanny: Women, Literature, and Interiority in *Mansfield Park*', *Texas Studies in Literature and Language*, 36, 3 (1994), p. 314.

Elaine Jordan argues that 'the obligations of patriarchy and its limits are one major theme of both play and novel. Both are also concerned with the position of women and this is something which has been masked by generalizing the play's issues in terms of romantic liberalism and individualism. Its libertarian impetus is very much to the advantage of women – the vindication of woman as victim, in Agatha the unmarried mother, and the vindication of woman as heroine, in Amelia's active initiation of courtship, regardless of class boundaries.' 'Pulpit, Stage, and Novel: *Mansfield Park* and Mrs Inchbald's *Lovers' Vows*', *Novel*, 20, 2 (Winter 1987), p. 146.

Marilyn Butler is the principal proponent of the view that Austen is using the play to criticise Rousseauistic individualism. As she comments, the overall effect of the play is that 'The individuals who have sampled what the play means, who have thrown off restraint, are the more likely to do the same again' (*War of Ideas*, p. 235).

21 This detail confirms Austen's familiarity with stage practices – the actual stage direction is less specific: '*He places chairs, and they sit.*'

22 Two letters from Eliza de Feuillide to Philadelphia Walter in November 1787 uncannily prefigure Fanny's trial here: 'You know we have long projected *acting* this Christmas in Hampshire [i.e. at Steventon parsonage] & this scheme would go on a vast deal better would you lend your assistance . . . Remember I *must* have a favourable answer.' 'I will only allow myself to take notice of the strong reluctance you express to what you call *appearing in Publick*. I assure you our performance is to be by no means a publick one, since only a select party of friends will be present.' Austen-Leigh, *Austen Papers*, pp. 127–8. Philadelphia remained firm in her refusal.

23 Austen's clear and ironical view of the social structure is neatly indicated in her narratorial comment, 'Miss Price had not been brought up to the

trade of *coming out*' (*MP*, p. 267). Nothing really differentiates the society lady's 'trade' from that of the actress (*MP*, p. 124) – or from the 'slave-trade', the other use of the pejorative term *trade* in the novel (*MP*, p. 198): in all cases, the (woman's) body is the commodity on display. This aspect of the novel is also discussed by Joseph Litvak in *Caught in the Act: Theatricality in the Nineteenth-Century English Novel* (Berkeley: University of California Press, 1992), pp. 1–27 (see note 27 below).

24  David Marshall, 'True Acting and the Language of Real Feeling: *Mansfield Park*', *Yale Journal of Criticism*, 3, 1 (1989), p. 88. He further remarks that 'there are also homoerotic currents in the veiled and mediated incestuous urges that circulate between Edmund, Fanny, Mary and Henry . . . [as] each woman becomes increasingly invested in her brother's or cousin's desire for the other, both the objects and the subjects of desire become confused' (p. 92). Patricia Rozema's 1999 film of *Mansfield Park* acutely embodies this point in the scene of lesbian flirtation between Mary and Fanny.

25  Inchbald, Preface to *Lovers' Vows*, reprinted in *MP*, pp. 477–8.

26  In a recent contribution to the critical rehabilitation of Elizabeth Inchbald, Jane Moody points out that 'the debate over Amelia's character which takes place in [*Mansfield Park*] is one whose moral positions had already been delineated in 1798 in the form of a dialogue between two women translators', Anne Plumptre and Elizabeth Inchbald. She reports that Plumptre, who had published a 'faithful' translation of the play as *The Natural Son*, was shocked when she went to see *Lovers' Vows* to find Amelia turned into a 'forward country hoyden'. 'Suicide and Translation in the Dramaturgy of Elizabeth Inchbald and Anne Plumptre', in Catherine Burroughs (ed.), *Women in British Romantic Theatre* (Cambridge University Press, 2000), p. 265.

27  The metaphor of 'infection' regarding theatre was something of a commonplace. Even the oddly asexual Tom, who as Paula Byrne points out, is the character 'with the most detailed and enthusiastic knowledge of the drama' (' "We must descend a little": *Mansfield Park* and the Comic Theatre', *Women's Writing*, 5, 1 (1998), pp. 91–102) finds himself – perhaps defensively – using the common metaphor of the anti-theatricalists: ' "This was, in fact, the origin of *our* acting," said Tom, after a moment's thought. "My friend Yates brought the infection from Ecclesford, and it spread as those things always spread, you know, Sir . . ." ' (*MP*, p. 184). Arguably, Tom is not cured of his theatrical fever until after he has undergone the full trials of the Prodigal Son, deserted by his male 'friends', ill and alone. Sir Thomas's attempts to disinfect Mansfield by removing all signs of the theatricals – he even burns every copy of the play he can find – cannot, however, rid the house of the theatricality intrinsic to its place in English society. Litvak's chapter on *Mansfield Park* is titled 'The Infection of Acting'; he cites Gisborne's *Enquiry into the Duties of the Female Sex* (1797), which criticises 'the infecting influence of a vicious character, adorned with polished manners, wit, fortitude, and generosity' in a drama (*Caught in the Act*, p. 6). He argues that 'the political order of *Mansfield Park* depends upon a certain theatricality' (p. 5); 'even before the Crawfords

arrive, Mansfield Park suffers from an overdose of theatricality. Indeed, the regime in question seems more like a parody of authority than like authority in the strict sense. Sir Thomas has delegated too much power to the officious Mrs Norris, who, with her "love of directing", views the household as a showcase for her own talents of management and domestic economy' (p. 14). The direction of the novel is to replace 'theatricality-as-subversion' with 'theatricality-as-convention' (p. 24): 'the aim of the authoritarian appropriation of theatricality [by Sir Thomas, particularly as regards Fanny in volumes II and III] is to demystify it, to shift its focus from glamorous excess to a more pedestrian trading in certain codified procedures . . . Once the more or less spectacular attack of the theatricals has subsided, the novel can address itself to the task of domesticating the theatrical Crawfords . . . in order to rob them of their subversive power' (p. 19). This analysis accords with my sense of the increasing coarseness of Mary's acting in these two volumes; but it does not, I think, adequately explain the complex and subtle behaviour of Henry, who takes the forestage in Fanny's story at this point. Litvak chooses to ignore Fanny's affective responses to her own 'coming-out' and to Henry's courtship of her with its powerful deployment of sexual charisma; I cannot agree that 'The burden of the middle section of the novel is to stage the theatricalization of the self in such a way that theatricality virtually disappears into that inner space, submerged in the form of rigorously inculcated habits of mind and modes of response' (p. 19).

28 *'Embracing him'*; *'Leans her head against his breast'*; *'Frederick . . . takes her hand and puts it to his heart'*; *'He embraces her'*; *'Presses him to her breast'*, *Lovers' Vows*, Act I. Hazlitt comments on the innovation of 'marginal directions to the players, in the manner of the German dramatists'. 'Mr Kean's Richard', in *View*, p. 32.

29 Cf. Sir Thomas's 'first appearance on any stage', when, watched by his theatre-mad elder son, he enters his billiard-room to find 'himself on the stage of a theatre, and opposed to a ranting young man'. 'It would be the last – in all probability the last scene on that stage; but he was sure there could not be a finer. The house would close with the greatest eclat', thinks the amused Tom (*MP*, p. 182), here as mouthpiece for an author determined that we shall note *all* characters' unavoidable implication in the theatricalised world.

30 Jane Austen to Cassandra: 'Henry [their brother] is going on with Mansfield Park; he admires H. Crawford – I mean properly – as a clever, pleasant Man.' *Letters*, 2–3 March 1814.

31 Frances Sheridan, *The Discovery*, Act I, scene v, in *Plays*, p. 50.

## 6 *EMMA*: PRIVATE THEATRICALS IN HIGHBURY

1 In *Letters*, 19 June 1799 Austen writes to Cassandra that they are going to 'The Play on Saturday . . . with Mrs Fellowes'. Hare's *Bath Calendar* confirms that they would have seen *The Birth-Day* and *Blue Beard*.

2 Kirkham, *Feminism and Fiction*, p. 122.

3  Act I, *The Birth-Day*, a Comedy in three acts as performed at the Theatre-Royal, Covent-garden. Altered from the German of Kotzebue, and adapted to the English Stage by Thomas Dibdin (London, 1800).

4  *Bath Herald and Reporter*, 29 June 1799, quoted in Tucker, *Jane Austen the Woman*, p. 96.

5  It is not just *Emma* that seems to have been anticipated in *The Birth-Day*. The two middle-aged brothers who are reconciled through Harry's agency bear the surname Bertram, and the housekeeper Mrs Moral is as grasping and faux-genteel as Mrs Norris. One of the brothers, Captain Bertram, is a navy man who prefigures the themes of *Persuasion*:

> England's gallant son, the bold and hardy tar,
> Brave and impetuous in the storm of war,
> Lull'd by the gentler gales of peace to rest,
> Feels all the milder virtues warm his breast.
>
> (Prologue)

The combination of patriotism, strong feeling, and respect for simple people whose goodness does not depend on wealth or rank, is characteristic of the early nineteenth-century English melodramas which in many respects the 'German drama' made possible. This genre will be examined in relation to *Persuasion* in chapter 7.

6  Charles Dibdin (who was also later a friend of Dickens) wrote a similar jingle-like role for Mathews, Dr Pother in *The Farmer's Wife*, which Austen saw in 1814 while she was working on *Emma*. Dr Pother is described by one of the other characters as 'this walking story-book, parish-register, and county chronicle' (Act I, scene v). That is, in writing Miss Bates's and Mrs Elton's idiosyncratic comic speeches, Austen draws on a specifically theatrical model of contemporary comedy.

7  Harris, *Jane Austen's Art of Memory*, pp. 169–87.

8  Paula R. Backscheider, editor of *The Plays of Elizabeth Inchbald*, 2 vols. (New York and London: Garland, 1980), comments that her plays of the late 1790s 'explore social problems that Ibsen and Shaw might have been reluctant to stage. Combining sentiment, strong moral principles, expert characterization, and well-executed plots, these plays consider such topics as adultery, revenge, domestic unhappiness, and loneliness' (Introduction, p. xvii).

9  Ibid., p. xvii. Interestingly, the role of Dorrillon was written for Quick, that of Bronzely for Lewis – the two actors mentioned in Austen's theatrical in-joke at the end of *Love and Friendship* (*MW*, p. 109).

10  Straub, *Sexual Suspects*, p. 5. Straub's work also seeks to contest this dominant reading of the gaze, 'to resist the notions of a monolithic masculinity as subject and a monolithic femininity as object'.

11  Barbara Freedman, *Staging the Gaze: Postmodernism, Psychoanalysis, and Shakespearean Comedy* (Ithaca: Cornell University Press, 1991), p. 73.

12  Mrs Elton's claim to female accomplishments is a broadly comic parody of Emma's queenliness:

'I do not ask whether you are musical, Mrs. Elton. Upon these occasions a lady's character generally precedes her; and Highbury has long known that you are a superior performer.'

'Oh! no, indeed; I must protest against any such idea. A superior performer! – very far from it, I assure you: consider from how partial a quarter your information came. I am dotingly fond of music – passionately fond; – and my friends say I am not entirely devoid of taste; but as to anything else, upon my honour my performance is *mediocre* to the last degree.' (*E*, p. 276)

13  This point is pursued with impressive cogency in Claudia L. Johnson's discussion of *Emma*'s 'remaking of English manliness' in *Equivocal Beings: Politics, Gender and Sentimentality in the 1790s* (University of Chicago Press, 1995), particularly in relation to the works of Wollstonecraft, Radcliffe, and Burney, with Edmund Burke's various treatises as a frequent point of reference in the politicised debate about gender. Joseph A. Kestner also deals interestingly with the issue in the context of figures such as Nelson and Wellington, in 'Jane Austen: Revolutionizing Masculinities', *Persuasions*, 16 (1994), pp. 147–60 (this article is further discussed in chapter 7). Kristina Straub offers a concise analysis and theorisation of the 'feminized erotic spectacle' of actors in the eighteenth century; this 'contributes to the definition of actors as sexually other to dominant masculinity' (*Sexual Suspects*, pp. 28–32). Austen seems to appropriate this discourse in her contrasting of Frank Churchill and Mr Knightley. Mr Knightley thinks Frank's handwriting 'too small – wants strength. It is like a woman's writing' (*E*, p. 297).

14  In the novel it is generally the morally suspect characters, such as Frank or Mrs Elton, who use faddish French words which had only recently made their way into English. When Mr Knightley uses a French word, as in this example, he does so in order to point out the moral and spiritual failings of the subject under discussion. *Manoeuvre* is imported from French in 1748 (as 'deceptive, elusive behaviour'); as a verb describing such behaviour its use dates from 1809). *Finessing* as a verb dates from 1746. Much later, when all is made clear, Mr Knightley comments that Frank has been 'playing a most dangerous game . . . his own mind full of *intrigue*, that he should suspect it in others. – Mystery; *Finesse* – how they pervert the understanding!' (*E*, p. 446). Emma considers Frank's secret engagement 'a system of hypocrisy and deceit, – *espionage*, and treachery' (*E*, p. 399): *espionage* only arrived in English in 1793, a word produced by the French Revolution. Roger Sales and Warren Roberts both comment on a similarly damning association with French language and behaviour in the Crawfords of *Mansfield Park*: Sales, *Jane Austen*, p. 91; Roberts, *Jane Austen and the French Revolution* (London: Macmillan, 1979), pp. 97–100. See also above, p. 136, for discussion of 'aimable/amiable'.

15  See note 7 above.

16  This point was first made by Alistair M. Duckworth in *The Improvement of the Estate: A Study of Jane Austen's Novels* (Baltimore: Johns Hopkins University Press, 1971): 'With Churchill's entrance, Emma is no longer the

puppet-mistress of Highbury but instead becomes a marionette in Churchill's more subtle show ... a dramaturgical vocabulary is inevitable with Churchill, for if he reminds us of any other character in Jane Austen's fiction it is the histrionic Henry Crawford. Like that actor, Churchill is an impresario of some ability' (p. 163). Duckworth cites his plans for the ball as those of an 'improver': 'There are no actual theatricals in *Emma*, but the theme is continued in minor key in the preparations for the ball and in the children's games which are a curious feature of the novel' (p. 163). Duckworth's analysis of this theme is helpful, but he does not pursue the narratological implications.

17 'Although well into the 1780s the entertainment at Astley's Amphitheatre consisted largely of horsemanship and variety acts such as tumblers, rope-dancers, trained dogs, learned pigs, and famous monkeys, along with music and dancing, pantomime with its appeal to the visual sense took an increasingly prominent place ... equestrian and military spectacle, especially if dealing with topical subjects, had become a principal attraction at Astley's by the last decade of the century.' Donohue, 'The London Theatre', pp. 358–9. Austen did go to Astley's at least once, aged twenty (*Letters*, 23 August 1796).

18 *OED*: 'Sensation: A condition of excited feeling produced in a community by some occurrence ... [;] 1779, Earl Malmesbury: What had passed already caused a great sensation in foreign courts. 1818, Southey: His death produced what in the phraseology of the present day is called, a great sensation.' *OED* might well have cited Austen two years earlier on this usage.

19 Frank's adopted surname misleadingly recalls the national hero, John Churchill, first Duke of Marlborough, who defeated the French in the War of the Spanish Succession.

20 Mrs Weston stands for them all in this late narratorial comment on the proposed marriage: 'Mrs. Weston was *acting no part*, feigning no feelings in all that she said to him in favour of the event' (*E*, p. 467; my emphasis).

## 7 *PERSUASION* AND MELODRAMA

1 These cancelled chapters are printed at the end of the 3rd edition of vol. v of the Oxford Illustrated Jane Austen, *'Northanger Abbey' and 'Persuasion'*, ed. R.W. Chapman (Oxford University Press, 1969 [1933]), pp. 258–73. Page references are to this edition.

2 Melodramatic rhetoric 'tends toward the inflated and the sententious. Its typical figures are hyperbole, antithesis, and oxymoron: those figures, precisely, that evidence a refusal of nuance and the insistence on dealing in pure, integral concepts.' Peter Brooks, *The Melodramatic Imagination* (New York: Columbia University Press, 1985), p. 41. Brooks discusses nineteenth-century fiction in more detail than he does drama.

3 Ibid., p. 41.

4 The plot of *The Mouth of the Nile* is a variation on the topos of the girl who disguises herself as a sailor in order to fight alongside her beloved:

midshipman William's messmate turns out to be his 'dear Susan'. There may
be an echo of this popular theme in Mrs Croft's declaration, 'I can safely say,
that the happiest part of my life has been spent on board a ship. While we
were together, you know, there was nothing to be feared' (*P*, p. 70).

5 For further details of the naval spectaculars, see Gillian Russell, *The Theatres
of War: Performance, Politics, and Society, 1793–1815* (Oxford: Clarendon Press,
1995), esp. chapter 3.

6 Terence M. Freeman, *Dramatic Representations of British Soldiers and Sailors on the
London Stage, 1660–1800: Britons, Strike Home* (Lampeter: The Edwin Mellen
Press, 1995). This admirable study, correcting standard misapprehensions
that 'redcoats and tars' were only ever subjects for satire on the eighteenth-
century stage, also contains a useful descriptive appendix of plays featuring
soldiers and sailors in the period.

7 The manuscript of Sheridan's *Pizarro*, his version of Kotzebue's *Die Spanier
in Peru*, contains a significant note: 'By the side of the line, "they fight for
wretched Gold, we for our King and country", Sheridan has jotted down
one word: "Nelson". . . . on a later occasion, [he] inserted at this point the
famous patriotic harangue of Rolla to the Peruvians that served, between 1799
and 1809, to rally public feeling in England against the French.' Cecil Price,
Introduction to *Pizarro*, in *Works*, vol. II, p. 645. Joseph Kestner gives details
of the contemporary iconisation of Nelson in 'Jane Austen: Revolutionizing
Masculinities' (pp. 147–60). He argues persuasively that Austen's sailor figures
'appropriate this paradigm and democratize it, that is, . . . instantiate this
paradigm into domestic and quotidian contexts' (p. 148). However, he seems
unaware of the widespread dissemination of this image through the popular
drama. (Conversely, the less successful army is not flatteringly represented in
this period, though there are plenty of brave colonels and heroic ensigns in
the comedies up to the 1780s.)

8 Juliet McMaster has drawn my attention to 'the *Times* first report of Trafalgar,
an item on a heroic young sailor called Price, who was offered as a model', as
a possible source for his (and Fanny's) apt surname. (Private communication.)

9 Scene iii of the play is simply scripted as 'The Sea Fight'. In scene iv, back
at the rural cottage, the sailor Ben recounts in song what the audience is
supposed to have seen: 'But love, avast! my heart is Oak / Howe's daring
signal floats on high; / I see through roaring cannon's smoke – / Their
Awful line subdued and broke / They strike they sink they fly.' In conclusion:
'Now (danger past) we'll drink and Joke, / sing "Rule Britannia"; "Hearts of
Oak!" / And Toast before each Martial tune – / Howe and the Glorious first
of June.' Sheridan, *Works*, vol. II, pp. 772–3.

10 Michael R. Booth points out that the fully developed nautical melodrama
'did not become a vogue until the 1820s' (*English Melodrama*, London: Herbert
Jenkins, 1965, p. 104).

11 Russell, *Theatres of War*, p. 85.

12 Freeman (*Britons, Strike Home*, pp. 115–25) lists many more songs in praise
of the British sailor from earlier in the century – most notably 'Black-eyed
Susan' (1731) and Boyce and Garrick's 'Heart of Oak' (1759).

13 A counter to this sentimental image was provided by the folksongs and ballads originating with press-ganged seamen and their devastated families: A. L. Lloyd in *Folk Song in England* (London: Panther Books, 1969, pp. 266–78) quotes a number of these, and argues that they more accurately reflected the sentiments that were to lead to the mutinies at Spithead and the Nore, e.g. 'Jack Tar''s: 'For your damned rogues of officers, they use men so cruel, / That a man-o'-war's worse than hell or the devil' (p. 272). Lloyd also points out that 'some folk songs of the sea were made by landsmen and are embellished with fanciful detail that would baffle a sailor' (p. 277).

14 Kirkham, *Feminism and Fiction*, p. 152.

15 Quoted in Freeman, *Britons, Strike Home*, p. 315.

16 John Genest quoted in Henry Saxe Wyndham, *The Annals of Covent Garden Theatre*, vol. 1 (London: Chatto & Windus, 1906), p. 289. The first English play to bear the label 'melodrama' was Holcroft's *A Tale of Mystery* (1802, based on the French of Pixerécourt, *Coelina*, 1800). Like most of the early melodramas, it was set in the vaguely medieval or renaissance past; the plot retains the familiar murders and mysteries of the Gothic drama.

17 Simon Shepherd and Peter Womack, *English Drama: A Cultural History* (Oxford: Blackwell, 1996), p. 196.

18 Ibid., pp. 199, 201.

19 Mrs Austen's comment in a letter of 1806 from Bath regarding a concert which Jane probably also attended suggests the atmosphere of such events: 'Rauzzini's Concert last night (when Mrs. Billington sang for the last time) was very full & very hot.' Austen-Leigh, *Austen Papers*, p. 238. The prologue to Dibdin's *Mouth of the Nile* (1798), written by Richard Cumberland, includes this patriotic and pertinent observation: 'Soft thrilling quavers cannot suit the throat, / Which Nelson tunes to triumph's loudest note. / If quavers are your taste, good folks, you'll meet / Enough of them, perchance, in t'other fleet; / Whilst our brave tars struck up their favourite lay, / Of *Rule Britannia*, on that glorious day.'

20 Hence the disconcerting rightness of the irruption of a circus procession in the background as Anne and Wentworth finally embrace in the colonnaded Bath Street in Roger Michell's 1995 film.

21 Christine Gledhill (ed.), *Home is Where the Heart is: Studies in Melodrama and the Woman's Film* (London: BFI, 1987), p. 22.

22 Nick Dear, *Persuasion, by Jane Austen, a Screenplay* (London: Methuen, 1996), p. 90. The direction follows: 'surprise amongst the party' – a melodrama response. Wentworth's interruption in this scene in the film is of course completely indecorous and wrong for the period (the lady always 'fixed the date').

# Bibliography

A Lady of Distinction, *Regency Etiquette: The Mirror of Graces (1811)*, Mendocino, CA: R.L. Shep, 1997.

Askwith, Betty, 'Jane Austen and the Theatre', in the Jane Austen Society, *Report for the Year 1983*, Overton: The Jane Austen Society, 268–84.

Austen, Jane, *The Novels of Jane Austen*, R.W. Chapman (ed.), 3rd edn, 5 vols., Oxford University Press, 1932–4; vol. VI, *Minor Works*, 1954, revised B.C. Southam, Oxford University Press, 1975.

Austen-Leigh, R.A. (ed.), *Austen Papers, 1704–1856*, London: privately printed, 1942.

Backscheider, Paula, *Spectacular Politics: Theatrical Power and Mass Culture in Early Modern England*, Baltimore: Johns Hopkins University Press, 1993.

Baer, Marc, *Theatre and Disorder in Late Georgian London*, Oxford: Clarendon Press, 1992.

Baillie, Joanna, *Plays on the Passions*, series 3, London, 1812.

Barish, Jonas, *The Anti-Theatrical Prejudice*, Berkeley and Los Angeles: University of California Press, 1981.

*Bell's British Theatre*, 90 vols., London, 1793.

Benedict, Barbara M., *Framing Feeling: Sentiment and Style in English Prose Fiction 1745–1800*, New York: AMS Press, 1994.

Bevis, Richard W., *The Laughing Tradition: Stage Comedy in Garrick's Day*, Athens, OH: University of Georgia Press, 1980.

*English Drama: Restoration and Eighteenth Century, 1660–1789*, London and New York: Longman, 1990.

Boaden, James, *Fontainville Forest*, a Play in Five Acts (Founded on the Romance of the Forest,) as performed at the Theatre-Royal Covent-Garden, London: Printed for Hookham and Carpenter, New Bond Street, 1794.

*Memoirs of the Life of John Philip Kemble*, 2 vols., London, 1825.

Bolton, Betsy, *Women, Nationalism and the Romantic Stage*, Cambridge University Press, 2001.

Booth, Michael R., *English Melodrama*, London: Herbert Jenkins, 1965.

'Sarah Siddons', in Booth, John Stokes, and Susan Bassnett, *Three Tragic Actresses: Siddons, Rachel, Ristori*, Cambridge University Press, 1996, 10–65.

Brooks, Peter, *The Melodramatic Imagination*, New York: Columbia University Press, 1985.

Brown, Bruce Alan, *Gluck and the French Theatre in Vienna*, Oxford: Clarendon Press, 1991.

Burney, Frances, *Evelina*, Harmondsworth: Penguin, 1994.

Burroughs, Catherine B., *Closet Stages: Joanna Baillie and the Theater Theory of British Romantic Writers*, Philadelphia: University of Pennsylvania Press, 1997.

Butler, Judith, 'Performative Acts and Gender Constitution: An Essay in Phenomenology and Feminist Theory', in Katie Conboy, Nadia Medina, and Sarah Stanbury (eds.), *Writing on the Body: Female Embodiment and Feminist Theory*, New York: University of Columbia Press, 1997, 401–25.

Butler, Marilyn, *Jane Austen and the War of Ideas*, Oxford: Clarendon Press, 1975.

Byrne, Paula, '"We must descend a little": *Mansfield Park* and the Comic Theatre', *Women's Writing*, 5, 1 (1998), 91–102.

Carlson, Julie A., *In the Theatre of Romanticism*, Cambridge University Press, 1994.

Castle, Terry, *Masquerade and Civilization*, Stanford University Press, 1986.

Conger, Syndy McMillen, 'Reading *Lovers' Vows*: Jane Austen's Reflections on English Sense and German Sensibility', *Studies in Philology*, 85 (1988), 92–113.

Copeland, Edward and McMaster, Juliet (eds.), *The Cambridge Companion to Jane Austen*, Cambridge University Press, 1997.

Cowley, Hannah, *The Plays of Hannah Cowley*, Frederick M. Link (ed.), 2 vols., New York and London: Garland, 1979.

Cumberland, Richard, *Memoirs*, London, 1806.

Dear, Nick, *Persuasion, by Jane Austen, a Screenplay*, London: Methuen, 1996.

Delpini, C., *Don Juan; or, The Libertine Destroy'd*, A Tragic Pantomimical Entertainment, in Two Acts; as performed at the Royalty-Theatre, Well-Street, Goodman's Fields, London: Printed for Mr. Delpini, n.d. [1789?].

Diamond, Elin, 'The Violence of "We": Politicizing Identification', in Janelle G. Reinelt and Joseph R. Roach (eds.), *Critical Theory and Performance*, Ann Arbor: University of Michigan Press (1992), 390–8.

Dibdin, Thomas, *The Birth-Day*, a Comedy in three acts as performed at the Theatre-Royal, Covent-garden. Altered from the German of Kotzebue, and adapted to the English Stage, London, 1800.

Dircks, Phyllis T., 'Garrick's Fail-Safe Musical Venture', in G.W. Stone (ed.), *The Stage and the Page: London's 'Whole Show' in the Eighteenth-Century Theatre*, Berkeley: University of California Press, 1981, 136–47.

Donkin, Ellen, *Getting into the Act: Women Playwrights in London, 1776–1829*, London: Routledge, 1995.

Donohue, Joseph W., *Dramatic Character in the English Romantic Age*, Princeton University Press, 1970.

'The London Theatre at the End of the Eighteenth Century', in Robert D. Hume (ed.), *The London Theatre World, 1660–1800*, London and Amsterdam: Southern Illinois University Press, 1980, 337–70.

Doody, Margaret Anne, *A Natural Passion: A Study of the Novels of Samuel Richardson*, Oxford: Clarendon Press, 1974.

Duckworth, Alistair M., *The Improvement of the Estate: A Study of Jane Austen's Novels*, Baltimore: Johns Hopkins University Press, 1971.

*English Drama* Full-Text Database, Literature Online, Cambridge: Chadwyck-Healey, 1997.

Fawcett, Trevor, *Bath Entertain'd: Amusements, Recreations and Gambling at the 18th-Century Spa*, Bath: Ruton, 1998.

 (ed.), *Voices of Eighteenth-Century Bath*, Bath: Ruton, 1995.

Fisher, Judith Warner, 'All the "Write" Moves: or, Theatrical Gesture in *Sense and Sensibility*', *Persuasions*, 9 (1987), 17–23.

Freedman, Barbara, *Staging the Gaze: Postmodernism, Psychoanalysis, and Shakespearean Comedy*, Ithaca: Cornell University Press, 1991.

Freeman, Terence M., *Dramatic Representations of British Soldiers and Sailors on the London Stage, 1660–1800: Britons, Strike Home*, Lampeter: The Edwin Mellen Press, 1995.

Gay, Penelope, 'Theatricals and Theatricality in *Mansfield Park*', *Sydney Studies in English*, 13 (1987–8), 61–73.

Genest, John, *Some Account of the English Stage*, 10 vols., Bath, 1832.

Gledhill, Christine (ed.), *Home is Where the Heart is: Studies in Melodrama and the Woman's Film*, London: BFI, 1987.

Goldsmith, Oliver, *Collected Works of Oliver Goldsmith*, Arthur Friedman (ed.), 5 vols., Oxford: Clarendon Press, 1966.

Green, F.C. (ed.), *Diderot's Writings on the Theatre*, Cambridge University Press, 1936.

Greenfield, Susan C., 'Fanny's Misreading and the Misreading of Fanny: Women, Literature, and Interiority in *Mansfield Park*', *Texas Studies in Literature and Language*, 36, 3 (1994), 306–27.

Hare, Arnold (ed.), *Theatre Royal, Bath: A Calendar of Performances at the Orchard Street Theatre 1750–1805*, Bath: Kingsmead Press, 1977.

Harris, Jocelyn, *Jane Austen's Art of Memory*, Cambridge University Press, 1989.

*Samuel Richardson's Published Commentary on Clarissa 1747–65*, London: Pickering & Chatto, 1998.

Hazlitt, William, *The Selected Writings of William Hazlitt*, vol. III, *A View of the English Stage*, Duncan Wu (ed.), London: Pickering & Chatto, 1998.

Highfill, Philip H., Burnim, Kalman A. and Langhans, Edward A., *A Biographical Dictionary of Actors, Actresses, Musicians, Dancers, Managers and Other Stage Personnel in London, 1660–1800*, 16 vols., Carbondale and Edwardsville, IL: Southern Illinois University Press, 1973–93.

Hogan, Charles Beecher, *The London Stage, Part 5: 1776–1800*, 3 vols., Carbondale, IL: Southern Illinois University Press, 1968.

Hume, Robert D., 'The Multifarious Forms of Eighteenth-Century Comedy', in G.W. Stone (ed.), *The Stage and the Page: London's 'Whole Show' in the Eighteenth-Century Theatre*, Berkeley: University of California Press, 1981, 3–32.

Hunt, Leigh, *Leigh Hunt's Dramatic Criticism 1808–1831*, Laurence Huston Houtchens and Carolyn Washburn Houtchens (eds.), New York: Columbia University Press, 1949.

Inchbald, Elizabeth, *A Collection of Farces*, 7 vols., London, 1815.

*The Plays of Elizabeth Inchbald*, Paula R. Backscheider (ed.), 2 vols., New York and London: Garland, 1980.

(ed.), *The British Theatre*, 25 vols., London, 1808.

(ed.), *The Modern Theatre*, 10 vols., London, 1811.

Jackson, Russell, 'Johanna Schopenhauer's Journal: A German View of the London Theatre Scene, 1803–5', *Theatre Notebook*, 52, 3 (1998), 142–60.

Johnson, Claudia, *Jane Austen: Women, Politics and the Novel*, University of Chicago Press, 1988.

*Equivocal Beings: Politics, Gender and Sentimentality in the 1790s*, University of Chicago Press, 1995.

(ed.), *Mansfield Park*, Norton Critical Edition, New York and London: W.W. Norton, 1998.

Jordan, Elaine, 'Pulpit, Stage, and Novel: *Mansfield Park* and Mrs Inchbald's *Lovers' Vows*', *Novel*, 20, 2 (Winter 1987), 138–48.

Kestner, Joseph A., 'Jane Austen: Revolutionizing Masculinities', *Persuasions*, 16 (1994), 147–60.

'Jane Austen: Revolutionising Masculinities – The Sailor and the Dandy in *Mansfield Park*', *Sensibilities*, 15 (1997), 71–87.

Kirkham, Margaret, *Jane Austen, Feminism and Fiction*, 2nd edn, London: Athlone Press, 1997.

Knapp, Mary E., *Prologues and Epilogues of the Eighteenth Century*, New Haven: Yale University Press, 1961.

Le Faye, Deirdre, *Jane Austen: A Family Record*, London: The British Library, 1989.

(ed.), *Jane Austen's Letters*, 3rd edn, Oxford University Press, 1995.

Litvak, Joseph, *Caught in the Act: Theatricality in the Nineteenth-Century English Novel*, Berkeley: University of California Press, 1992.

Lloyd, A.L., *Folk Song in England*, London: Panther Books, 1969.

Macready, W.C., *Reminiscences*, Sir Frederick Pollock (ed.), New York: Macmillan Co., 1875.

Marshall, David, 'True Acting and the Language of Real Feeling: *Mansfield Park*', *Yale Journal of Criticism*, 3, 1 (1989), 87–106.

McMaster, Juliet, *Jane Austen the Novelist*, London: Macmillan, 1996.

'From *Laura and Augustus* to *Love and Freindship*', *Thalia: Studies in Literary Humor*, 16, 1 & 2 (1996), 16–26.

Moody, Jane, *Illegitimate Theatre in London, 1770–1840*, Cambridge University Press, 2000.

'Suicide and Translation in the Dramaturgy of Elizabeth Inchbald and Anne Plumptre', in Catherine Burroughs (ed.), *Women in British Romantic Theatre*, Cambridge University Press, 2000, 257–84.

More, Hannah, *Strictures on the Modern System of Female Education*, 2 vols. London and New York: Garland, 1974 (facsimile of 1st edn, London, 1799).

Mullin, Donald C., 'Theatre Structure and its Effect on Production', in G.W. Stone (ed.), *The Stage and the Page: London's 'Whole Show' in the Eighteenth-Century Theatre*, Berkeley, University of California Press, 1981, 73–89.

Murray, Venetia, *High Society in the Regency Period 1788–1830*, Harmondsworth: Penguin, 1999.

Nagler, A.M. (ed.), *A Source Book in Theatrical History*, New York: Dover, 1959.

Page, Norman, *The Language of Jane Austen*, Oxford: Basil Blackwell, 1972.

Radcliffe, Ann, *The Italian*, Oxford University Press, 1981.

*The Romance of the Forest*, Oxford University Press, 1986.

Ranger, Paul, *'Terror and Pity reign in every Breast': Gothic Drama in the London Patent Theatres, 1750–1820*, London: Society for Theatre Research, 1991.

Roach, Joseph R., *The Player's Passion: Studies in the Science of Acting*, Ann Arbor: University of Michigan Press, 1993 [1985].

Roberts, Warren, *Jane Austen and the French Revolution*, London: Macmillan, 1979.

Rosenfeld, Sybil, 'Jane Austen and Private Theatricals', *Essays and Studies*, n.s., 15 (1962), 40–51.

'Landscape in English Scenery in the Eighteenth Century', in Kenneth Richards and Peter Thomson (eds.), *The Eighteenth-Century English Stage*, London: Methuen, 1972, 171–8.

Russell, Gillian, *The Theatres of War: Performance, Politics, and Society, 1793–1815*, Oxford: Clarendon Press, 1995.

Sales, Roger, *Jane Austen and Representations of Regency England*, London and New York: Routledge, 1994.

Salgado, Gamini, *Eyewitnesses of Shakespeare*, London: Sussex University Press, 1975.

Saxe Wyndham, Henry, *The Annals of Covent Garden Theatre*, 2 vols., London: Chatto & Windus, 1906.

Scott, Sir Walter, 'Essay on the Drama', in *The Prose Works of Sir Walter Scott, Bart.*, 28 vols., Edinburgh: Robert Cadell, 1849, vol. VI, 217–395.

Shepherd, Simon and Womack, Peter, *English Drama: A Cultural History*, Oxford: Blackwell, 1996.

Sheridan, Frances, *The Plays of Frances Sheridan*, Robert Hogan and Jerry C. Beasley (eds.), London and Toronto: Associated University Presses, 1984.

Sheridan, R.B., *The Dramatic Works of Richard Brinsley Sheridan*, Cecil Price (ed.), 2 vols., Oxford: Clarendon Press, 1973.

Southam, Brian (ed.), *Jane Austen's 'Sir Charles Grandison'*, Oxford: Clarendon Press, 1980.

Stone, George Winchester, *The London Stage, Part 4: 1747–76*, 3 vols., Carbondale, IL: Southern Illinois University Press, 1962.

(ed.) *The Stage and the Page: London's 'Whole Show' in the Eighteenth-Century Theatre*, Berkeley: University of California Press, 1981.

Straub, Kristina, *Sexual Suspects: Eighteenth-Century Players and Sexual Identity*, Princeton University Press, 1992.

Thomas, David and Hare, Arnold (compilers), *Restoration and Georgian England, 1660–1788*, Theatre in Europe: a Documentary History, Cambridge University Press, 1989.

Thompson, Emma, *Sense and Sensibility: The Screenplay and Diaries*, London: Bloomsbury, 1995.

Tomalin, Claire, *Mrs Jordan's Profession*, London: Viking, 1995.

*Jane Austen: A Life*, London: Viking, 1997.

Tucker, George Holbert, *Jane Austen the Woman: Some Biographical Insights*, London: Robert Hale, 1994.

Van Thal, Herbert (ed.), *Solo Recital: The Reminiscences of Michael Kelly*, London: The Folio Society, 1972.

West, Shearer, *The Image of the Actor: Verbal and Visual Representation in the Age of Garrick and Kemble*, London: Pinter Publishers, 1991.

Worthen, William B., *The Idea of the Actor: Drama and the Ethics of Performance*, Princeton University Press, 1984.

# Index